Maximum Boost

Designing, Testing, and Installing Turbocharger Systems

by Corky Bell

www.
B BentleyPublishers
.com

Maximum Boost
Designing, Testing, and Installing Turbocharger Systems

Introduction

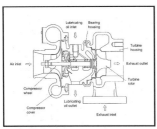

Page 23 Turbo selection

Page 73 Intercooling

Page 81 Intake design

CONTENTS

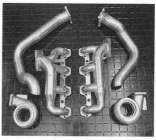

Page 121 Exhaust design manifold

Page 132 Exhaust piping

Page 181 Turbo developments

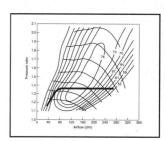

Page 201 Designing a system

Page 221 Installing a system

Copies of this book may be purchased from selected booksellers, or directly from the publisher by mail. The publisher encourages comments from the reader of this book. These communications have been and will be considered in the preparation of this and other manuals. Please write to Robert Bentley, Inc., Publishers at the address listed on the bottom of this page.

Library of Congress Cataloging-in-Publication Data

Bell, Corky.
   Maximum boost : designing, testing, and installing turbocharger systems / by Corky Bell.
      p.   cm.
   Includes index.
   ISBN 0-8376-0160-6 (alk. paper)
   1. Automobiles--Motors--Turbochargers.   I. Title.
TL214.T87B45   1997
629.25'04--dc21   97-9087
                                                                CIP

Bentley Stock No. GTUR

05 04 03 02   12 11 10 9 8 7

The paper used in this publication is acid free and meets the requirements of the National Standard for Information Sciences-Permanence of Paper for Printed Library Materials. ∞

Maximum Boost: Designing, Testing, and Installing Turbocharger Systems, by Corky Bell

Front cover: Photo by John Thawley.

Back cover: (clockwise from top center) a) Turbocharger cutaway courtesy of Mitsubishi; b) installing an aftermarket turbo on a Mazda Miata, photo by the author; c, d) Volkswagen Cabrio turbocharged by New Dimensions, photos by Robert A. Fredrich; e, f) turbo Honda CRX courtesy of "Turbo and High Performance" magazine, photos by Evan Griffey; g, h) bi-turbocharged Porsche Carerra, photos by Ian Kuah; i) turbocharged BMW 535i engine, courtesy of Dinan.

BENTLEY PUBLISHERS | Automotive Books & Manuals

Bentley Publishers, a division of Robert Bentley, Inc.
1734 Massachusetts Avenue
Cambridge, MA 02138 USA   Information that makes
800-423-4595 / 617-547-4170   the difference®
www.
BentleyPublishers
.com

INTRODUCTION

Author Corky Bell

A turbocharger is a simple device. It is nothing more than an air pump driven by energy remaining in the exhaust gases as they exit an engine. Of the energy released in the combustion process, approximately one-third goes into the cooling system, one-third becomes power down the crankshaft, and one-third is dumped out the tailpipe as heat. It is this last third that we can use to power the turbo. Consider that a 200 bhp engine dumps approximately 70 bhp equivalent of raw heat straight out the tailpipe. That is a tremendous amount of energy that could be put to better use. By comparison, when was the last time you saw an air fan operated at 70 horsepower? Thus, it is not so hard to imagine the turbo's potential for moving huge amounts of air.

A turbocharger system consists of a turbocharger and the parts necessary to integrate it into the engine's operation. A turbocharger system is not a simple device. Nowhere in these pages, however, do I discuss such things as the shapes of vortices created by the tips of the compressor wheel. Therefore, you may read on with confidence that this is not an engineering treatise on the mysteries of the inner workings of the turbocharger. The specific contribution I intend this book to make is as a handbook on the practical aspects of applying the turbocharger to the internal combustion engine. The turbocharger

An intercooled twin-turbo big-block is a serious power proposition. The big Pontiac V-8 has a liquid-to-air intercooler and came within 1 mph of exceeding 300 mph with a stock Firebird body.

has, pure and simple, greater potential for improving the power output of an engine than any other device.

What the turbo is, how it does its magic, and the equipment necessary to civilize it are the focal points around which this book is written.

A modern fuel-injected twin turbo system created by Ivan Tull of San Antonio for the small-block Chevy. The system features Gale Banks exhaust manifolds, Garrett AiResearch turbos, Dean Moon cross-flow intake manifold, and TWM throttle bodies. This level of preparation (incl. intercooler, not shown) is capable of 800+ bhp on street gasoline.

The Indy car is today's best example of engineering of turbocharged power plants within the restrictive rules of the racing-series sanctioning clubs.

1

AN ENGINEERING LOOK
AT THE BASICS

The power-enhancing capability of the turbocharger has been most thoroughly demonstrated by the Grand Prix racing cars of the 1977 to 1988 era of Formula 1.

The comparison of the power output of a top fuel dragster with that of a Formula 1 race car will establish the turbo's credentials. Current output of top fuel cars with 500 cid (cubic inch displacement) engines is suggested to be in the 5000–6000 bhp range, which calculates to around 10 bhp per cid. These numbers are not favorable compared to the 1300–1400 bhp, 90 cid qualifying engines of the 1987 Formula 1 cars. These outputs represent 14 to 15 bhp per cubic inch. That the champion is crowned is obvious even to casual observers. However, for the potential street turbo user, large questions remain. Answers to these questions will indicate why turbocharging is equally useful to the fast car enthusiast who relies on his car for daily commuting, to the racer, and even to the outer fringe of street power freaks.

Turbo Power Output

Why does the turbo produce more power than other forms of enhancement?

The power output potential of any supercharger is measured by the amount of airflow the device creates after factoring out the power required to drive it and the extent to which it heats up the air while creating the flow and pressure. While it might appear that the turbo does not drain power from the engine, since the exhaust energy is lost anyway, this is far from correct. Heat and airflow drive the turbine. When air is forced through the turbine section of a turbo, reduced-flow areas inherent in the design create back pressure. This

Fig. 1-1. *Porsche TAG turbo Formula 1 engine*

1

causes a small loss in power that would not occur if the turbo had a power source other than the engine into which it is pumping. The power loss increases as the size of the turbo decreases, because the decreased size creates greater back pressure. Conversely, larger turbos create much less back pressure and therefore less power loss. The power loss inherent in a turbocharged engine is substantially less than the loss incurred by driving a supercharger with a belt or by some other means.

That an air pump always heats air it compresses is a thermodynamic fact with which we are stuck. Different kinds of air pumps heat air different amounts for the same flow rates and pressure ratios. These differences are due largely to the different efficiencies of various types of pumps. The classic Roots-type supercharger usually rates efficiencies of about 50%, whereas the turbo runs efficiencies in the mid-70s. The higher the efficiency, the less the heating effect on the air. Efficiency is of paramount importance to the real power enthusiast, since heat in the intake charge is the enemy of performance. The density of an intake charge is less as the temperature rises; thus, an engine actually consumes less air at the higher temperature, even if the pressures are the same. A second problem is that higher temperatures promote detonation of the air/fuel mixture. Engines cannot withstand the thermal and pressure shocks of detonation for more than very short periods.

Withstanding Power Output

How can the engine structure withstand these huge power outputs?

To understand why the structure of an engine is not seriously affected by the increased power output permitted, within logical limits, by the turbo, it is necessary to look at the basic loads in an engine while it is in operation. Two basic loads are relevant to engine structure: inertial load and power load. Inertial loads can be tensile (produced by pulling) or compressive (produced by pushing). Power loads can only be compressive. They must be understood both individually and in their interaction. This is necessary for a clear view of why the turbo does not send the crank south.

INERTIAL LOAD. An inertial load results from an object's resistance to motion. To examine the inertial loads, it is convenient to divide a cylinder assembly into an upper half and a lower half. Imagine the two halves separated by an imaginary line called the center stroke.

The piston always accelerates toward the center stroke, even when traveling away from the center stroke. In other words, when the piston is above the

Fig. 1-2. The relationship of engine loads to engine components has three significant piston/crankshaft positions.

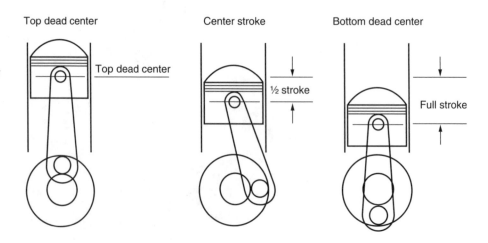

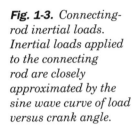

***Fig. 1-3.** Connecting-rod inertial loads. Inertial loads applied to the connecting rod are closely approximated by the sine wave curve of load versus crank angle.*

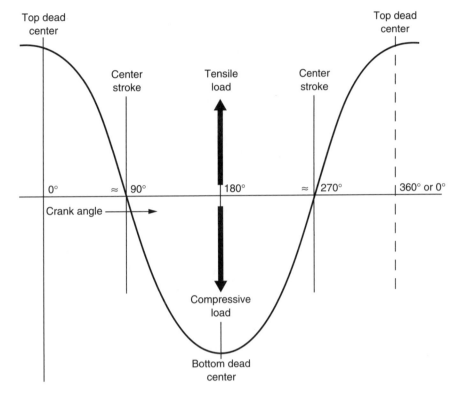

center stroke, it will always be accelerating downward. When it is below the center stroke, even at bottom dead center, it will be accelerating upward. Acceleration is greatest at top dead center and bottom dead center, when the piston is actually sitting still. When acceleration is greatest, the loads will be highest. Similarly, acceleration is zero and velocity is greatest as the piston passes the center stroke.

The size of the loads generated by these motions is proportional to the rpm of the engine squared. For example, if engine speed is increased threefold, the inertial load will be nine times as great. The action of the piston's being pulled (forced to accelerate) to a stop at top dead center and then pulled down the bore toward the center stroke will put a tensile inertial load into the con-rod/piston assembly. Similarly, as the piston is pushed to a stop at bottom dead center and then pushed back up the bore toward the center stroke, the inertial load will be compressive. Thus, any time the piston is above the center stroke the inertial load will be tensile, and below the center stroke, it will be compressive. The largest tensile load induced into a con rod is at top dead center on the exhaust stroke (because at top dead center on the compression stroke, the gas is already burning and creating combustion pressure to oppose the inertial load). The largest compressive load is generally at bottom dead center after either the intake or power stroke.

These inertial loads are huge. A large-displacement engine running 7000 rpm can develop con-rod inertial loads greater than 4000 pounds. (That's like a Cadillac sitting on your rod bearing.)

POWER LOAD. A power load results from the pressure of the burning gases applied to the piston. An example would be the compressive load put into a connecting rod as the burning gases force the piston down the bore of the cylinder.

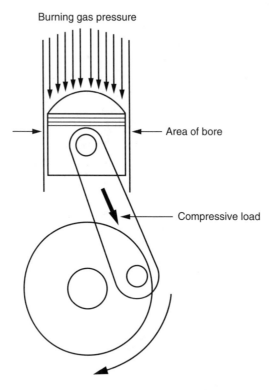

Fig. 1-4. Burning gas induces a compressive load in the connecting rod.

Pressure created by the expansion of the burning gases applies a force to the top of the piston equal to the area of the bore times the chamber pressure. For example, a cylinder with a bore area of 10 square inches (3.569-inch bore) with 800 psi of pressure would be subjected to a compressive power load of 8000 pounds.

Fig. 1-5. Combined power and inertial loads. Note that power and inertial loads generally subtract from one another.

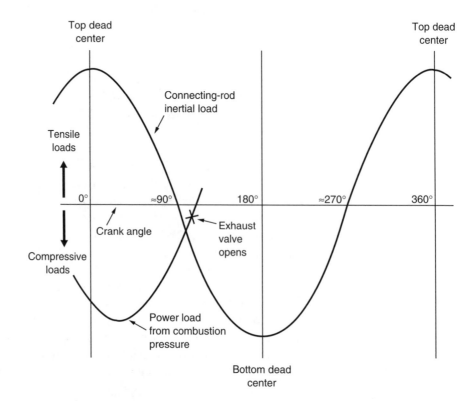

The peculiar relationship of the inertial and power loads is of most interest in the upper half of the power stroke. Here we have the odd circumstance that the two loads acting on the con rod are doing so in different directions. Remember that an inertial load is tensile above the center stroke, while a power load is compressive in all cases. Power load peaks at the torque peak and fades a little as rpm increases but is generally greater than the inertial load. The difference between these two loads is the real load in the con rod (fig. 1-5).

Clearly, the inertial load offsets some of the power load. It is further apparent, as indicated above, that on the exhaust stroke, when the con-rod/piston reaches top dead center and is unopposed by combustion pressure (because both valves are open), the highest tensile load is reached. This load is the most damaging of all, because tensile loads induce fatigue failure, whereas compressive loads do not. For this reason, when a designer sits down to do the stress analysis on the con rod and con-rod bolts, the top dead center and bottom dead center inertial loads are virtually the only ones he is interested in knowing.

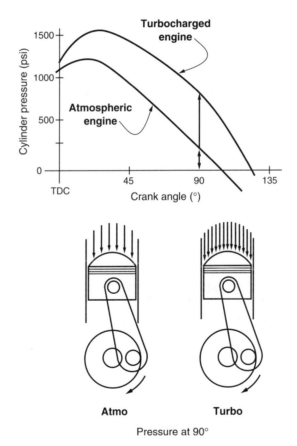

Fig. 1-6. *Torque input into the crankshaft versus crank angle at approximately two atmospheres of pressure. Note that for the turbo engine, maximum pressure occurs at about 20° ATDC, yet only about 20% of the mixture will have burned. Even with high boost pressures, the small amount burned will not result in large maximum pressure changes. As the burn nears completion, the greater mixture density can raise the pressure three- to fourfold at crank angles near 90°, such that torque input to the crank at that position can be twice as great.*

The thought of doubling an engine's torque (doubling the power at the same rpm) easily gives one the idea that the power load will double. Thank goodness this is not true. To show how power can double without the combustion chamber pressure's doubling is much easier done graphically. Any significant design load changes would be based on peak pressure in the chambers, and it can be seen in figure 1-6 that with twice the mixture in the chamber, peak pressure is up only about 20%. There are two reasons for this disparity.

First, power is a function of the average pressure over the entire stroke of the piston, not just peak pressure. The average pressure can be dramatically increased due to the much higher relative pressures near the middle or end of the stroke, while the peak does not gain significantly.

Second, peak pressure is generally reached after only 18–20% of the mixture has burned. If the mixture quantity is doubled, 18-20% of it, too, will have burned by the time peak pressure is reached. Since the total chamber pressure consists of the compression pressure plus the burning gas pressure, it is impossible to double the total pressure by doubling only one of its constituents. (Clearly, mother nature has a soft spot in her heart for con rods and con-rod bearings.)

A careful study of figure 1-6 will show that at crank angles nearing 90°, chamber pressure is perhaps three to four times as great when operating under boost. This is, however, noticeably less than peak pressure. Therefore, it does not create a damaging load. The part of the power stroke near 90° is where the real turbo engine power increases take place. If a physics type looks at the graph, he will tell you that the area under the respective curves represents the power. Thus, the difference in the two areas represents power gain due to the turbocharger. It certainly is a neat deal that we can double the power but not the load!

The preceding discussion establishes that the increased combustion chamber pressure due to a turbo, and thus the power load, will have only a moderate adverse effect on the structure of the engine.

☞ **RULE:** Power loads generally won't tickle the engine structure's tummy.

Long-Term Durability

Long-term durability: Is it there, and how is it attained? The answer to "Is it there?" is relatively easy to show by citing a few examples. Someone at Porsche once stated that a racing mile was about equivalent in wear and tear to 1000 street miles. Porsche's turbocharged race cars have won so many twenty-four-hour endurance races that only a racing historian can keep up with the number. These cars generally cover over three thousand miles in such races. A street car with three million miles on it may seem to be stretching the point, but the idea doesn't fail to impress. To stand along the banking at Daytona when a Porsche 962 turbo comes whistling by in excess of 200 mph can easily leave one aghast to think that these things are going to do this for twenty-four hours. The violence and speed can give the initial impression that nobody will finish this race. Yet, chances are a turbocharged racer will take the checker first. This book is primarily about street turbocharging, not race cars, but the problems are the same, even if different in magnitude. Street cars, by comparison, are a piece of cake. Chrysler even put a 70,000-mile warranty on some of its turbo cars.

How durability is attained is not quite so easy to answer as is the question of whether it exists. In a broad sense, durability boils down to the control of heat in the engine/turbo system. Each aspect of the system in which heat plays a part is a candidate for the Achilles' heel. For long-term durability, each of these factors must be optimized. They include turbo compressor efficiency, intercooling, control of end-gas temperatures, turbine bearing temperatures, and many others, and will be discussed in the following chapters. We should call the answer to the entire heat problem "thermal management." In reading this book, it will prove useful to keep uppermost in mind that virtually the entire success of a turbo/engine system lies in thermal management.

Power Gain Where does the power gain come from? What is the equation for the power of any given engine, and how does the turbo influence that equation? (Don't let equations scare you off—these are both neat and easy.)

It is revealing to examine the simple equation that relates power to the parameters describing the internal combustion engine.

$$Power = P \times L \times A \times N$$

P is brake mean effective pressure, or bmep. An easy way to imagine bmep is as an average pressure pushing the piston down the bore.

L is the length of the stroke. This tells you how far the pressure is going to push the piston.

A is the area of the bore. This is, of course, the area the pressure has to work on.

N is the number of putts the engine makes in one minute. This represents how fast the engine is running and how many cylinders it has.

$$N = number\ of\ cylinders \times \frac{rpm}{2}$$

(For a 4-stroke engine, the rpm is divided by 2 because each cylinder fires only on alternate revolutions.)

Now, there are several interesting relationships here! For example, take the *P* and multiply by the *A* and you have a pressure times an area, which is nothing more complicated than the average force pushing down on the piston. Now multiply the *PA* (force) by the length of the stroke, *L* (distance), and you have a number that represents the torque output of the cylinder. Then take this figure and multiply by the *N* (how fast the job is getting done), and the result is *Power*, the thing we are really after.

Please note that this means

$$Power = torque \times rpm$$

Fig. 1-7. "PLAN" is the key to the source of all power output.

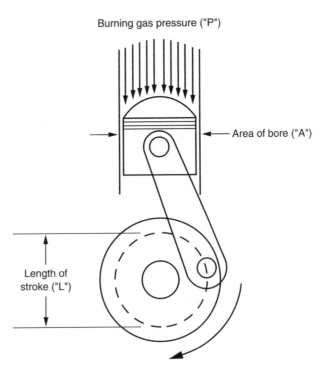

Burning gas pressure ("P")

Area of bore ("A")

Length of stroke ("L")

Since the whole purpose of this exercise is to get more power, let's examine what this *PLAN* gives us to work with.

First, let's check out what working with the *N* can yield. There are two ways to get more putts per minute: add more cylinders or rev the engine higher. That leaves little to work with, as the whole field of endeavor known as blueprinting is almost solely for the purpose of allowing higher rpm with some degree of safety. Consider that those nasty inertial loads go up with the square of the rpm increase. That means that at 7200 rpm, the inertial load will be 144% greater than at 6000 rpm. Wear and tear lies up there. Ultimately, it is neither cheap, pleasant, nor durable long-term to increase power output by increasing the *N*. Since we cannot, for practical reasons, increase power significantly with *N*, the only remaining choice is to increase torque by doing something with the *PLA*.

So we must go back and look at the *PLA* a bit more. We can change the *A*. Bored, it's called, but how much does it help? Change *A* by an eighth of an inch and maybe you'll gain 10%. Not worth the trouble. We can also change *L*. Stroked. Another 10%, maybe. Obviously, then, if we're pursuing real power, the *A* and the *L* don't hold much promise. Changing *P* becomes our only hope.

How to successfully change *P* is the crux of this book. *P* can be changed by factors of 1.2, 1.5, 2, 3, 4, 5. . . . The real potential is not known, since engineer types push the envelope every year. The Grand Prix racing cars of the '87 season took turbo development to the highest levels ever achieved, with power outputs of nearly 15 bhp per cubic inch. Suffice it to say, then, that doubling the power of a street engine, while not exactly child's play, is well within our reasonable expectations.

It is essential here to make clear the fact that we are dramatically increasing power without changing rpm. Therefore, it is torque *(PLA)* that we are really changing.

☞ **RULE:** Turbos make torque, and torque makes fun.

Driveability Limitations

What are the driveability limitations of a turbocharged engine?

The nice driveability of most cars today is something we have grown to expect under all conditions. Get in, turn on, drive off smoothly. Nothing else is acceptable anymore—exactly as the situation should be. It is often perceived

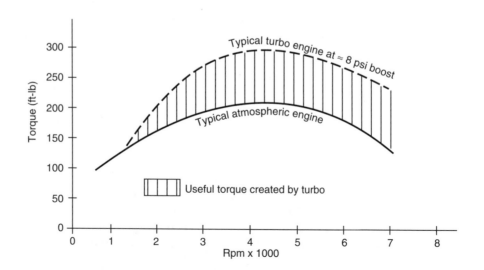

Fig. 1-8. *One typical example of the difference in torque curves for a turbocharged and an atmospheric engine.*

that real power and nice driveability are not compatible in the same automobile. This is frequently true in atmospheric engines but decidedly not true in turbocharged engines.

Consider the facets of an engine that create driveability: conservative camshaft profiles, small intake ports, fuel system flexibility and calibration. A proper turbo engine has a short-duration, low-overlap cam, generally referred to as an "economy cam." Port sizes are usually small, to create good cylinder filling at low speeds and to let the turbo pack it in when high pressure is wanted. Fuel system calibration must always be spot on, at least with electronic fuel injection. Obviously, then, the factors creating nice driveability are present in turbocharged cars. The fact that a turbo is available to push more air in when desired has no influence on "Get in, turn on, drive off smoothly."

Two factors affecting driveability do come into play when the turbo is in use: boost threshold and lag. These do not significantly degrade atmo engine performance, since the cam, compression, ignition timing, and fuel mixture remain virtually the same. If you stick a rock under the throttle and go for a trip around the block, you just can't tell the difference.

BOOST THRESHOLD. Boost threshold, defined in the glossary, is essentially the lowest engine rpm at which the turbo will produce boost pressure when full throttle is applied. Below that rpm, the turbo simply is not supplied with enough exhaust gas energy to spin fast enough to produce above-atmospheric pressures in the intake manifold (see fig. 1-8). Up to the boost threshold, the engine's torque curve remains virtually the same as that of an atmospheric engine. To accelerate through this range at full throttle, the driver would feel a surge in power as the torque curve takes an upward swing at the boost threshold. If full throttle is not used, the turbo makes no contribution to the torque curve, and acceleration continues the same as with a non-turbo engine.

The nonboosted torque curve can sometimes be compromised by an unreasonable reduction in the compression ratio (displacement volume plus clearance volume, divided by clearance volume), causing a soggy feel at low speeds when not under boost. It is here that some of the automotive manufacturers have made a serious engineering (or economic) error, by not fitting suitable intercooling systems to remove enough heat from the intake charge. This would permit the use of higher compression ratios, retaining that sweet, low-speed response of an engine with an adequate compression ratio. If you are shopping for a turbo car, have some fun and ask the salesperson to tell you the efficiency of the intercooler. That is, of course, after you ask if it has one. It is certainly reasonable to assume that low-speed driveability is superior if the vehicle is fitted with an intercooler and the compression ratio is kept over 8 to 1.

Judging the merit of a turbo system solely on a low boost threshold is a serious error. It would be tough to argue that boost at low rpm is a bad thing, but it is easy to argue that boost at low speeds achieved by small turbos is a potential problem, due to higher exhaust gas back pressure. A well-designed system that has had great attention paid to all its parameters will display good low-speed boost as one of its features.

Small turbochargers frequently produce an annoying response when the throttle is applied in small increments. This distinctly affects driveability, in that a small motion of the throttle will produce a quick and usually unwanted small surge of boost that upsets the smoothness of the car. To some extent, this causes a passenger to think the driver inept. This small surge frequently gives the driver the impression the car will really fly when full throttle is finally reached. Instead, he realizes sadly that the small surge was all the surge the little wimp could make. OEMs do this to us hoping we will think the car has instant response and gobs of low-end torque. They have generally overlooked the fact that it was raw power we really were after. This OEM phenomenon has left many journalists, writers, would-be fast drivers, and other social outcasts wondering "Where's the beef?"

☞ **RULE:** In general, OEM turbo applications are a long way from what enthusiasts and engineers would pronounce fast, fun, and first class. Let us call OEM turbos conservative.

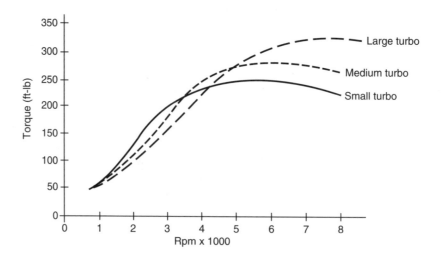

Fig. 1-9. *Comparison graph of the torque-increasing capability of small, medium, and large turbos applied to the same engine*

LAG. Seldom are turbos discussed without the mention of lag. Equally seldom, it seems, are discussion participants really talking about lag. Usually they are talking about boost threshold. Please read the definitions of lag, boost threshold, and throttle response in the glossary. In the day-to-day use of a turbo, sure, lag essentially means how long you have to wait to get boost after you nail the throttle. By definition, then, it is a bad thing. But lag has nothing to do with throttle response. Throttle response remains the same, turbo or no turbo.

Consider that if you did not have a turbo, the brief lag would be followed by no boost at all. Reasonable to say, then, that lag would extend from the point at which you apply throttle all the way to the redline. What fun that would be! The situation boils down to some tolerance for lag with a huge torque increase as opposed to no tolerance for lag accompanied by no torque increase.

Lag decreases as rpm rises. While lag can be as much as a second or more at low rpm, the delay in boost rise virtually disappears at revs of about 4000 or greater. For example, in a properly configured turbo system, boost rise will follow the position of your foot any time the revs are above 4000 rpm. Response here is virtually instantaneous.

☞ **RULE:** If you have no lag, you have no turbo. You also have no huge torque increase to look forward to.

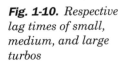

Fig. 1-10. *Respective lag times of small, medium, and large turbos*

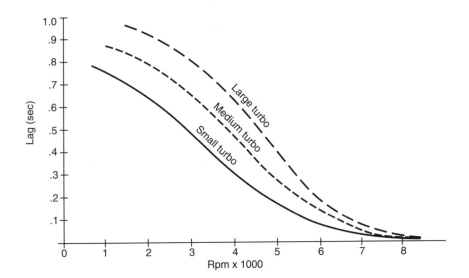

The shape of the torque curve of a turbo engine is different enough from that of an atmo engine that driveability of a turbo is only slightly affected. Torque peaks are virtually always at lower rpm on turbo engines. Chart all the published data and no other conclusion is possible. The more performance-oriented the atmo engine, the greater the difference. The net effect on the driver is that he or she need not rev the turbo engine as much to move rapidly. This is quite contrary to popular opinion but is indeed fact.

Hot and cold starting are frequently perceived to be problems of high-performance engines. To some extent this is true in carbureted turbo systems, but these are few and far between. Fuel injection systems depend solely on various engine-temperature sensors for all cold- and hot-start air/fuel mixtures and are completely automatic. Cold starting is particularly a problem for engines with lower compression ratios. If an engine has a problem in this respect without a turbo, it will likely have the same problem with a turbo, since the turbo does not influence these temperatures or the electronics. Either way, the difficulty is not related to the turbo.

CRUISING. The turbo is out of the picture in all cruise conditions except those that must have boost pressure to achieve a particular speed. Consider that a given vehicle may have a top speed of say, 130 mph, no turbo. Now add a turbo. It is reasonable to say that the vehicle will still reach approximately 130 without the need for additional power; hence, no boost is required. For all practical purposes, even the wildest imaginable cruise speeds are unlikely to require any boost pressure to sustain.

The idea that a superpowerful, maximum-effort turbo car would be fun to drive at full throttle but be a bit of a cantankerous beast at low speeds is not unreasonable on the surface. This idea does not, however, hold up under closer scrutiny. To create an effective high-pressure turbo car, one need only do more of the same required to produce the turbo car in the first place: reject more heat, increase fuel flows, raise the octane, and be certain the structure of the engine is adequate. The factors that are the basis of good low-speed behavior—conservative cam profiles, small intake ports, and fuel system calibration—are unchanged by higher boost pressures. All other things remaining equal, merely turning the screw on the boost knob does not alter driveability. It is most unreasonable to claim that a 500 bhp street turbo car—which, given full throttle in second gear, has the ability to create tire marks in directions perhaps other than those intended—has a driveability problem.

AND FURTHERMORE . . .

How much power can I expect from a turbocharged engine?

With currently available fuels, 7 to 12 psi boost is a practical upper limit for stock engines (at sea-level elevation). Intercooling permits this when elaborately and properly done. Certainly not all turbo kits or systems will perform the same, due to widely varying engineering efforts on the above items. Special preparation of engines specifically for turbo applications can frequently permit boost pressures of 15 to 20 psi. To claim, calculate, or estimate a specific figure for power from a turbo engine can be precarious indeed.

Of known dyno runs on piston engines with a variety of turbo systems, the lowest output we have achieved is .052 bhp/cid psi and the highest is .077 bhp/cid psi. The variance is due to the engines' basic designs. To guess at the output of your own engine, choose a logical boost level and multiply each of the two values by both displacement in cubic inches and boost pressure plus 14.7.

Example: A 350 cid engine with 10 psi boost

$Lower\ value\ =\ 0.052 \times 350 \times (10 + 14.7) =\ 449\ bhp$

$Higher\ value\ =\ 0.077 \times 350 \times (10 + 14.7) =\ 666\ bhp$

Does the rated boost of a kit have any merit?

It does if, and only if, the conditions required to achieve that boost are defined and accurate. For example:

- Was the gasoline used commercially available pump gas?
- Were octane boosters used?
- Was detonation present?
- What was intake air temperature?
- Is this the same boost-pressure setting the buyer will receive?

Considering the large power increases offered by the turbocharger, what keeps the entire structure of the engine from going south?

A proper answer to this question is a complete analysis of the inertial, power, and thermal loads before and after turbo installation. If this is performed, the conclusion will be two interesting bits of information:

- The inertial loads in a modern internal combustion street engine are so large at maximum power that the power component of the total load is of little significance. For example, to induce as much power load into a conrod bearing as the bearing already sees from inertial loads, the actual power of the engine would need to increase approximately 50%.
- The thermal load in an engine not originally designed for a turbocharger will cause an increase in component and cooling-system temperatures when operating under boost. The components and cooling system can handle the temperature increase for a limited period. This is true for Buicks, Porsches, Saabs, Volvos, Nissans, etc. It is also true for all aftermarket turbo kits. The time limit is subject to many judgments and conditions. Experience has led me to believe that the time limit at full boost is on the order of 20 to 25 seconds. This is an operational restriction

but not one of any consequence. Consider, for example: How fast will you be traveling if you hold full throttle in a 325 bhp Toyota Supra for twenty seconds? The answer is obviously an impractically high rate of speed.

When should the turbo start producing boost?

In most cases, there are trade-offs between a low boost threshold and maximum power. To bias the turbo size toward low-speed boost capability generally means operating the turbo in a very inefficient flow range at the engine's top end. Conversely, if maximum power is to be achieved, the turbo will usually be so large that no boost will be available until the last half of the rev range. Compromise is obviously necessary. I believe the reasonable balance between low-speed response and top-end power is to size the turbo such that it begins producing boost at about 30% of the redline rpm.

How will the turbocharger affect driveability?

Driveability of fuel-injected engines will remain the same. Driveability of blow-through carbureted engines will remain virtually the same. The starting of carbureted engines will be degraded slightly. Please note that draw-through units will virtually always degrade driveability and starting somewhat, with cold weather proving the Achilles' heel of a draw-through system.

Will the turbocharger hurt my mileage?

Yes. The turbo, when installed as an aftermarket item on a spark-ignition engine, is not an economizer and cannot be construed as such. There is no engineering basis for making such claims. If you are led into purchasing a turbo under the premise of improving your fuel mileage, be sure to get a written guarantee. When not operating under boost, a turbocharger is a small system restriction. This restriction causes a small loss in volumetric efficiency. Volumetric efficiency and fuel economy are definitely tied together. If your driving habits are about the same as most, your mileage will drop about 10% city and 5% highway. No miracles here.

Will the turbocharger affect engine wear and maintenance?

Certainly the turbo will affect engine wear. Do you really expect to add power and not increase wear? No miracles here either. If you drive vigorously but with some respect for the equipment, you can expect about 90% of normal engine life.

Will the transmission and drivetrain be adversely affected?

Very unlikely. Consider that the drivetrain endures more torque in first gear from the stock engine than almost any turbo can produce in second gear. Occasionally a clutch comes along that won't do the extra duty. Most clutch problems are going to crop up when shifting habits are less than acceptable. Not to worry.

What does it feel like to drive a properly set up turbo car?

A turbo can justifiably be called a torque multiplier: the more boost, the more torque. This situation is analogous to gear ratios. For example, a third gear with a tranny ratio of 1.4 will develop 40% more torque at the rear wheels than a fourth-gear ratio of 1.0. A boost pressure of 6 psi will increase torque by about 40% (using an intercooler). Thus you can see that 6 psi boost will produce fourth-gear acceleration virtually equal to a stock automobile's third-gear capability. Imagine what the proper turbo car will do in second gear! Another reasonable comparison is that a proper turbo car operating at 10 psi boost will do 0–60 in two-thirds the original time; i.e., 6 seconds versus 9 seconds.

2

ACQUIRING A TURBOCHARGED VEHICLE

The essence of this book, if such exists, is to provide the performance car enthusiast interested in turbocharging with a body of information that can be used to evaluate system designs, whether of a factory turbo system or an aftermarket kit. This book is also intended as a design guide for the hobbyist who wants to build his own turbocharger system. Three viable methods exist to acquire a turbocharged vehicle:

- buy an OEM-turbocharged automobile
- buy an aftermarket kit, if available, for your specific application
- build your own turbo system

The rationale behind the decision that suits your needs and requirements best is no more than a logical summary of the following:

- What is the intended use of the vehicle?
- What is the legality with respect to state and federal law and the year of the car?
- How much power is required?
- Is fear of a failure such that a factory warranty is required?
- Can you make a reasonable judgment with respect to the engineering of an aftermarket kit?
- Do you have the skills, time, patience, and equipment to build your own?

Fig. 2-1. The Mitsubishi 3000GT turbocharged 24-valve V-6. Two turbos, two intercoolers, four-wheel drive, and 183 cid give the 3000GT extraordinary potential.

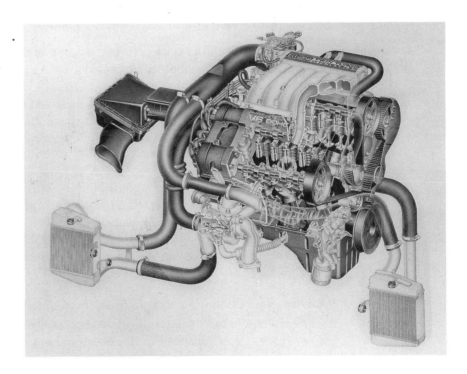

OEM-Turbocharged Automobile

Automobile manufacturers have built a variety of turbo cars in the last decade. One can easily wonder how some decisions are made. On one hand we have the Ford EXP Turbo, most Chryslers, and the Nissan NX Turbo. The other hand holds something like the Porsche 944, Buick GNX, and Lotus Esprit turbo. Members of the radical middle are large in number, relatively nondescript, and not entirely without merit. In most circumstances, the factory turbo engine is conservative in power output—easily understandable in view of warranties, liabilities, and emissions requirements. Generally speaking, OEMs will not equip a turbocharger system with optimum-configuration parts. Virtually all OEM designs will have some shortcoming, whether in turbo size, intercooler capability, or restrictive exhausts. Occasionally the shortcoming is just a different design, based on the OEM's perception of its buyers' requirements. Finding and fixing these weak links then becomes the focus of attention in efforts at greater performance.

☞ **RULE:** OEMs will generally provide you with a vehicle that functions nicely but is blessed with enough shortcomings that performance is far from optimum.

The first step in pursuing more performance is a complete analysis of the system design. Chapter 14, Testing the System, is your starting point. With those data accumulated and analyzed and the weak links identified, you can set out to find the necessary components to improve the system. Keep in mind that the issue here is to improve efficiency, thereby opening up the potential for huge gains in power. Increasing boost pressure is also a consideration, but without efficiency improvements, this path to power is fraught with mechanical risk. Once the system has been tested and the merit of each feature has been determined, start the improvement process with the weakest link. Here is where foresight becomes important. For example, an intercooler that loses only 2 psi at the factory-rated boost can be judged okay. It is okay, but only for the factory-rated boost. Likely it will lose 3 or 4 psi at any significantly increased airflow. That kind of loss is not acceptable.

Aftermarket Turbo Kit

The purchase of an aftermarket turbocharger system is an ideal occasion to employ this book as the guide it is intended to be. An investigation is necessary to determine the system that will meet your needs. Before a reasonable decision can be made, answers to a variety of questions must be both sought and understood. The following samples will get you on the right track:

Does the system provide a correct air/fuel ratio at all operational conditions?

The air/fuel ratio is a basic building block of a turbo system. It needs to be maintained over the boost range that the manufacturer claims for the kit. It is not to be expected that the air/fuel ratio will stay correct if the system's design limits are exceeded. In all circumstances, it is necessary to avoid discussing "fuel enrichment." Either an air/fuel ratio is correct or it isn't—no "enrichment" required.

Does the system provide a margin of safety on detonation?

The attempt here is to determine whether the system installed and operated per instructions will yield useful boost and not be subject to detonation problems.

*Fig. 2-2. This compre-
hensive and complete
aftermarket system for
Honda CRX cars easily
shows HKS's custom-
ary attention to detail.
Although non-inter-
cooled, for reasons of
cost, the system enjoyed
many excellent features,
a superb exhaust mani-
fold design, fuel con-
trols, and compressor
bypass valving.*

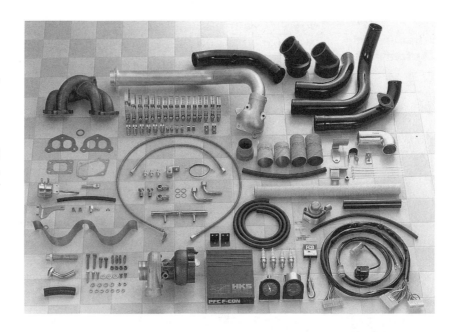

*Fig. 2-3. The idea of a
complete system takes
on significance with the
HKS Supra turbo. Note
the oil cooler, flywheel,
clutch, fuel injectors,
spark plugs, and the
entire exhaust system.*

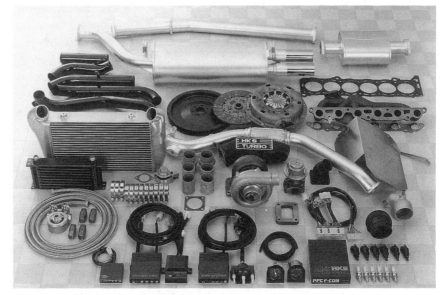

*Does the system provide the necessary thermal controls to operate at the stat-
ed boost pressures?*

Ask for a description and explanation of these controls.

What efforts are extended toward quality control?

Fit and finish are obvious. Material selections, methods of welding, surface
finishes, and other fabrication procedures should also be checked out.

Do the components carry a reasonable warranty?

Although warranties on performance-oriented components are frequently
subject to severe limitations, the buyer cannot be hung out to dry. It is useful to
discuss with the kit maker the warranty limitations and procedures necessary
to establish the best warranty terms.

Are proper instructions offered with the system?

Instructions should provide all the necessary information to install, check out, and subsequently operate and service the turbo vehicle.

Will consulting be provided after the sale?

This is where the maturity of a turbo system manufacturer will truly show.

If the system is to be used on a public highway, is it designed with all emissions-related equipment in proper order, and/or is the system on EPA- or CARB exemption-order status?

In all states, the emission question will be the most important one.

When the answers to the above questions are satisfactory, it is time to get down to the fun details, such as compressor efficiency with respect to the system flow rates and boost pressures.

☞ **RULE:** All kit makers will try to represent their systems as the most powerful. Absolute power is the last reason to make a decision.

Building Your Own Turbo System

Any reasonably able fabricator should have no serious difficulty designing and building his own turbocharger system. Forethought, planning, calculating, sketching, and measuring, all done in considerable detail, will be the keys to the success of the project. Perhaps the single greatest problem facing the do-it-yourselfer is avoiding getting stuck. Getting stuck is the phenomenon of "You can't get there from here." For example, you can't ever hope to intercool your turbo system if you build a draw-through carb type. Creating a high-performance piece for a 454 cid V-8 with a single turbo where a twin is clearly dictated will decidedly put you in a position where you are stuck. Avoid going down these paths leading to "stuck." The first requirement is to determine the power level desired. Translate that figure into a boost pressure necessary to get the job done. That, in itself, will determine the equipment needed. The remainder of the project is the sum of the experience contained in this book.

Fig. 2-4. The Callaway twin-turbo Corvette featured a thoroughly prepared engine, two Roto-Master Compact turbos, and intercooling. Note the low oil drains, collector sump, and belt-driven scavenge pump located at the lower right corner of the engine.

AND FURTHERMORE . . .

Why is a correct air/fuel ratio necessary?

Basically, a correct afr means the engine is getting all the fuel it can efficiently burn, but not an excess. If you err on the rich side (the safer side), performance declines, because a rich condition louses up combustion temperatures. Lean mixtures lead to higher charge (in-cylinder) temperatures, promoting detonation.

What does "fuel enrichment" mean?

"Fuel enrichment" means, in every aftermarket sense ever expressed, an indiscriminate dump of fuel into the system. It is indiscriminate because it does not care what the actual airflow is. Any kit maker who uses the phrase will usually supply the indiscriminate dump device. Don't ever ask a kit maker what he uses for fuel enrichment; rather, ask, "How have you managed to maintain a correct afr, to how high a boost level, and can you prove it to me?" Every kit maker will respond that the necessary equipment to maintain a correct afr is in the kit. Not necessarily so. Be sure the answers are correct, as this facet of turbocharging is of the greatest importance.

Fig. 2-5. *The BMW 2002 is a superb street rod when equipped with a water-based intercooled turbo and two blow-through Mikuni 44s. Ten psi boost created 210 bhp and stock vehicle driveability.*

What are some of the devices for maintaining a correct air/fuel ratio?

The worst device is none. It is perhaps the most popular. It is also the easiest to install. Another equally bad device is the boost-pressure-sensitive switch that sends a false water-temperature signal to the EFI brain. This is a wholly unworkable gizmo. It attempts to add fuel when under boost by lengthening injector pulse duration. While it can double fuel flow at mid-range rpm, it can add only about 10% more fuel at the redline. The nature of timed injection (like EFI) results in a situation where the length of an injector pulse for a maximum torque cycle remains essentially constant, regardless of rpm. That fixed injector pulse length becomes a greater percentage of engine cycle time as rpm increases. The point is finally reached where engine cycle time is the same as the maximum-torque injector pulse time, and then the injector is open continually. This is why an injector duration increase, by any device whatsoever, cannot supply enough fuel for a turbo engine at any upper-range rpm.

Further, all additions or subtractions of fuel are instantaneous incremental changes as the switch is activated, and nothing with a large instantaneous change in the afr can be correct. The result of the "fuel enrichment switch" is at best a poorly running, detonation-prone engine. The EFI fuel enrichment switch is the source of perhaps 75% of turbo-related horror stories. Avoid it.

Another popular scheme is to proportion "fuel enrichment" according to boost pressure. While this sounds better and is better, it is still technical nonsense. The situation is created wherein the same amount of fuel would be added at 3000 rpm and 5 psi boost as at 6000 rpm and 5 psi boost. Obviously, fuel requirements would double at twice the rpm, but the boost-proportioned fueler would deliver the same quantity of fuel regardless of rpm. Not a workable mechanism.

The change to larger injectors is a valid approach to adding fuel. This generally requires other changes to reduce the larger injectors' flow at low speeds, so off-boost operation will not be too rich. This can be done by reprogramming the ecu or altering flowmeter signals. With boost pressures greater than 8 to 10 psi, the larger-injector approach is a necessity.

Another popular device is to send the lambda (tailpipe oxygen sensor) system to full rich when under boost. Lambda systems have control of approximately 8% of the fuel delivery. Combine that with 50% more air (7 psi boost) and the engine becomes intolerably lean. This method is unfortunate, at best.

Fig. 2-6. *A straightforward, low-cost design from Performance Techniques for the Mazda Miata. The absence of an intercooler and compressor bypass valve keep boost down and the cost more affordable.*

What is compressor surge, and how can it be countered?

Compressor surge is the rapid fluctuation of turbine speed caused by the throttle's being closed under boost. Rapidly spinning air compressors (turbos) can go unstable briefly when this occurs. The fluctuating speed can be damaging to the turbo, and the accompanying noise is obnoxious. The condition can be alleviated with a compressor bypass valve that opens as the throttle closes and allows air exiting the turbo to vent back to the front. This keeps the flow up. Many modern turbo cars are equipped with such valving, but seldom are they big enough to handle high-flow, high-boost systems. A useful fringe benefit to these valves is that they reduce lag and perceptibly increase fuel economy.

What is a reasonable price to pay for a turbocharger system?

The lowest-priced system that offers

- a correctly sized turbo
- a correct air/fuel ratio under boost
- boost control by controlling turbine speed
- proper ignition timing
- proper thermal controls
- a margin of safety on detonation
- quality components

Such a system can put together a good argument for being the best value. It is popular to believe that you get what you pay for, but there are turbo kits costing nearly $4500 that do not have a correct air/fuel ratio or even an iron exhaust manifold. Conversely, kits are available that have all the above at a price less than $2500. A reasonable price? This must remain the prospective buyer's decision, based on a thorough knowledge of what he gets for his money.

What paperwork should be included with a turbo kit?

Instructions and warranty are self-explanatory. Cautions and operating procedures must be well detailed and conservative.

What are the warranty implications of installing a turbo in a new automobile?

All factory warranty on drivetrain components will be voided. There are, however, several circumstances to consider. You can purchase an aftermarket warranty to cover your vehicle for all non-turbo-induced or -related problems. It is currently in vogue to sell these policies with turbo systems under the in-

Fig. 2-7. A simple, effective, low-boost system for the small-block Chevy. Note the additional fuel injectors, lack of intercooling, and warm-air pickup for the filter.

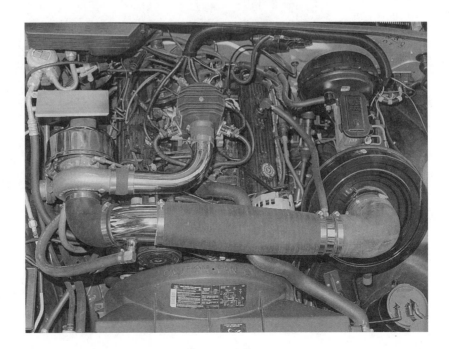

tended misconception that your drivetrain is warranted against "turbo-induced" failures. Not so.

If one breaks his turbo engine, it is not going to be paid for by anyone's warranty—exactly the same situation as waiting until the factory warranty expires and then adding the turbo. Which means that waiting out the factory warranty before installing a turbo accomplishes nothing except insuring that the mechanism is one-third used up pre-turbo. Furthermore, it eliminates the fun of ever owning a nice new automobile with enhanced power. It is rare for a modern automobile to have an engine/drivetrain problem within the warranty duration. Those problems that do appear are generally minor and will likely cost under a hundred dollars to repair. To preserve the warranty for many thousands of miles to avoid a possible hundred-dollar component failure rather than enjoying the extra performance seems to me the poorer choice. To assuage your concerns, call the car maker's regional office and discuss with a service rep the areas of the drivetrain that have been a warranty problem.

Fig. 2-8. *Turbo Engineering produced this low-mounted turbo specifically for the Chevy Camaro. With intercooling, a large series TO4 turbocharger and generous flow paths, this system could offer power levels in excess of 500 bhp.*

3

SELECTING THE TURBOCHARGER

The size of the turbo selected for a given application will strongly influence the degree of success enjoyed by the system. It is not at all a case of only one size working in a specific situation; rather, there is just one that will work best. The trade-offs of lag, boost threshold, heat, low-speed torque, and power are the variables in the decision process of matching the turbo to the requirements. To optimize the trade-offs, the requirements must be defined first. These requirements can be spelled out by listing the performance objectives for the particular vehicle.

Objectives can vary for day-to-day commuter cars, Bonneville maximum-speed cars, drag cars, super-performance street cars, real race cars, and even for the outer fringe of vehicles called pickup trucks. Specific performance objectives will be items such as desired boost threshold, torque peak, and estimated power output. Higher-speed vehicles require larger turbos, street cars respond well to mid-range torque, and low-speed vehicles need smaller turbos. How to select the right turbo for the job and how to choose some of the more advantageous features are discussed in the following paragraphs.

To illustrate the degree to which turbo sizing can vary for the particular job, compare the 1988 Nissan 300ZX Turbo and the Porsche 911 Turbo. These two cars are similar in size, weight, and engine displacement, yet the turbos are vastly different in size. From the size of the Porsche's turbo, it is relatively easy to conclude that the Porsche design staff did exactly what they needed to do. They fitted a large turbo to the 911, for three specific reasons:

Fig. 3-1. The classic turbocharger: a very simple, highly engineered, high-quality, precisely manufactured air pump.

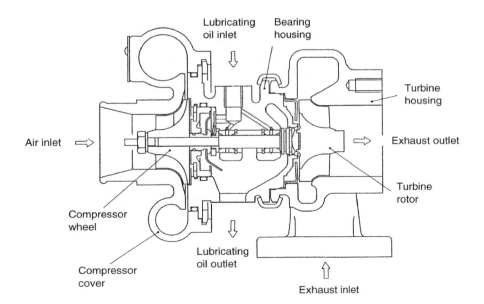

- When operating at maximum load, the large compressor puts less heat into the intake charge.
- The large turbine creates less exhaust manifold back pressure, further reducing the heat load.
- The design staff wanted a powerful automobile.

The Nissan staff, on the other hand, with a much more heat-tolerant engine (water-cooled), was free to use a small turbo for virtually immediate off-idle response. This small turbo gives quick boost response at the extreme expense of high back pressure and high intake-charge temperatures. Nissan was obviously not looking for serious power, as they did not see fit to offset these high temperatures with any form of intercooling. Their objective appears to have been aimed at a 0–30 mph performance car. Certainly they had a different buyer in mind from Porsche. Although the Porsche has been proclaimed by all its road testers the prime example of a high turbo-lag design, it had to be that way because of the low heat allowables. A small turbo could not have been used on the 911 because of the thermal restrictions of the air-cooled engine, and certainly not when serious power is an objective. Porsche, therefore, should be credited with doing a fine job. Nissan should be credited with selling a large number of cars to a large number of people.

☞ **RULE:** Never send a child to do an adult's job.

General Guidelines

The influence of compressor and turbine sizes on system performance will generally follow these guidelines:

COMPRESSOR. A compressor has a particular combination of airflow and boost pressure at which it is most efficient. The trick in choosing optimum compressor size lies in positioning the point of maximum efficiency at the most useful part of the rev range. Choosing the most useful part of the rev range is where some judgment needs to be exercised. Keep in mind at all times that when efficiency drops off, heat produced by the turbo goes up. If a turbo were sized such that maximum efficiency occurred at one-third of the rev range, efficiency at or near the redline would taper off to where the charge temperature would be scorching hot. At the other extreme, if maximum efficiency were at the redline, mid-range temperatures could get out of hand. This particular size would then be useful only for running flat out at that rpm; i.e., the Bonneville car. Somewhere in the middle of the useful rev range of the engine lies the best place to locate the maximum efficiency point.

Larger or smaller compressors do not have a huge effect on turbo lag or boost threshold. The compressor wheel is the lightest rotating part of the turbo; hence, its contribution to the total inertia of the rotating assembly is fairly low. Boost threshold is mostly a function of the turbo's speed, which is controlled by the turbine.

Often, a choice of turbo(s) is influenced by factors other than those optimized by thermodynamics or maximum power. Vehicle cost can determine the number of turbos, for example. One would not expect to see a Ferrari V-12 with one turbo and a Mazda Miata with two. Cost also plays a large part in designing a system. If low cost is imperative, perhaps even the water-cooled bearing feature would be deleted in favor of more frequent oil changes.

Ultimately, the value of the equipment selected will not lie just with cost, power, thermodynamic factors, or the number of turbos. Rather, it will be de-

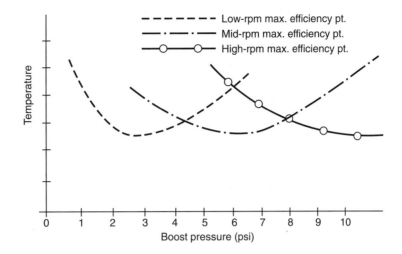

Fig. 3-2. *With a small turbo, the maximum efficiency point peaks early, and temperatures will be lowest at low boost pressures. To keep temperatures down at high power outputs, a large turbo is clearly necessary.*

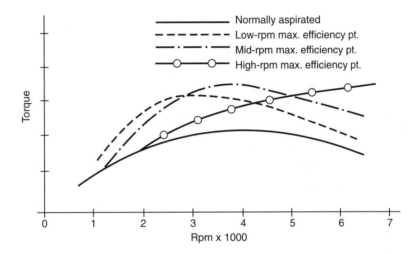

Fig. 3-3. *As the maximum efficiency point occurs at higher and higher rpm, cooler temperatures also occur. Cooler temperatures mean denser air, which keeps torque peaks at higher rpm.*

termined by the way this baby behaves on the road. Is it actually fast, and does it feel fast? Does it feel responsive and eager to run? Is it crisp and sharp? Does it pull smoothly with ease and grace to the redline? Does it make you smile when no one is around to see?

Start by selecting two or three candidates whose pressure ratio and cfm appear, from their flow maps, to be in the right range, with efficiency not below 60%. Once this is accomplished, it is necessary to perform calculations to choose between them. (See Chapter 17 for an example of these calculations applied to a specific installation.)

TURBINE. The turbine's role is to power the compressor. In doing so, it must make the compressor spin fast enough to produce the desired airflow rates at the designated boost pressures. A small turbine will spin faster than a larger turbine, given the same exhaust gas energy to work with. Further, a small turbine will offer, in essence, a greater restriction to the flow of the exhaust gases. This restriction causes back pressure between the turbine and the combustion chamber. This back pressure is an evil side effect of the turbocharger and must be dealt with accordingly. In reality, then, selection of the turbine must focus on the principles of spinning the turbine fast enough to produce the desired response and boost pressures yet keeping back pressure to an absolute minimum.

**Selecting
Compressor
Size**

A few fundamentals must be understood prior to the actual process of choosing compressor size. It is necessary to develop a feel for the concepts of pressure ratio, airflow rate, density ratio, and compressor efficiency before one can be comfortable with the logic behind choosing a compressor size.

PRESSURE RATIO. The pressure ratio is the total absolute pressure produced by the turbo divided by atmospheric pressure. Absolute pressure means the amount of pressure above nothing at all. Nothing at all is zero absolute, so atmospheric is 14.7 absolute. Two psi boost becomes 16.7 absolute, 5 psi boost is 19.7 absolute, and so on. Total absolute pressure is then whatever the gauge reads plus 14.7. The pressure ratio thus becomes a reflection of the number of atmospheres of pressure generated.

$$Pressure\ ratio\ = \frac{14.7 + boost}{14.7}$$

Example:
For 5 psi boost:

$$PR = \frac{14.7 + 5}{14.7} = 1.34$$

In this example, approximately 34% more air will go into the engine than the engine could have consumed by itself.

For 12 psi boost:

$$PR = \frac{14.7 + 12}{14.7} = 1.82$$

Here, approximately 82% more air will be going through the system. Pressure is also measured in *bar*, short for *bar*ometric (1 bar = 14.7 psi). In the above example, a pressure ratio of 1.82 equates to an intake pressure of 1.82 bar. This term is used in high-class turbo circles (which explains why it does not appear again in this book).

Fig. 3-4. Compressor density ratio versus pressure ratio. Density is degraded by temperature; therefore, actual air-mass increase is always less than that indicated by the pressure ratio.

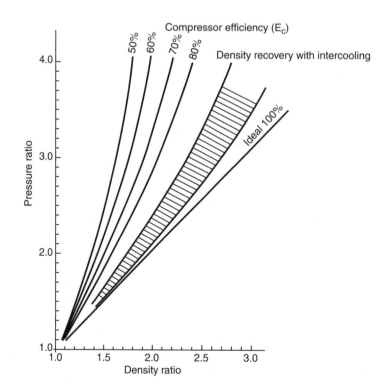

DENSITY RATIO. Ultimately, power produced by turbocharging depends on the number of air molecules packed into each cubic inch of volume. This is referred to as the density of the air charge. This density takes a bit of a beating in passing through the turbocharger system. When the air molecules are forced closer together by the turbo to a certain pressure ratio, density does not increase by the same ratio. This is because compression makes the temperature rise, and the air molecules expand back apart, based on how hot the air gets. Although the air charge winds up denser, density is always less than the pressure ratio, as indicated in figure 3-4. (Since the air intake system is not a fixed volume, air density can decrease without the pressure ratio decreasing.) The effort expended by a designer to use efficient compressors and intercoolers allows the density ratio to get closer and closer to the pressure ratio but never quite reach it.

AIRFLOW RATE. The airflow rate through an engine is usually referred to as cubic feet per minute (cfm) of air at standard atmospheric pressure. The technically correct but less-used term is pounds of air per minute. This book will use the semi-incorrect term "cfm."

To calculate the airflow rate of an engine without a turbo—i.e. no boost:

$$Airflow\ rate\ =\ \frac{cid \times rpm \times 0.5 \times E_v}{1728}$$

Here, flow rate is in cfm and displacement is in cubic inches. The .5 is due to the fact that a four-stroke-cycle engine fills its cylinders only on one-half the revolutions. E_v is volumetric efficiency. The 1728 converts cubic inches to cubic feet.

Example:
In a small-block Ford, let size = 302 cid, rpm = 5500, and E_v = 85%.
Then

$$Airflow\ rate\ =\ \frac{302 \times 5500 \times 0.5 \times 0.85}{1728}\ =\ 408\ cfm$$

Fig. 3-5. The volume rate of flow (cfm) for four-stroke-cycle engines. Choose an engine size (the x-axis) and an rpm, and the cfm is shown on the y-axis.

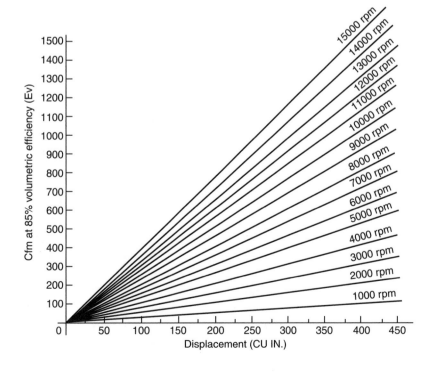

With the basic engine flow rate established, the flow rate under boost can be determined. The pressure ratio times the basic engine flow rate then becomes the approximate flow rate under boost (neglecting volumetric efficiency): the number we're really after. In the small-block Ford operating at 12 psi boost:

$$Airflow\ rate\ =\ pressure\ ratio \times basic\ engine\ cfm$$
$$=\ 1.82 \times 408\ =\ 743\ cfm$$

To convert cfm to the more correct term of pounds of air per minute, cfm must be multiplied by the density of air at the working altitude (see table 3-1).

COMPRESSOR EFFICIENCY. In concept, compressor efficiency is a measure of how well the compressor wheel can pump air without heating the air more than thermodynamic law says it should. Thermodynamics says the air temperature should rise a certain amount based on the pressure ratio. That temperature rise would be called the ideal temperature rise. When the temperature is actually measured, it is always higher than the thermodynamic calculation indicates it should be. The measured temperature rise is, of course, the real temperature rise. The efficiency is the calculated temperature rise divided by the real temperature rise. In essence, efficiency is how well the compressor really behaves with respect to how well thermodynamics says it should behave.

All compressor wheels operate with peak percentage efficiencies in the seventies. Choosing compressor size becomes mostly a question of where that compressor's efficiency peaks with respect to the flow capabilities of the engine/turbo system.

With an understanding of the terms pressure ratio, density ratio, airflow rate, and compressor efficiency, the basic information necessary to select a compressor for a given application is at hand. In general, under 7 psi is low boost, 7–12 psi is medium boost, and over 12 psi is high boost. Working through the example of the small-block Ford with several choices of compressors will illustrate the process of calculation as well as the importance of placement of the efficiency peak. A study of Fig. 3-6 indicates the effect of a compressor's efficiency on charge temperatures. In general, compressor effi-

Table 3-1. Variation of air pressure and temperature with altitude

Altitude (ft)	Air pressure (in. hg)	Temperature (°F)	Relative density
Sea level	29.92	59.00	1.00
1000	28.86	55.43	.997
2000	27.82	51.87	.993
3000	26.81	48.30	.989
4000	25.84	44.74	.986
5000	24.90	41.17	.982
6000	23.98	37.61	.979
7000	23.09	34.05	.975
8000	22.23	30.48	.972
9000	21.39	26.92	.969
10,000	20.58	23.36	.965
11,000	19.80	19.79	.962
12,000	19.03	16.23	.958
13,000	18.30	12.67	.954
14,000	17.58	9.11	.951
15,000	16.89	5.55	.947

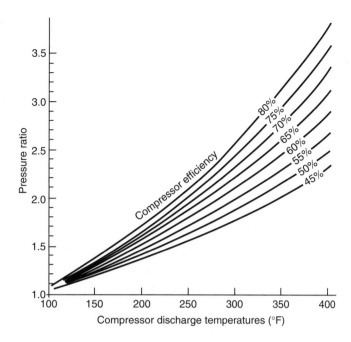

Fig. 3-6. *Compressor discharge temperature versus pressure ratio. Why one wants to secure the highest compressor efficiency possible: the greater the efficiency, the lower the temperature.*

ciency without an intercooler should be at least 60%. If the system includes an intercooler, minimum efficiency can be somewhat less (see Chapter 5).

With the calculated values of the cfm and pressure ratio for the Ford 302 example, one is ready to go to the compressor maps to check where the efficiencies lie in order to determine a suitable compressor. Plot the calculated data of cfm = 743 and PR = 1.82 on the axes of the compressor maps. The intersection of the two lines represents the maximum flow the compressor can produce at the pressure ratio for this application, and that point falls into a particular efficiency percentile on each map. It is largely the efficiency at this point that establishes the suitability of that compressor for the particular application. In figure 3-7, the intersection of these points falls along the 67% line. In figure 3-8, the intersection falls to the right of the 60% line, which indicates that the efficiency will be somewhat less—perhaps 50–55%. Therefore, the H-3 would be a less satisfactory choice for this application.

The surge characteristics of the compressor with regard to the application must also be examined before finalizing a selection. This can be approximated in a simple manner. Assume that the desired pressure ratio is reached at 50% of the redline rpm and plot this point on the compressor map. The above example with rpm = 2750 then establishes a point at cfm = 371 and PR = 1.82. Draw a line from this point to a point at PR = 1 and cfm = 20% of maximum, or 149 cfm in this example. It is imperative that this line lie completely to the right of the line on the flow map called the surge limit. Surge limits are not always labeled on flow maps, but you can assume they are the leftmost line. This example indicates that the 60-1 compressor, at 67% efficiency, is better suited for this application than the H-3, at 55%.

Selecting Turbine Size

The intended use of the engine/turbo system is again the primary influence on selection of turbine size. Intended use dictates a choice of low-speed, mid-range, or top-end torque. The choice can easily encompass two of these ranges.

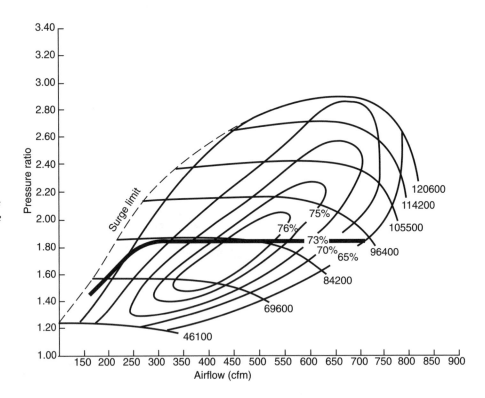

Fig. 3-7. *Nearly 900 cfm are available from the Turbonetics 60-1 compressor with a pressure ratio of 2.8. The steep incline of the surge limit line clearly indicates that the 60-1 will produce high boost pressures at low cfm before surge is produced The numbers at the extreme right are the turbine rpm.*

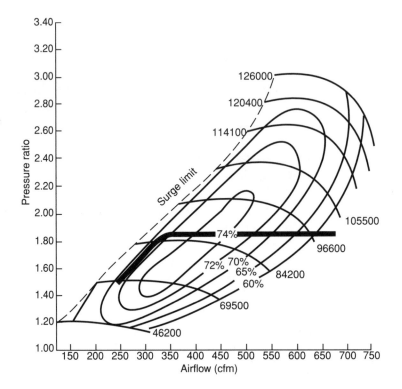

Fig. 3-8. *The Turbonetics H-3 compressor will produce 750 cfm at a pressure ratio of 2.8, but this yields an efficiency of only 60%. Note how the surge line leans sharply to the right, indicating that the H-3 will not work at high boost pressures at low airflow rates.*

Fig. 3-9. *Definition of the exducer bore*

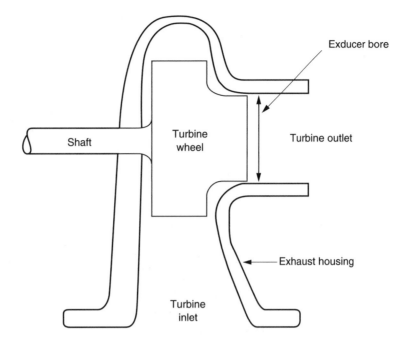

In making this selection, two quantities must be dealt with: basic turbine size and area/radius (A/R) ratio.

BASIC TURBINE SIZE. Consider basic turbine size a measure of the turbine's ability to generate the shaft power required to drive the compressor at the flow rates desired. Larger turbines, therefore, generally offer higher power outputs than smaller turbines. For a large measure of simplicity, turbine size can generally be judged by the turbine's exducer bore. While this is a gross simplification of the science of turbines, it is nevertheless a reasonable representation of the turbine's flow capability.

The graph of exducer bore versus intake cfm is not a selection tool but an approximate size indicator. A reasonable turbine selection method is to con-

Fig. 3-10. *Approximate exducer bore required to power a compressor to a given flow rate*

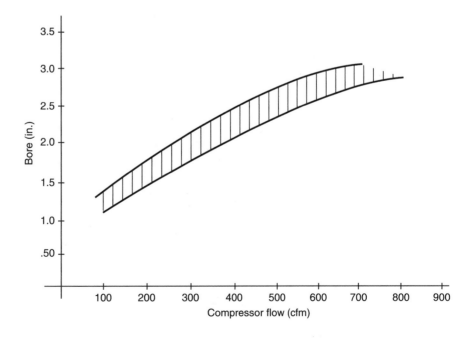

sult the source from whom you are purchasing the turbocharger. Certainly a choice will exist whether to err on the high side or the low side. Again, this choice falls within the scope of the original objectives of the turbo system. I will go for the higher side every time.

CHOOSING AN A/R RATIO. While basic turbine size reflects a measure of the turbine's flow capability, the A/R ratio is a method of fine tuning between basic sizes. To easily grasp the idea of an A/R ratio, imagine the turbine housing as nothing more than a cone wrapped around a shaft to look like a snail. Unwrap this cone and cut off the small end a short distance from the tip. The hole in the end of the cone is the discharge area. The area of this hole is the *A* of the A/R ratio. The size of the hole is significant, as it determines the velocity with which exhaust gases exit the turbine scroll and enter the turbine blades. For any given rate of flow, a smaller exit will require that the gases flow faster. Thus, the area of the exit is important in controlling the velocity of the gases as they enter the turbine blades. This velocity has much to do with controlling the actual speed of the turbine. It is necessary to keep in mind that the area of this exit is the controlling factor in the bad side-effect of exhaust gas back pressure and, thus, reversion into the combustion chambers.

The *R* of the A/R ratio is the distance from the center of the section area in the cone to the center of the turbine shaft. All *A*s divided by their respective *R*s will give the same dividend:

$$\frac{A_1}{R_1} = \frac{A_2}{R_2} = \frac{A_3}{R_3} = \frac{A_4}{R_4} = \frac{A_5}{R_5} = \frac{A_6}{R_6}$$

or

$$\frac{Area}{Radius} = constant$$

The *R* also has a strong influence in controlling turbine speed. If one imagines that the turbine blade tips will travel about as fast as the gas is moving

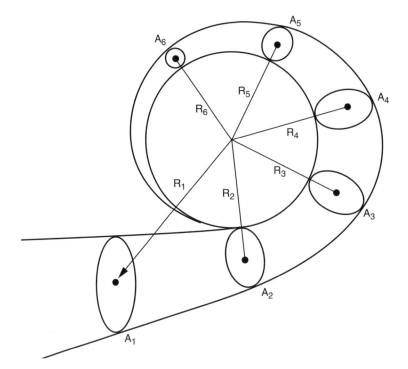

Fig. 3-11. *Definition of the A/R ratio*

when it enters the tip area, it is easy to see that a smaller R will impart a higher rotating speed to the turbine.

Fig. 3-12. To increase turbine speed, which varies with changes of the A/R ratio, it is almost always the discharge area that is changed, with the radius remaining constant.

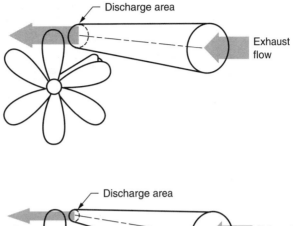

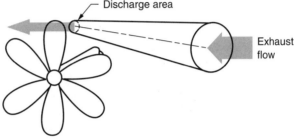

It is of further value to note that a larger R will effectively give the turbine shaft greater torque with which to drive the compressor wheel. The same force (exhaust gas) applied with a greater lever arm (R) puts more torque into the shaft. This, on occasion, can allow a bigger compressor wheel if conditions so require. In practice, however, it is almost always the A that is changed, while the radius remains constant. A simplified approach to choosing the A/R ratio is summed up in Fig. 3-13.

Selecting what appears to be a logical starting point for an A/R ratio is one thing, but actually getting the right one is yet another. Trial and error is usually necessary. A reasonable choice can be judged by the numbers, or to some extent by performance and response. Judging by the numbers requires measurement of exhaust manifold pressure, or turbine inlet pressure, and comparison with boost pressure.

The seat-of-the-pants feel of an improper A/R selection is sluggish boost rise if the ratio is too large. The ratio can be so big as to keep the turbo from turning fast enough to produce the desired boost. If the ratio is on the small side, the turbo response can be so quick as to seem jumpy and difficult to drive smoothly. It will also show up as fading power in the upper third of the engine's rev range. The feel is similar to that of a normally aspirated engine with a very small carburetor. "Choked" is a reasonable description.

Split-Inlet Exhaust Housing

A split-inlet exhaust housing permits the exhaust pulses to be grouped (or separated) by cylinder all the way to the turbine. The merit of doing this is in keeping the individual package of energy, an exhaust putt, intact and unmolested by other putts all the way to the turbine. This can give the turbine a little better kick to get it moving. When you consider the absolute barrage of pulses and energy coming down the tube from an eight-cylinder engine, the

Fig. 3-13. The effect of varying the A/R ratio, all other factors remaining constant

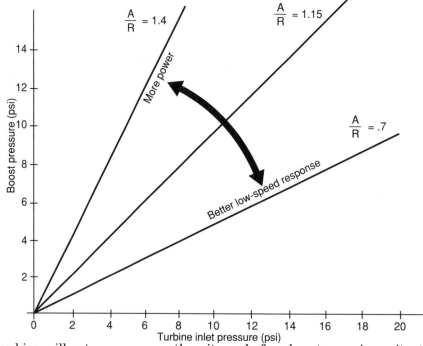

turbine will get more energy than it needs for almost any given situation. Thus, a split housing will make zip for improvement on a single-turbo V-8. A four-cylinder, by comparison, which sees only one putt every 180° of crank rotation, needs all the energy it can get from each pulse. Keeping them separate and undisturbed will therefore pay some dividends.

Fig. 3-14. The split-inlet exhaust housing theoretically offers a small performance advantage by keeping exhaust pulses in a tight bundle all the way to the turbine. This is more effective for engines with fewer cylinders, and thus fewer pulses, per engine cycle.

Two Turbos or One? Several reasons exist for giving false consideration to using two turbos where one might otherwise do the job. Probably the most popular notion of the advantage of two turbos is reduced lag. This notion is generally hard to justify. Half the exhaust energy put through each of two turbines, with inertia proportional to the square and flow proportional to the cube, is not necessarily conducive to producing less lag. Multiple turbos imply more power. Power is, in part, a function of efficiencies. All other things equal, a big turbo is more efficient than a small one. Pizzazz is a reasonable consideration when turbocharging a Ferrari, but the same logic cannot be applied to a turbo installation on a pickup truck. Good reasons do exist for using two turbos. This is particularly true with respect to V-style or horizontally opposed cylinder layouts.

Exhaust manifold design is one of the keys to high power output, and the two-turbo layout inherently offers superior manifold design. The heat loss of the cross tube in V-style engines can be considerable. Remember, it is in part this heat that powers the turbine.

A two-turbo design will usually require two wastegates. Other than the minor problem of synchronizing the two gates, much greater control of turbine speed at low boost pressures can be achieved. The stability of boost pressure at high flow rates is also improved. If remote wastegates are used rather than integrals, the actual exhaust gas flow area can be enlarged by giving the gates their own tailpipes.

Greater turbine discharge area is always an improvement to the system. Turbine discharge pipes from two turbos will virtually always give a large flow increase. For example, two 2 1/4-inch-diameter tubes offer substantially more flow area than just one of 3 inches.

A further reason two turbos offer superiority under certain conditions is that the heat is divided between two mechanisms, allowing each to operate with lower heat input. The heat absorbed into the materials of the turbo is proportional to the temperature of the gases and their mass rate of flow. The temperature will remain the same, but the mass rate of flow will be halved. Thus the operating temperature of the turbo will be reduced, and its life expectancy somewhat improved.

Desirable Features

WATER-COOLED BEARING SECTIONS. The water-cooled bearing is a feature that probably extends the average turbo's useful life by a factor of two. The presence of water flow through a jacket surrounding the bearing chamber greatly reduces temperature rise of the lubricating oil as it passes through the bearings. The reduced temperatures keep the oil from looking like Brand X in the Mobil 1 commercials. Charred oil residue accumulating inside the turbo and eventually blocking the oil flow, thus killing the turbo, is the dread disease called "coked-up bearings." (See chapter 4.) The water-cooled bearing was created because too many end users refused to change oil on a schedule dictated by the turbo. Ironically, the presence of the water-cooled bearing does not offer serious extension of oil-change intervals. Go straight to the best combination possible: water-cooled bearings and frequent oil changes.

TURBO SECTION CLOCKING. The rotation of one turbo section relative to another is called clocking. Although integral wastegates offer a measure of convenience in the design of noncompetition turbo systems, they usually do not allow the three sections of the turbo (turbine, bearing, and compressor) to be rotated 360° with respect to each other. Restrictions on clocking can seriously handicap packaging the turbo system into an engine compartment.

CONNECTIONS TO THE TURBO. The flanges on the turbine housing that connect the turbo to the exhaust manifold and tailpipe are two of the most common failure locations in the entire system. Heat-induced warpage, fastener, and gasket problems are relatively common. In general, flange configurations with more fasteners and thicker sections will endure the heat with fewer problems. Some turbos use a material called Ni-Resist for the exhaust housing. Ni-Resist is high in nickel and offers a worthwhile improvement in high-temperature stability, and thus durability, of the exhaust housing.

The compressor outlet is almost always a hose-style connection. Flexibility in this joint is usually desirable, to accommodate the moving around of the turbo caused by a stack-up of thermal expansions. High-boost-pressure systems may still need to add a connecting bar to the discharge tube, to keep the hose connection intact under the high tensile loads caused by higher boost levels.

Compressor inlets are also generally configured with hose connections. These prove entirely adequate where fuel is not introduced before the turbo. In a draw-through carb application, the use of any hose between the carb and the turbo should be avoided, as fuel will puddle at the hose. A large-diameter hose boss permits a larger-diameter inlet system. Large-diameter, low-flow-loss inlets to the compressor are vital. Insure that all hoses are sufficiently stiff to avoid collapse due to the small vacuum created by the air filter and any associated air flowmeters.

AND FURTHERMORE . . .

How important is turbocharger sizing?

The turbo has got to be the right one for the job. The right turbo will offer a low rpm boost threshold, low system restriction, low charge temperatures, and low exhaust manifold pressure. Anyone with the ability to read and use a telephone can arrive at the right size turbo. No science, no magic, just a little R&D. For example, do you want the very lowest boost threshold? Well, maybe, if you drive only in five o'clock traffic. That is the only value a low boost threshold has. Be assured, the lower the boost threshold, the less the horsepower. On the other hand, if maximum power is your bag, the turbo size required probably

Fig. 3-15. *The turbo bearing section with a water jacket offers extended turbo life and longer oil-change intervals.*

won't produce any boost until the upper half of the rev range. This is impractical for the flexible requirements of a street turbo. Compromise at both ends is necessary. Don't fall for the journalistic gag that the merit of a turbocharger system is how soon it will produce boost.

Does the brand of turbocharger affect performance?

No. Virtually all turbo units are durable, responsive, and efficient. The performance of a kit is in no way related to the turbo brand unless that brand is the only proper size available for the application. Some designs feature integral wastegates. These wastegates tend to require a bit more work to make them as effective as remote wastegates. In that situation the brand affects performance, but it's because of the integral wastegate.

Do twin turbos offer any advantage?

Sometimes. An engine with flow capabilities greater than 300 cfm (roughly 180 cid) can benefit from two turbos. Two little turbos can slightly cut turbo lag, as opposed to one large turbo, and allow a better balance of low-speed and top-end boost performance. Over 350 cid, twin turbos become a virtual necessity. Do not accept the idea that twin turbos are inherently more powerful, as too many other factors are involved.

What does compressor efficiency mean, and why is it important?

Compressor efficiency means nothing more than the real temperature of the air coming out of the turbo under boost relative to a calculated number based on thermodynamic equations. Calculate one, measure the other, divide the calculated by the measured, and you have compressor efficiency. Matching a compressor's efficiency to a particular engine is important, in that getting maximum efficiency somewhere near the power peak or maximum rpm means that the compressor has induced the lowest possible thermal load. "Highly efficient" is a goofy expression invented by casual writers about turbos to mean nothing more than that whatever vehicle a turbo is on gets boost at low speeds. If something can be exactly wrong, this is an example of it. Low-speed boost means small compressors that are inefficient at high speed. Thus, they produce high temperatures and are quite the opposite of "highly efficient."

Does exhaust manifold pressure influence performance?

Yes. Exhaust manifold pressure is a measure of how well the turbine unit is sized for the engine. Exhaust manifold pressure should not exceed approximately two and a half times the boost pressure. It is tempting for kit makers to use turbines too small for the job just to show a psi of boost at low rpm. Low rpm boost can be nice, but to overdo it means a severe (20% or so) loss of power above mid-range rpm. A proper balance of low versus top end is a development problem every kit maker should go through. Generally, less exhaust manifold pressure means more bhp. In other words, bigger turbines go faster.

4 TURBOCHARGER LUBRICATION

The problem of lubricating a shaft spinning inside a sleeve-type journal bearing was solved many years ago. No new science was necessary when the turbocharger came along, even though it presented a couple of new twists. The new twists were the tremendous heat in the turbine side and the cumulative damage to the oil by the migration of this heat into the bearing section. The heat deteriorates the oil and quickly makes it unusable. Solutions to these new twists on the oiling problem have always been readily available but have just recently been implemented. Reasons for delay, one presumes, were economics and fear of sales resistance. The economic aspect of the oil problem was the OEMs' reluctance to increase prices by the amount necessary to put a water-cooling jacket around the bearing section. The sales problem was the reluctance of the sales department to tell the consumer he must change the engine oil with greater frequency—fear, I suppose, that the end user would shy away from what incorrectly appeared to be a high-maintenance product. It's just another example of the sad state of affairs when sales and accounting overrule sound engineering. The story ends on an upbeat note, however, as virtually all OEM turbo cars now have water-cooled bearings and the recommendation of frequent oil changes. Had this state of affairs existed from the start of production of OEM turbos, the English language would be missing the less-than-colorful phrase "coked-up turbo bearings." Pity.

Fig. 4-1. A bearing section and shaft with heavy deposits of charred oil can expect an imminent demise. A coked-up bearing is the result of using oil with insufficient high-temperature stability and/or not changing oil with sufficient frequency.

What Causes a Coked-up Bearing?

Coking is nothing more than charred oil residue accumulating in the turbo bearing section to such an extent that the proper flow of oil to the bearing is eventually blocked. The seriously compromised oil flow will kill the turbo in short order. Four things gang up on the turbo to cause a coking problem:

- Oil with inadequate high-temperature capability
- Oil with a wide multiviscosity range
- Extended oil-change intervals
- Excessive heat in the bearing section

Dealing with these problems and the mechanics of a clean, cool oil supply is the focus of this chapter.

☞ **RULE:** If your turbo suffers a coked bearing failure, check your own maintenance diligence before cursing the turbo.

Selecting a Lubricating Oil

The selection of a type, grade, and brand of engine oil should be done with some forethought and perhaps even a little R&D. Please weed out all old family biases toward Rosie's Red Re-Refined 'cause Dad used it back on the farm and wouldn't hear of usin' nothin' else. Dad may not have changed much over the years, but engine oil and tractors have made progress measured in orders of magnitude.

Here's what you need to do: First, get a feel for what the lubricant is supposed to do for your engine and what special requirements your situation imposes on the lube. These data will tell you what type of oil will best fit your needs. Second, consider the climate and operating conditions the lube must endure. This info tells you what viscosity and level of severity (grade) lube will do the best job for you. In general, it is best to avoid wide-range, multiviscosity oils, as the materials added that create the multiviscosity capability are the same materials that cause the coking. Thus 20W–50 is clearly better turbo oil than 10W–50. A straight viscosity is best of all, with a ten-point higher viscosity in summer. If it is possible to determine the detergent rating and antioxidizing rating, good turbo oil will be high in these two categories.

Now you know the type and grade of lube that is your best choice. The one remaining factor is the brand to buy. This boils down to availability, price, and what your R&D efforts tell you is truly *the* lubricant for your engine. One can be relatively certain that an oil formulated for turbo use, and so advertised, will be an adequate lubricant.

Types of Lubricants

There are two choices here: synthetic-based or mineral-based lube.

Synthetic lubes are manufactured fluids (not necessarily from oil) in which the basic structure of the lube is much more rigidly controlled than in standard hydrocarbon oils. The resultant product is a very consistent, stable fluid with uniform molecular structure, whose properties are highly predictable. Synthetics have clearly demonstrated their capability with respect to frictional losses, high-temperature stability, and basic toughness of the molecular structure. Mineral-based lubes are less expensive and more likely to coke.

Water-Cooled Bearing Housings

The turbo bearing housing with a water jacket around the bearing chamber has virtually eliminated the problem of oil coking. The cooling capability of the water is such that the oil seldom reaches the temperature at which it begins to break down. Of course, all oil subject to high-temperature use breaks down slowly over time, so the need for periodic oil changes still exists. The oil-change interval thus becomes only slightly less than with an atmospheric engine.

Fig. 4-2. A water jacket incorporated into the turbo bearing housing and connected to the engine cooling system carries away most of the heat that migrates from the exhaust side to the bearing section. Lubricating oil is guarded from temperature levels high enough to cause coking.

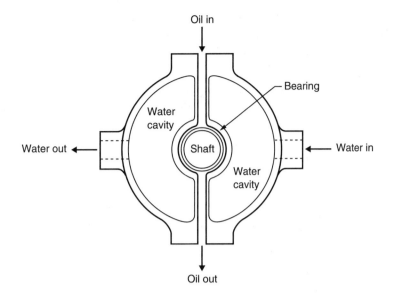

Fig. 4-3. Temperature comparison of water-cooled and non-water-cooled bearings, illustrating temperature magnitudes and distributions in the turbo bearing section. The non-water-cooled housing can cause some constant damage to the oil. With 2000-mile oil change intervals, the damaged particles of oil will be removed and not cause coking.

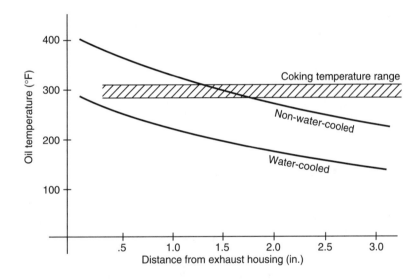

Oil Flow and Pressure Requirements

The turbo survives with surprisingly low oil pressure and flow. It is virtually certain that all engines in production today have enough excess oil-pumping capacity to adequately take on the additional requirement of lubricating the turbo. If you know a particular engine was shortchanged in the oiling area on original design, it is certainly a good idea to fix it. However, fix it for the engine's sake and not for the additional burden of the turbo. Observe the basic lower limits of oil pressure and flow published by the turbo manufacturer and you can't go wrong as far as lubrication is concerned.

Too much oil pressure can create problems with turbos. It is possible to force oil past oil seals that are in perfect condition if oil pressure exceeds 65 to 70 psi at the turbo. If a particular engine creates more oil pressure than the seals can handle, it may be necessary to install a restrictor or bypass system to reduce pressure at the turbo.

Problems of oil pressure overpowering the seal are evident in a frequent if not quite constant smoking problem. Anytime oil pressure exceeds the 65–70

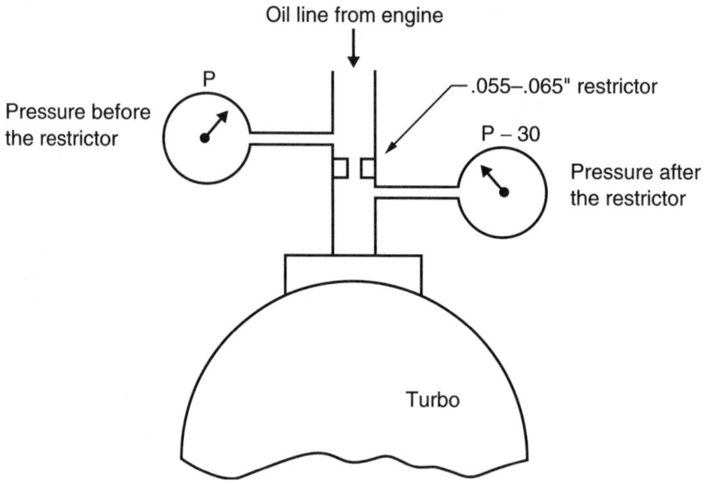

Fig. 4-4. *Oil pressure reduction at the turbo by a restrictor. Use of a restrictor requires that pressure available to the turbo bearings be measured and proven adequate.*

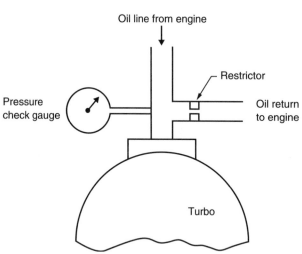

Fig. 4-5. *Oil pressure reduction at the turbo by a bypass. This is more reliable than a restrictor in the oil feed line, but the pressure at the bearings must still be known.*

psi range and smoking persists, a restrictor or bypass should be installed prior to any other changes.

These are good guidelines for virtually all turbos:

	Min. pressure (psi)	**Min. flow** (gal/min)
Idle, hot	5	0.1
Maximum load	25	0.5

Oil Coolers

Adding an oil cooler to a high-performance engine is often contemplated in the expectation of improving engine durability. Although it usually does, don't be too hasty to rush out and buy a huge oil cooler without investigating the real requirements of your engine. Oil prefers to operate in a given temperature range that supplies the viscosity needs for protecting the engine, doesn't overheat the oil on the high end and, when cool, doesn't add more drag to the system than necessary. These requirements are all easily met by the right oil type and viscosity operating in the correct temperature range.

Mineral-based oils are not as tolerant of high temperatures as are synthetic oils. For street engines, both synthetic and mineral-based oils have the same lower temperature requirement (150°F minimum), but synthetics can operate to about 40°F higher (270°F versus 230°F for mineral-based). Therefore, you

Fig. 4-6. Oil system fittings and lines must withstand high temperatures and pressures, the hydrocarbon environment, and vibration. This oil feed-line installation, with insulation and supporting bracket removed, reveals the sturdiness required, such that oil feed to the turbo is never a problem.

may need an oil cooler if you use mineral-based oil and perhaps not if you use synthetic.

It needs to be understood that oil temperatures below these minimums will degrade durability just as surely as exceeding the maximums. The installation of an oil temperature gauge will tell the whole story. Do that before installing an expensive oil cooler system. There are occasions when both oil and water temperatures are on the high side but neither is out of bounds. This situation is ideal for an oil cooler, which will remove enough extra heat from the entire system to also reduce the water temperature. The presence of a good oil cooler can easily drop the water temperature by 15°. The thermostatically controlled oil system is a good idea: the oil must reach a certain preset temperature before the thermostat diverts it to the oil cooler. Do keep in mind that unlike water cooling systems, the thermostatically controlled oil system will *not* require the oil to reach the minimum acceptable operating temperature, because the oil thermostat does not block the oil flow but merely diverts it. It has nothing to do with the maximum temperatures either.

Oil Filters

The turbo creates no special filtering requirements. It is certainly within the acceptable range of reason, however, that the real motorhead may want to care for his high-performance engine a bit better than relying on the stock filtration equipment. A wide variety of good components are available.

Oil to and from the Turbo

The plumbing that feeds oil to the turbo and drains it back to the engine is perhaps the weak link in the entire scheme of turbocharging. This is definitely the place for a fifteen-cent part to fail and take out a seven-hundred-dollar turbo —or, worse yet, an engine bearing. The following should be considered minimum requirements. Do a thorough job, and don't hesitate a minute to spend even more $ attempting to establish bragging rights on building the fail-safe turbo lube system.

The oil lines feeding the turbo must meet the requirements of pressure and temperature (use twice the oil-temperature maximum allowable) and be hydrocarbon-proof. Metal-braid-protected lines are highly desirable from the standpoint of abrasion, chafing, and vibration resistance. Use caution in allowing the metal braid line to touch anything, as it will frequently damage the other item if relative motion exists. For example, a stainless steel braid line rubbing on an aluminum valve cover will abrade a slot right into the cover. Anchor the oil line in several places to eliminate relative motion, and support the

Fig. 4-7. Top: *The oil-line brace at the frame forces the oil line and fittings to carry loads induced by engine rocking. The motion must be absorbed by the short distance "A"; therefore, the loads are potentially large and damaging.* **Bottom:** *With the brace attached to the engine, the fittings will not experience any bending load. All flexing of the oil line occurs over the long, flexible portion "B", inducing only low stresses and helping to eliminate failures.*

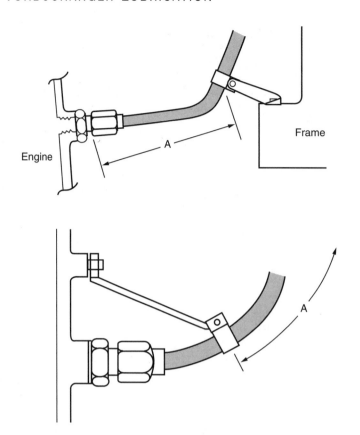

end fittings. Support of the oil lines near the end fittings will eliminate fatigue-induced failures of these fittings.

Oil Drain System

Oil return line design is even more stringent than oil feed line design. Even the position of the turbo relative to the engine should take into account the requirements of positioning the oil drain line. The turbo must be positioned high enough to allow a downhill drain to the oil sump. The focus of the problem is that the oil seals in the turbo do not operate well if they are completely bathed in oil. Oil that has passed through the turbo bearings must be free to drain out quickly and without any serious restriction. Gravity is the only force available to rid the bearing section of oil, and gravity is, by all relative standards, a wimp.

The layout of the oil drain system has a few fundamentals that should be observed:

EXIT ANGLE FROM THE TURBO. Virtually all turbos allow a 360° rotation of the bearing section relative to the exhaust and intake housings. This is to permit a near-vertical downward alignment of the oil drain hole. Vertical is the ideal alignment, but where necessary, the deviation may be as great as 30°.

SIZE OF DRAIN HOSE. Where possible, a minimum inside diameter of 1/2 inch should be observed. It is frequently necessary to compromise the 1/2-inch ID, and this is permissible when other factors are favorable. For example, a 1/4-inch ID restriction at the fitting where the oil passes back into the engine may work just fine, but it is unlikely to work at all at the turbo end of the line. Keep in mind that no oil pressure exists after the bearing, and low-pressure flow requires much greater flow area for equal flow rates.

ROUTING OF THE DRAIN HOSE. Ideally, the drain hose should swoop smoothly downward and arc gently over into the oil pan with no kinks, sharp bends, or rises. Equipment hanging off the side of the engine rarely permits the ideal to

Fig. 4-8. Oil inlet and outlet drain positions. These must always be within 30° of vertical to assure a gravity drain from the bearing section back to the oil sump.

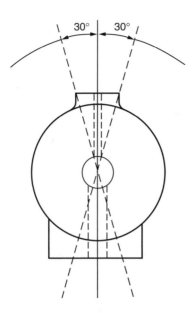

Fig. 4-9. A variety of methods exist to attach the oil drain fitting to the sump. Sturdiness and the least number of parts determine the joint's merit.

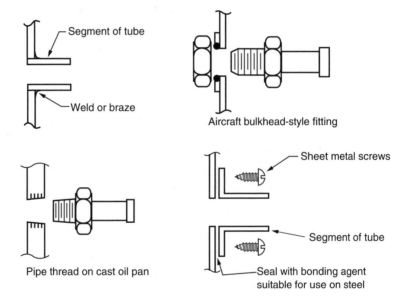

be achieved. Effort and forethought are necessary here. Keep the hose clear of heat radiated from the exhaust housing and manifolding. Insure that it is not subject to damage from road debris or is suitably protected.

Special Requirements for Low-Mounted Turbos

Situations frequently dictate mounting the turbo so low in the chassis that gravity drain back to the oil pan is out of the question. While gravity is still the prime mover to get the oil out of the bearing cavity, a sump or small reservoir immediately below the turbo will be necessary to collect the oil, which can then be returned to the engine oil sump via a pump system. Perhaps the cleverest device in this circumstance is the oil-pressure- powered scavenge pump. The oil flow to the turbo is used to power a pump that in turn scavenges the oil sump.

Oil System Aids

A wide variety of devices on the market endeavor to provide oil flow to the turbo bearings when the engine is not running. These mechanisms are attempting to solve three basic problems, as perceived by their designers:

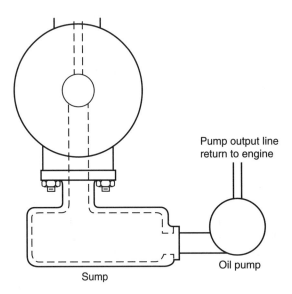

Fig. 4-10. An oil sump is required for a low-mounted turbo when a gravity drain is not possible. Electrical and mechanical pumps can do the job well. High flow capability should be avoided, as the risk of cavitation will be greater.

Pump output line return to engine

Oil pump

Sump

- supplying lubricant to the turbo prior to start-up, to replace oil that drains away while the turbo is stationary
- supplying lubricant to the turbo after engine shut-off stops the oil pump
- pumping a given amount of oil through the turbo after shut-off, to help remove heat from the bearing cavity, reducing the oil's tendency to coke

While all these intentions are honorable enough, there are a few flaws in the scheme:

- All of the oil does not flow out of the turbo bearing. Further, the turbo does not leap into action on start-up. Rather, it achieves a rotational speed at idle similar to that of your ceiling fan.
- When an engine is turned off, the instant the spark is discontinued, heat available to the turbo for its driving power is removed, and the turbo stops. Generally, the turbo will stop before the engine's rotation ceases. A nonrotating turbo needs no lubrication.
- Removing heat from the turbo is always a good idea. However, a turbo that is already air cooled, oil cooled, and probably water cooled is going to enjoy little extra benefit from one more quart or so of oil pumped through it to cool it. Not cost-effective.

Determine precisely what an oil system aid will do for you and for the manner in which you operate your automobile. If the aid suits your needs, buy it, and good luck to you.

AND FURTHERMORE . . .

What is all that jazz about coking your turbo bearings?

Although I tend to think journalists are responsible for coked turbo bearings, it might be that never changing the oil is a more likely culprit. In actual practice, if one lets the engine idle for 30 seconds before shutdown, changes the oil every 2000 miles, and uses high-quality oil, turbo lubrication failures aren't going to happen. Water-cooled bearings assure that bearing housing temperatures never reach the oil breakdown temperature. Please resist the idea of "oilers and lubers" (oil system aids) as the savior of turbo bearings. The advertised merit of these devices is based on fallacious information. In my opinion, they are worthless.

5 INTERCOOLING

$\mathbf{A}$n intercooler is slowly but surely becoming recognized as a fundamental part of a turbocharger system. It never has been, nor should ever be, considered icing on the cake. A proper intercooler is more cake.

The intercooler is a radiator—or, more correctly, a heat exchanger—positioned between the turbo and the intake manifold. Its sole purpose is to get the heat out of the intake charge that the turbo put into the charge while compressing it. On the surface then, the merit of an intercooler should be judged by its success in removing that heat. Unfortunately, this is only part of the story, as the mere presence of the intercooler creates a variety of other complications. Maximizing the merits of an intercooler while minimizing the problems it can bring is the engineering problem that must be solved before one can create an intercooled turbo system.

Fig. 5-1. General layout of the intercooled turbocharger system

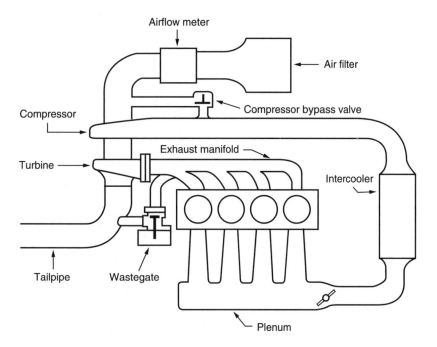

☞ **RULE:** It is absolutely incorrect to think that "any intercooler is better than no intercooler."

Removing heat from the intake charge has two huge areas of merit. First, the reduction of temperature makes the intake charge denser. The increase in density is proportional to the change in temperature (measured on the absolute scale). Denser intake charges make more power. Second, but no less important, is the terrific benefit to the combustion process brought about by

Fig. 5-2. *The front-mounted intercooler is a typical aftermarket replacement for the Buick GN/GNX series cars.*

reduced temperatures in the intake charge. Detonation is reduced by any reduction in intake temperatures. These two areas of merit are the reasons a proper intercooler can increase the power and/or margin of safety of the turbocharged engine. For a discussion of the testing procedures involved in evaluating an intercooler system, please refer to Chapter 14.

Design Criteria   Design criteria for creating an intercooler are many and varied. These criteria will outline the considerations for building an intercooler that maximizes heat removal and minimizes boost-pressure loss and any lag increases.

HEAT TRANSFER AREA. Heat transfer area is the sum of all the plates and shells in the heat exchanger core that are responsible for transmitting heat out of the system. Easy to see that the greater the heat transfer area, the more efficient the intercooler. This is not a case, however, where twice the area doubles the efficiency. A 10% increase in core will net you about 10% of the amount you did not get out the first time. Therefore, every 10% increase will become less and less important. For example, if an existing intercooler core measures 70% effi-

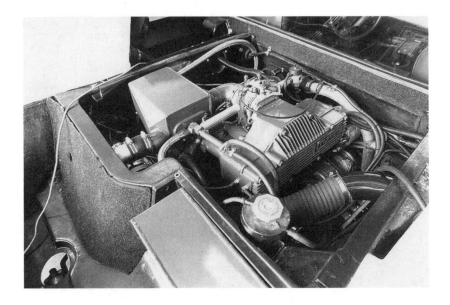

Fig. 5-3. *A water-based heat exchanger has been added to this Lotus Esprit.*

cient, a 10% core increase should yield about 10% of that missing 30%, or a new efficiency of 73%.

INTERNAL FLOW AREA. Streamlining inside a core is bad by design. The harder it is for air to find its way through a core, the more likely it will give up its heat—obviously the major objective. But the bad side is that this poor streamlining can cause large boost-pressure drops. To compensate for bad streamlining, the internal flow area must be made large enough to really slow the air down inside the intercooler, so as to reduce flow drag and keep pressure losses to acceptable levels.

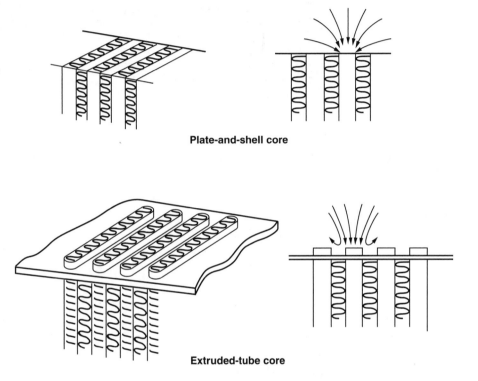

Fig. 5-4. The two most popular intercooler core styles are plate-and-shell (top) and extruded-tube (bottom). The plate style generally offers less flow resistance, whereas the extruded-tube style tends to be more efficient. The "tubes" are typically 1/4" wide by 1 1/2–3" long.

Plate-and-shell core

Extruded-tube core

☞ **RULE:** The single most important aspect of intercooler design is low internal pressure loss.

INTERNAL VOLUME. All of the volume internal to the intercooler system must be pressurized before that amount of pressure will exist in the intake manifold. Although this volume is not a large contribution to lag, it is nevertheless a design factor to optimize in the process of creating a good intercooler system. It is a good idea to keep track of the volume and constantly attempt to keep the excess down. A reasonable judgment of the volume's relationship to lag can be made by dividing the internal volume by the flow rate through the system at the rpm at which throttle is applied and multiplying by 2. (The factor of 2 results from the approximate doubling of airflow through the system when going from cruise to boost.) The approximate lag time is given by

$$Time = \frac{V}{flow\ rate} \times 2$$

Fig. 5-5. *An air duct can provide adequate ambient airflow to a horizontally mounted intercooler.*

Example:

Let volume of intake = 500 cu in. and flow rate = 150 cfm at a cruise speed of approximately 2000 rpm.

Then

$$Time = \frac{500\ in^3}{150\ \dfrac{ft^3}{min}} \times \frac{60\ \dfrac{sec}{min}}{1728\ \dfrac{in^3}{ft^3}} \times 2 = 0.23\ sec$$

It is distinctly possible to upset the basic throttle response if an engine is equipped with an airflow meter positioned too far from the throttle body. Opening the throttle causes a low-pressure pulse to be created that travels upstream toward the airflow meter. The time it takes this pulse to reach the flowmeter and cause it to react is indeed the delay in throttle response. Typically, such a pulse must travel from the throttle body to the intercooler, through the intercooler, back to the turbo, then to the flowmeter, in order for the flowmeter to register a response. It is not until the flowmeter receives this pulse that the air/fuel ratio can change to account for new load conditions in the engine. I should point out that there are exceptions here, based on the style of throttle-position sensor with which the engine is equipped. Nonetheless, it is generally true that the farther the throttle is from the airflow meter, the poorer the throttle response. Thus, this path length should receive some consideration in the design process.

When an engine is equipped with a speed density type of EFI system, wherein no airflow meter is utilized, or a blow-through carbureted turbo system, the length of the intake tract can extend into the next county with no negative results insofar as throttle response is concerned.

The overall problem in designing an intercooler system, then, lies in maximizing the ability of the system to remove heat from the compressed air while not adversely affecting boost pressure, losing throttle response, or contributing to any delay in boost rise.

Calculating the Value of an Intercooler

The change in density of the intake charge can be measured relative to the temperature change brought about by the intercooler. For example, suppose a turbo has a compressor discharge temperature of 200°F above atmospheric temperature, that is, about 740° absolute on an 80°F day. (Zero degrees absolute is about 460°F.; add 80° to get 540°; 200° above that temperature is, therefore, 740° absolute.) If we insert a 60% efficient intercooler into the system, we would remove $0.6 \times 200°\,\text{F} = 120°\text{F}$ from the system, leaving a gain of just $80°\text{F}$ rather than $200°\text{F}$, or an absolute of $540° + 80° = 620°$. The density change can then be determined by the ratio of the original absolute temperature to the final absolute temperature:

$$Density\ change\ =\ \frac{original\ absolute\ temperature}{final\ absolute\ temperature} - 1$$

$$=\frac{540+200}{540+80}-1\ =\ 0.19\ =\ 19\%$$

Therefore, this intercooler will yield a gain of about 19%. This means that 19% more air molecules will be in the combustion chamber than otherwise would have been. All other things remaining equal, one would expect a similar gain in power. This, unfortunately, doesn't come about, because of pressure losses caused by the aerodynamic drag inside the intercooler.

The corresponding power loss due to boost-pressure loss can be estimated by calculating the ratio of absolute pressure with the intercooler to that without the intercooler and subtracting it from 100%.

Example:

If 2 psi out of 10 are lost due to intercooler drag,

$$Power\ loss\ =\ 1-\frac{14.7+8}{14.7+10}\ =\ 0.08\ =\ 8\%$$

This indicates that flow losses through the intercooler amount to 8%.

The idea that the lost boost can easily be recovered by adjusting the wastegate, while attractive, is not quite correct. Certainly, if boost is increased the power will rise, but one consequence of this is that turbine inlet pressure will rise if you attempt to drive the turbo yet harder. More turbine inlet pressure creates more reversion, which creates more combustion chamber heat, which reduces charge densities—and on and on. Thus, one can see that to some extent, recovering lost power by turning up the boost is in part an exercise in chasing one's tail. 'Tis far superior to design and build the mythical zero-loss intercooler.

Fig. 5-6. Intercooling taken seriously.

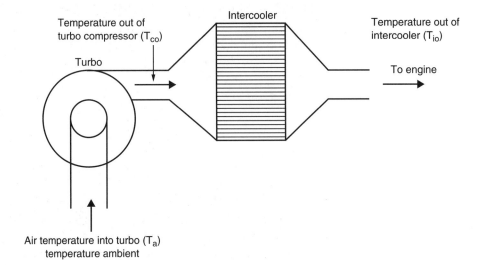

Fig. 5-7. Calculating intercooler efficiency

Calculating the Efficiency of an Intercooler

The idea here is to compare the temperature rise of the intake air caused by the turbo to the amount of heat removed by the intercooler.

Temperature rise through the compressor is compressor outlet temperature (T_{co}) minus ambient temperature (T_a).

$$Temperature\ rise\ =\ T_{co} - T_a$$

Heat removed by the intercooler is the temperature difference between air exiting the compressor (T_{co}) and air exiting the intercooler (T_{io}).

$$Temperature\ removed\ =\ T_{co} - T_{io}$$

Intercooler efficiency (E_i) is then the temperature removed divided by the temperature rise:

$$E_i = \frac{T_{co} - T_{io}}{T_{co} - T_a}$$

Fig. 5-8. An air/air intercooler mounted in the Nissan 280 ZX.

Fig. 5-9. *A water-based intercooler mounted in an '87 Mazda RX7.*

Example:
Let $T_a = 80°F$, $T_{co} = 250°F$, and $T_{io} = 110°F$.
Then

$$E_i = \frac{250 - 110}{250 - 80} = 0.824 = 82.4\%$$

Choosing the Type of Intercooler

Currently, there are two types of intercoolers suitable for street use, the air/air unit and the air/water unit. Each has its own areas of merit. The decision about which is most suitable for a particular application is based on the merits of each with regard to the configuration of the vehicle.

The air/air unit will generally have greater simplicity, greater thermal efficiency at high speeds, greater reliability, lower maintenance, and lower cost. The air/water unit will generally have better thermal efficiency at low speeds, better throttle response when a mass-flowmeter-equipped EFI system is present, lower boost-pressure loss, and less compressor surge. Space requirements or plumbing complications may dictate that an adequately sized air/air unit cannot be used. Thus the choice is sometimes made without any further consideration.

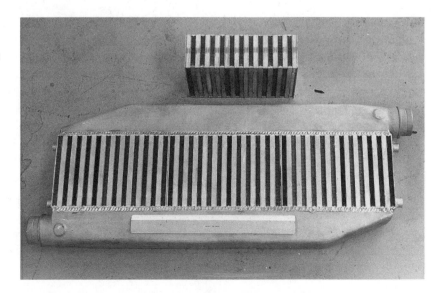

Fig. 5-10. *Plate-style intercooler cores offer a good balance of ambient vs. charge air flow areas.*

Design of the Air/Air Intercooler

A variety of factors must receive equal and adequate attention when configuring the air/air IC. A truly balanced and optimum design is just a case of working at the details until all facets of the layout are within the specifications outlined in the following paragraphs.

INTERNAL FLOW AREA. A large part of the pressure loss through the IC system is determined by the internal flow area of the heat exchanger cores.

$$Internal\ flow\ area\ =\ channel\ length\ \times channel\ width \times number\ of\ channels$$

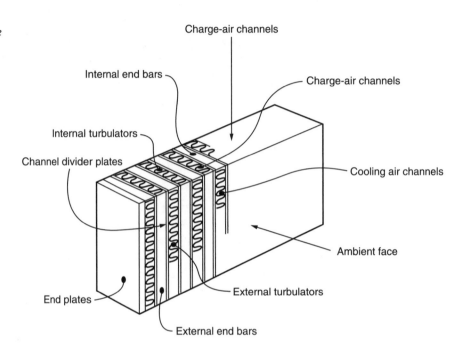

Fig.5-11. Nomenclature of the intercooler core. The charge air face receives charge air from the turbo. The ambient air face is positioned to receive oncoming cooling air. End bars and plates (typically 1/8" thick), brazed to the outside surfaces, provide spacing and rigidity. Turbulators promote exchange of heat from the tubes to the channel divider plates and from there to ambient air through the cooling air channels.

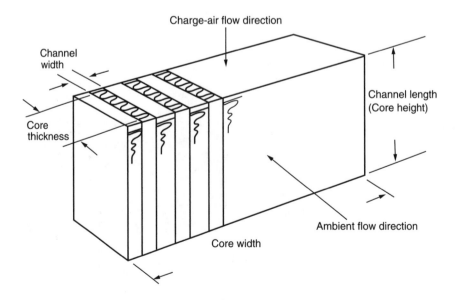

Fig.5-12. Measurement of core flow area

There is no magic formula for calculating a correct flow area for a given cfm capability, but experience has shown that figure 5-13 consistently yields satisfactory results.

If it were not for the turbulators, which are double-edged swords here, we could make do with much less flow area, but we would experience considerably less heat transfer. The turbulator's job is to see that no laminar flow ever exists inside the core. When this is done well, each charge air molecule will get its chance to snuggle up to the core walls and exchange its heat energy with the wall. If turbulators are dense, heat exchange is better, but flow loss is greater. Conversely, no turbulators at all would yield minimal flow losses, but heat exchange would be lousy. If space is available for a large amount of core material, one can logically choose a core with dense turbulators and trade high turbulator drag for large internal flow areas. The reverse is equally correct: where space is severely limited, a core with low-density turbulators should be selected.

CORE SIZING. Once internal flow area has been calculated, actual core size and shape can be determined. With most cores, approximately 45% of the charge air face is available for entry into the air tubes. To find the required area of the charge air face, divide the internal flow area by this 45% figure. Cores are typically available in thicknesses of 2 and 3 inches, channel lengths (heights) of 6, 8, 10, and 12 inches, and widths of 9, 18, and 24 inches (which can be cut to any intermediate width with a bandsaw). Cores with longer channels are available, but they tend to reduce internal flow area, as indicated in figs. 5-20 and 5-21.

Example:

Let flow rate = 500 cfm. Fig. 5-13 indicates that a typical intercooler would require an internal flow area of approximately 25 sq in.

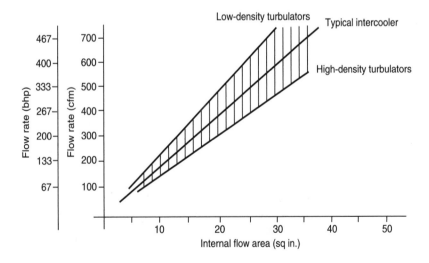

Fig. 5-13. *Estimating internal flow area required in the core*

Therefore,

$$Area\ of\ charge\ air\ face\ =\ \frac{25\ in.^2}{0.45}\ =\ 56\ in.^2$$

For a 3-inch-thick core,

$$Width\ =\ \frac{56\ in.^2}{3\ in.}\ =\ 19\ in.$$

For a 2-inch-thick core,

$$Width = \frac{56 \ in.^2}{2 \ in.} = 28 \ in.$$

If space is available for the 2-inch-thick core, efficiency will prove slightly superior, due to the greater width and consequent greater frontal area. Although the thinner core is a better choice, the thicker core is entirely adequate.

The length of the air channels (height) multiplied by the width of the core is the actual frontal area.

FRONTAL AREA. In many respects, frontal area reflects the amount of ambient air that goes through the core to cool the intake charge. The greater the mass of ambient air that can get through the core, the greater the cooling capability. The actual rate of flow is the product of the forward speed and the frontal area of the core.

Fig. 5-14. *Estimating cooling air available to the intercooler*

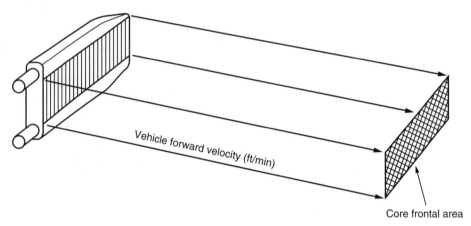

Core frontal area

$$Airflow \ rate = s \times a$$

Example:
Let $s = 60$ mph and $a = 2$ sq ft

$$Airflow \ rate = 60 \ \frac{mi}{hr} \times 2 \ ft^2 \times 5280 \ \frac{ft}{mi} \times \frac{1}{60} \ \frac{hr}{min} = 10,560 \ cfm$$

Thus, it is obvious that of two cores with virtually equal internal flow area, the one with the greater frontal area should prove superior.

CORE STREAMLINING. Streamlining represents the ease with which ambient air can get through the core. Certainly, the easier the air moves through the core, the greater will be the rate of flow and, hence, the greater the cooling effect. For example, if the charge air tubes in the core present a rounded edge to incoming ambient air, the rate of flow is likely to be somewhat greater. An engineering factor missing from all core data published is an ambient air drag coefficient.

DUCTS. A duct is, in a large sense, a form of streamlining of the core. The ducts present the air molecules with no alternative but to go on through the core. Do not underestimate the ability of a duct to improve the efficiency of the intercooler. I would suggest that an improvement of 20% is possible, good duct

Fig. 5-15. *This extruded tube style core is designed for the air/air intercooler application.*

Fig. 5-16. *Ambient airflow through the core is proportional to the external drag coefficient of the core. The rounded-edged extruded-type core will permit more cooling airflow.*

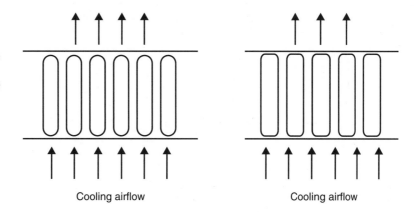

Cooling airflow   Cooling airflow

versus none. When constructing ducts, it is decidedly worth the extra effort to insure that the air molecules have no alternative but to go through the core. That is, seal all edges, corners, and joints.

It is not necessary for the duct inlet to be as big as the frontal area of the IC core. A rule of thumb is that the duct inlet should be at least one-fourth the core area. This rather strange situation is brought about by the fact that less

Fig. 5-17. *Minimum duct inlet area should not drop below one-quarter of the core area.*

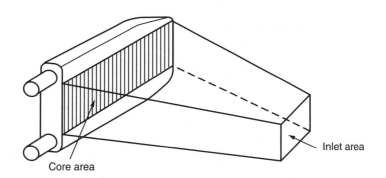

Core area   Inlet area

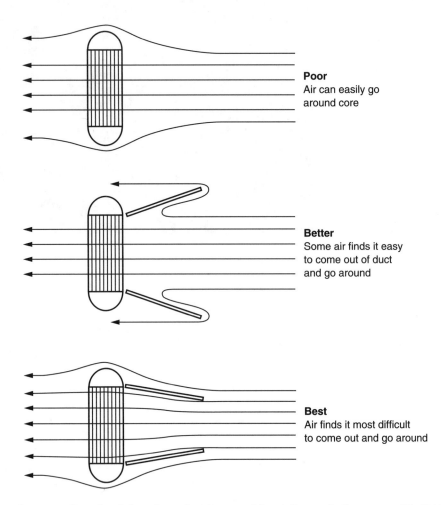

Fig. 5-18. Proper ducting will force more cooling air through the intercooler.

Poor
Air can easily go around core

Better
Some air finds it easy to come out of duct and go around

Best
Air finds it most difficult to come out and go around

than one-fourth of the air molecules would get through the core with little or no attention to ducting.

CORE THICKNESS. Choosing the thickness of the intercooler core is a bit of a juggling act similar to the turbulators. The juggling act is brought about by the fact that the second half of any core does only one-fourth the work.

Adding thickness to the core will indeed improve efficiency, but the gains become less and less. Another negative effect is brought into play by increasing the thickness: the increasing difficulty of getting the ambient air to pass through the core. Essentially, then, the drag coefficient of the core goes up as thickness increases. A clever way to package cores where frontal area is scarce and depth abundant is the staggered-core IC, discussed later.

☞ **RULE:** When viewing intercooler designs, regard thick core layouts as less than well thought out.

CORE FLOW DIRECTION. When adequate space exists for a large IC, the decision must be made about the direction in which to orient the core. Unless overwhelming reasons dictate otherwise, the core should always be constructed to provide the greatest possible internal flow area. The direction of flow is unimportant. For example, the ICs in figure 5-15 take up the same space, but the vertical-flow unit has more internal area and, hence, considerably less restriction.

Fig. 5-19. *Increasing core thickness does not proportionally increase heat transfer capability. Each increment of core thickness will receive hotter cooling air.*

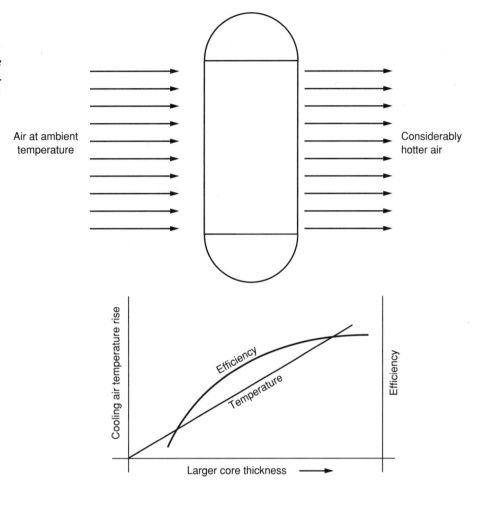

Air at ambient temperature

Considerably hotter air

Cooling air temperature rise

Efficiency

Temperature

Efficiency

Larger core thickness

Fig. 5-20. *The top and bottom cores have the same frontal area, heat transfer area, and efficiency, but the bottom core has much greater internal flow area, due to the larger number of tubes— and, therefore, lower pressure loss.*

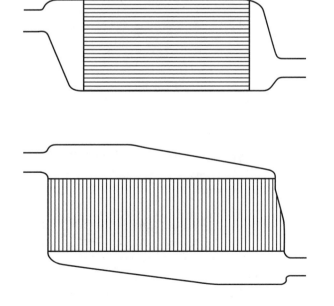

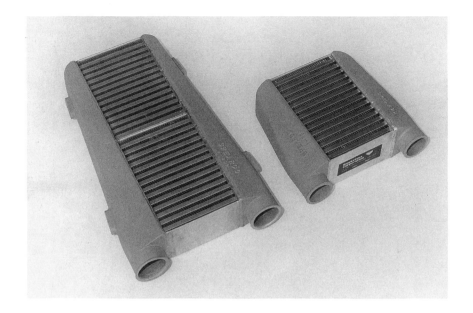

Fig. 5-21. *This is the proper way to make a bigger intercooler. Always increase the core area by adding a greater number of internal passageways. Do not just make the same number of passages longer.*

INTERCOOLER END TANK DESIGN.   Several details in the design of the end tanks fitted to the IC cores can both improve thermal efficiency and decrease flow losses. It is certainly *not* a good idea to suggest that all those molecules of air

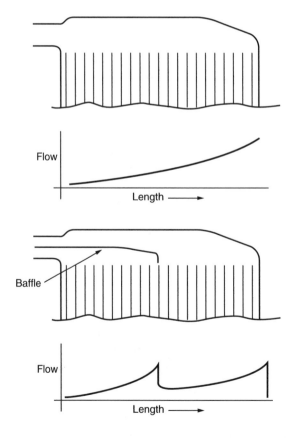

Fig. 5-22. *Proper internal baffling can create more uniform airflow distribution through the core and, thus, greater heat rejection. Add the baffle to force half the charge to go through the first half of the core and the remainder through the second half.*

can easily and conveniently find their own way into and out of the intercooler. Think in terms of herding sheep. Give them direction and guidance and make the journey easy for them.

IN-CAP DESIGN. It is fundamental that thermal efficiency will improve if we can get equal distribution of airflow through the core tubes. A serious attempt at accomplishing this can be made by suitable baffles built into the in-cap.

The position of the inlet to the in-cap should receive attention in several areas. Keep uppermost in mind the requirements of air distribution and ease of flow.

OUT-CAP DESIGN. After the distribution job is done by the in-cap, it is the out-cap's lot to gather up all the molecules and point them toward the engine. This must be done with equal attention to streamlining, to keep flow losses to a minimum. Point the sheep in the direction of the exit, give them room, and don't make them do anything sudden. Do not offer them any abrupt changes in direction.

Fig. 5-23. Good and bad end-cap designs

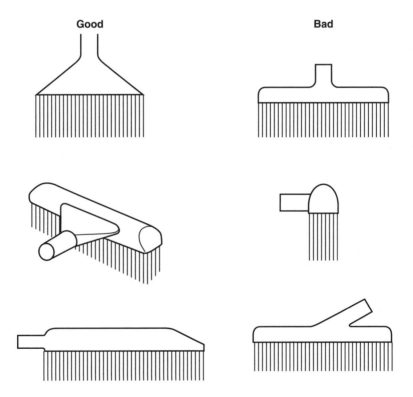

TUBE SIZES AND SHAPES. There is probably a magic number that airflow velocity in a tube should not exceed, for reasons of rapidly increasing drag and consequent flow losses. I suspect this number is around Mach .4, or about 450 feet per second, since drag, and therefore flow loss, increases significantly after this. Tube size can easily be checked by calculating the maximum airflow attainable, dividing by the area of the tube in square feet, and dividing again by 60 to convert to feet per second. An approximate value for maximum airflow can be obtained by multiplying the desired bhp by 1.5.

Example:

Let power = 400 bhp, for which maximum airflow is approximately 600 cfm, and air tube diameter = 2.5 in.

Then

$$Velocity = \frac{airflow}{area}$$

$$= \frac{600 \frac{ft^3}{min}}{\pi \left(\frac{2.5}{2}\right)^2 in.^2} \times \frac{\frac{1}{60} \frac{min}{sec}}{\frac{1}{144} \frac{ft^2}{in.^2}} = 293 \frac{ft}{sec}$$

The speed of sound is approximately 1100 feet per second. Therefore,

$$Mach = \frac{293}{1100} = 0.27$$

Thus, the 2.5-inch-diameter tube will be adequate to flow 600 cfm without unreasonable drag.

Resist the temptation to use larger diameter tubes than necessary, as little drag is created in smooth tubes with gentle bends. Larger tubes will only add to the volume of the IC system, and that is not a good thing to do.

☞ **RULE:** A large tube is not necessarily better than a small tube.

BENDS AND SECTION CHANGES. Any bend in a tube or sudden change of cross section must be viewed as a potential flow loss or source of increased drag. It would be reasonable to estimate that every time the airflow must turn 90°, a loss of 1% of the flow will occur. Three 30° bends will add up to a 90. Always use

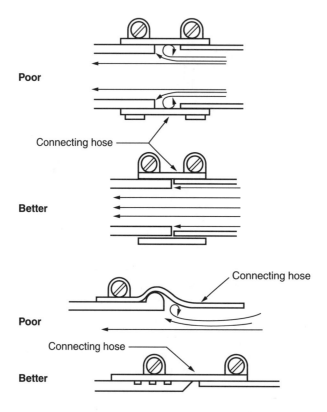

Fig. 5-24. *Minor flow interruptions can exist at tube intersections.*

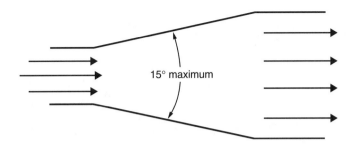

Fig. 5-25. *A cone angle greater than 15° can cause disruption of the air stream's boundary layer, increasing drag.*

15° maximum

the largest possible radius for any change of direction. Certainly a short-radius 90° bend will lose more flow than a large 90. The change from one size tube to another is frequently necessary for purposes of getting into a throttle body, out of the turbo, and into and out of the intercooler. These changes of section upset smooth flow and create losses.

Gradual changes of section can best be created by conical segments. A reasonable rule of thumb for the angle of the cone would be one diameter change in four diameter lengths.

HOSES AND CONNECTIONS. All hoses and connections spell trouble. At the outset of designing a turbo system, consider all hoses and connections the weak links of the intake system. Failure of a hose connection will certainly mean a loss of boost pressure. However, where a mass-flowmeter-controlled EFI is used, the engine will no longer run. When a hose fails, the engine can get air around the mass flowmeter, and thus the meter loses its ability to generate the proper signal. Without the proper signal, the engine will run poorly or not at all. The problem with hose joints stems from the fact that each joint has a load trying to

Fig. 5-26. *Tie bars on intercooler tubes relieve tension on the connecting hose.*

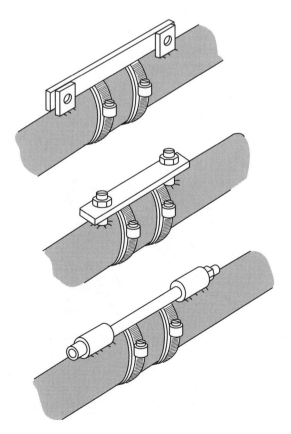

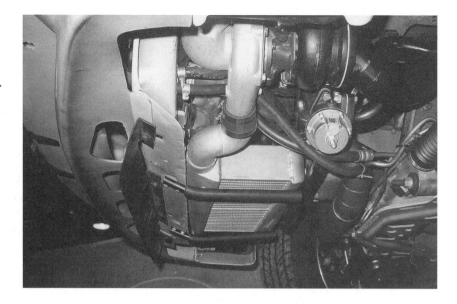

Fig. 5-27. *Adequate airflow to an air/air intercooler is a must for good efficiency. This intercooler would benefit from a scoop rather than the air dam.*

push it apart equal to the cross-sectional area of the tube times the boost pressure. If a system runs 20 psi boost through a 2-inch ID hose joint, it will have 63 pounds of force trying to pull the joint apart. This load will pull a hose off a tube unless some form of barrier is presented to the hose or the load is forced to take another path. In many instances the hose may stay attached to the tube, only to have the hose worked over so badly that the hose itself fails. An easy cure for this is a tie bar between tubes to carry the load, rather than letting the hose carry it. The hose's life then becomes a much simpler proposition.

The poor hose is trying to do all this load-carrying in a hot, hydrocarbon-fuel-rich environment. It is necessary, then, to seek hose material impervious to hydrocarbon fuels and exhibiting little degradation at the temperatures involved. Such hoses are generally made of silicone-based material.

PLACEMENT OF THE INTERCOOLER. The place to put an intercooler so often boils down to finding available space for a big enough unit. That doesn't take much science. A few rules, however, should receive some forethought. Try hard not to put an air/air intercooler in the same compartment as the engine. Placing it behind the cooling system radiator is also out. Consider that air having passed

Fig. 5-28. *Devious plumbing is sometimes required to fit an air/air intercooler into the system. Keep tubes a little larger and the number of bends to a minimum.*

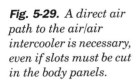

Fig. 5-29. *A direct air path to the air/air intercooler is necessary, even if slots must be cut in the body panels.*

through the cooling system radiator is generally 40°F, or more, hotter than ambient and therefore does a lousy job of trying to cool anything.

Indeed, the turbo, in low boost ranges, may not heat the intake charge up to the temperature level of the underhood air that is being asked to cool the intake charge. When this happens, the intercooler becomes an "interheater"—not a good turbo part. When the boost rises to the point that the temperature of the charge exceeds the underhood temperature, the IC will begin doing some work but will forever suffer from a severe efficiency loss. Not what we want. Underhood radiation of heat to the IC can also be a problem. Insulation and ducting can help these problems, but, fundamentally, the engine compartment is no place for an intercooler.

☞ **RULE:** Always be on the lookout for the villain called the "interheater."

Staggered-Core Intercooler

In a situation where frontal area space for an IC is limited but abundant depth exists, the staggered-core IC should be considered. Basically, the staggered-core IC is just a thick core unit with the back half moved aft a bit. Some fresh air is ducted to it, while the used air from the front core is sent around the sec-

Fig. 5-30. *The all-conquering Toyota GTP car from Dan Gurney's shops. Endurance racers will always tend toward air/air intercooling.*

ond core. A compact, high-flow IC can be built with the staggered-core concept. Efficiency can be high, because the rear half of the IC is made to do its share of the workload.

Fig. 5-31. Front watercoolers for a water-based intercooler system

Air-to-Water Intercooler

The water-based intercooler system becomes an attractive alternative to the air/air unit when space or plumbing restrictions preclude use of the latter. The logic behind most of the design criteria for the air/air IC applies as well to the water-based IC. Obviously, there are different considerations for handling the water. Although complex, the water-based IC enjoys the one terrific advantage of the far greater (fourteenfold) heat transfer coefficient between water and aluminum than between air and aluminum. This huge difference is of huge

Fig. 5-32. This installation of the water-based intercooler onto the Maserati bi-turbo clearly illustrates its compactness.

Fig. 5-33. *General layout of a water-based intercooler*

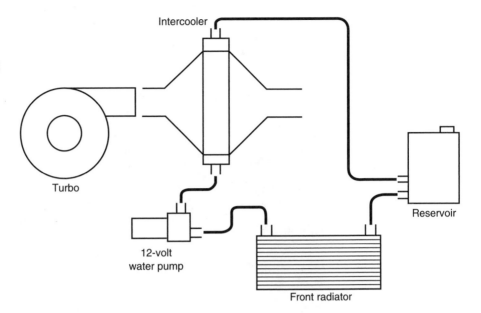

Fig. 5-33. *General layout of a water-based intercooler*

value only if all the heat transfer barriers can be optimized such that the 14-to-1 rate can be of benefit. This is the path to the intercooler system that exceeds 100% for thermal efficiency. Presently this is not practical for any situation except a drag car, Bonneville runner, or marine application. The solution to the problem is in need of the services of a genius inventor type. Without any ingenious solutions, the water-based IC reverts to nothing more than an air/air unit in which the intake charge heat is carried to the front of the vehicle for exchange into the atmosphere by water rather than by the intake charge itself.

The focus of the problems on handling the water is largely centered around rate of water flow, amount of water in the system, and the subsequent removal of heat from the water.

CHARGE-AIR HEAT EXCHANGER. It is easy to get a large internal flow area inside the water IC, since the most usable cores for this purpose are often air units with the flow reversed.

Fig. 5-34. *When using a typical air/air core as a water heat exchanger, reverse the direction of charge air flow to obtain greater flow area.*

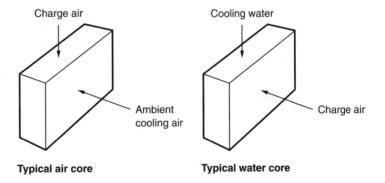

Although aluminum is by far the most convenient material to use in any IC application, copper core elements, should the situation allow them, can yield a greater heat transfer rate. The large flow areas usually associated with the water IC readily suggest that core thickness should be expanded as far as space permits.

Fig. 5-35. *A variation on a water-based intercooler. The copper-element heat exchanger is inside the plenum.*

Water will likely find equal access to all the core tubes, but attention should be given to trapped air in the top regions of the core. A simple air bleed can prevent air pockets. A better answer is to put the water in at the low point and take it out at the high point.

Small air leaks in an air/air unit are unimportant, but *any* water leak in the main heat exchanger core can be a disaster. Thus it is imperative that the unit be pressure checked for leakage prior to use. Ten psi with the core underwater is adequate. Don't be surprised to see air bubbles coming right through cast aluminum.

WATER PUMPS. Easily the most usable pumps are 12-volt marine bilge pumps. These can be ganged in series or parallel, depending on pressure and flow capability of the pumps. The fundamental should not be overlooked that the more water circulated, the greater the IC efficiency. Consider a water flow rate of 10 gallons per minute a reasonable minimum. There is a trade-off in pump life versus IC efficiency if the pumps are required to run all the time. With performance the focus of all this work, the answer should be that the pumps run continuously. If the pumps run continuously, the interesting thing happens that when off boost, the intake air will be cooling the water in the IC.

Wiring the pumps to a switched 12-volt source will permit an audible inspection of their function every time the ignition is turned on. The pumps should be mounted as the low points of the IC system, so that they will always be primed and thus preclude the chance of their running dry.

COOLANT. Water is by far the best cooling medium. Glycol and other antifreeze materials degrade the ability of water to transport heat and should be

Fig. 5-36. *An offshore racing boat is the ideal situation for a water-based intercooler. The seawater coolant with a temperature below ambient air offers the megahorsepower racing boats an intercooler with the potential to exceed 100% efficiency. This unit was designed for a 1500 bhp twin-turbo, big-block Chevy.*

used only in quantities required to prevent freezing and corrosion. Essentially, put the same ratio of water and antifreeze into the IC that is used in the engine cooling system. Use of a modern coolant can offer the further benefit of protection from aluminum corrosion. Distilled or demineralized water will keep the system clean.

RESERVOIRS. The size of the reservoir is of prime importance to the efficiency of the water-based IC. Consider that most applications of boost will last only a few seconds—say, 15 as a high average. Then it is reasonable to be sure in this interval that any given piece of water will not see the IC unit twice. A pump capability of 10 gallons per minute will move 2.5 gallons in 15 seconds; thus, the ideal size of the reservoir here is 2.5 gallons. Unreasonably large, obviously, but the point is made that the bigger the reservoir, the greater the time until the water takes its second lap through the IC. It is not too difficult to see that as a larger reservoir is used, the need for a front cooler decreases. Consider that the greater the mass of water, the greater the thermal inertia.

FRONT COOLER. The front cooler is the least important part of the IC system, as it is doing most of its work when the vehicle is not operating under boost. At the start of a boost run, the entire system will be at approximately ambient temperature. As boost rises, heating the water in the main core, this heated water must get to the front core before it has any temperature difference with which to drive the heat out. This time delay can be as long as 7 or 8 seconds, depending on the size of the reservoir. That amount of time is typical of a boost application. It is clear, then, that the front cooler will do most of its work after the boost run. Since the temperature difference between the water and the front core is small compared to the temperature difference between the boost charge and the water, the time required to cool the water down is much greater than the time required to heat it up. This is another reason for running the water pumps all the time. The front core does not need to be as big as it may seem at first glance, because the relative cfm rates through the two cores will usually be heavily biased toward the front cooler. For example, a forward velocity of just 60 mph could potentially put 5280 cfm through a cooler of 1 square foot area. Surely it is another case of bigger is better, but not really enough better to get carried away with huge front coolers.

Fig. 5-37. *The water-based intercooler must have a front-mounted heat exchanger. The compactness and efficiency of oil coolers makes them ideal for this application.*

Water Spray onto Intercoolers

Spraying water onto an IC core, presumably an air/air unit, is a method of improving thermal efficiency of the IC. Preliminary testing of such a mechanism has been shown to offer an easy improvement of 5 to 10%. The design and use of any cooling system based on a consumable fluid is best considered for special events only.

Water Injector

The water injector is not a very interesting device. It has little place in a properly conceived turbo system. Two circumstances are viable for a water injector: a 1970 home-built Vega turbo with a draw-through carb, or a Roots supercharger sitting between a huge engine and two huger (really big) carburetors. To stake the margin of safety of a turbocharged engine on an inherently unreliable device is an idea whose time has long since passed. RIP.

> ☞ **RULE:** A water injector on a turbo car is a poor-excuse band-aid for not doing the job correctly the first time.

One-Shot Intercooler

Special-purpose events like drag racing or top-speed trials lend a note of keen interest to the one-shot, superefficient intercooler. While not yet practical for everyday use, intercoolers operating well in excess of 100% efficiency can easily be created and used to great advantage for short durations. The principle behind the 100+% efficient intercooler is that of providing a cooling medium for the heat exchanger core that is either below ambient temperature or that can absorb huge amounts of heat by the evaporation process when in contact with the core. Examples of each would be an ice-water-bathed core or one sprayed with liquid nitrogen. Keep in mind that whatever the cooling medium, it must be kept in motion at all times, to avoid boundary layer formation. A stationary boundary layer will get warm and severely restrict the flow of heat from the core. Don't get carried away with gleeful thoughts of how great a 100+% intercooler will be and overlook that equally important design aspect of pressure loss through the core.

Fig. 5-38. *An ice-chest heat exchanger for a one-shot intercooler for drag racing. Ice is packed around the water tubes, and the container is then filled with water.*

AND FURTHERMORE. . .

What is an intercooler, and why is it of merit?

The intercooler is a heat exchanger (radiator) placed on the turbo compressor outlet. Its purpose is to reduce the temperature of the compressed air coming out of the turbo, increasing air density and allowing higher boost pressures.

This change in temperature has two distinct advantages: it increases power and it staves off detonation to considerably higher boost pressures. Cooling a gas makes it denser—i.e., more molecules per cubic inch. The density increase will generally be around 10 to 15%, depending on boost level and cooler efficiency. Power increases proportional to density. This is certainly a useful increase in power but nowhere near all that is safely available. The increased margin of safely on detonation is so great, due to the temperature reduction, that a portion of that margin of increase can be used to raise the operating boost level. In my experience, detonation will be suppressed a further 4 to 5 psi boost with a proper intercooler (provided a correct air/fuel ratio is present). Operating boost pressures can and should then be raised 3 or 4 psi. The improvement in performance as a result of this additional 3–4 psi intercooled is approximately the same as the performance provided by the first 5–6 psi of boost.

However, there can be pitfalls, First, it is currently in vogue to offer an intercooler as a substitute for a correct air/fuel ratio. Can't do it. A correct air/fu-

Fig. 5-39. *Increased intercooling for factory turbo cars should be accompanied by modest boost increases.*

el ratio is imperative. Must have. If your choice is one or the other, you must choose the correct air/fuel ratio. Both are the best situation, by far.

Second, too great a pressure loss pumping through an intercooler can raise exhaust manifold pressure by such a large amount as to demolish virtually all the power increase offered by the intercooler. A zero-resistance intercooler is ideal. Get as close as you can. Know what you buy. Ask what the pressure drop is at 1.5 times the cfm rating of your engine, It should be less than 2 psi. Few will be, OEM included.

What configurations do intercoolers come in?

There are two basic styles of intercoolers: air-to-air and air-to-water. Each has distinct merit, yet each has some problems. Air-to-air is the simplest. It

Fig. 5-40. *An elaborate yet effective water-based intercooler built by Jim McFarland, Mechtech Motorsports, for his unique Nissan V-6 twin-turbo-powered four-seater sand car.*

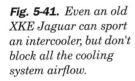

Fig. 5-41. *Even an old XKE Jaguar can sport an intercooler, but don't block all the cooling system airflow.*

has no moving parts and is as reliable as a brick. Heat-transfer capability is adequate, but pressure losses can be high, particularly with the small cores generally used. A given pressure loss through the intercooler will show up as an increase of twice that in the exhaust manifold pressure—one of the devils of turbocharging. All in all, a good unit if sized for adequate heat rejection and minimum pressure loss.

The air-to-water unit suffers a bit from complexity, but it does perform. It is composed of two radiators, one between the turbo and the engine and a smaller one in front of the standard cooling-system radiator. The water is circulated by an electric pump.

Decisions on which unit to use must be based on the engine, available space, fuel injection flow sensors, and a variety of other factors. An example of each: the obvious choice for 6-cylinder BMWs is a water-based unit, since no space exists for adequately sized air/air cores. Further complicating the air/air unit in the BMW 6 is a complete lack of high-velocity air in the only space where even a small core will fit. On the other hand, the Ford Mustang GT offers an ideal situation for the air/air unit in all respects. The space exists for a truly huge air/air unit (three full cores), and it sits in a great airflow spot.

What is water injection, and when is it needed?

Water injection is the spraying of a fine stream of H_2O into the intake system. Heat absorbed upon vaporization of the water has a strong cooling effect on the hot compressed air exiting the turbo. The reduction in intake air temperature reduces the tendency to knock.

Don't be too hasty to create a margin of safety on detonation based on an unreliable device. Water injection is best used when boost levels over 6 psi are desired but no intercooler is present. Do not allow a situation to exist where the water injector is used as an excuse for improper air/fuel ratios. All things considered, you would be far ahead never to have heard of a water injector.

6 INTAKE MANIFOLD

Guidance of airflow into the cylinder head is the job of the intake manifold. Control of the amount of flow is the function of the throttle.

A fuel-injection-equipped engine will usually flow an air/fuel mixture over a short portion of the intake manifold passages, whereas a carbureted engine will flow the air/fuel mixture through the entire length of the manifold. These two different characteristics create vastly different design requirements.

FUEL INJECTION MANIFOLD

The basic layout of the fuel injection manifold will be determined by its application. A racing application will generally tend toward a design with one throttle plate per cylinder. Typically, a street manifold will employ just one throttle plate or one multiple-plate progressive throttle body, attached to a plenum that will feed all cylinders. The one-plate-per-cylinder style will exhibit lower flow loss and is thus more suitable for maximum power. With just one plate total (or one progressive throttle body), a considerably crisper intake manifold vacuum signal is generated. This greatly increases the accuracy with which low-speed fuel and ignition can be calibrated and is thus better suited to a

Fig. 6-1. The Cosworth V-8 is one of the greatest racing engines in history. In its turbocharged Indy car form, it shows the way to high-performance intake manifolding, throttling, and plenum sizes and shapes. Note the throttle position at the lower front of the plenum. The throttle inlet sweeps upward into the center of the plenum.

Fig. 6-2. Top: *Log-style intake manifold with a single throttle inlet.* **Bottom:** *Plenum manifold with multiple throttle plates*

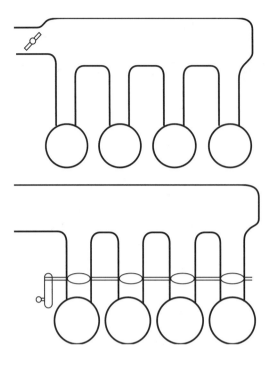

street-driven automobile. Synchronizing the flow, cylinder to cylinder, through multiple throttle plates is another matter altogether.

The two vastly different applications have many features in common. Both require an ideal shape for air inlets into the runners to the combustion chambers. Both require considerable thought as to the rate of taper of the port runners. In all applications, it is desirable to accelerate air toward the combustion chamber. This is done by gradually reducing the section area of the runner as it nears the chamber. Accelerating the air to a reasonably high velocity is beneficial, because it promotes chamber turbulence, yielding better combustion. Better chamber filling, which creates more power, will also occur.

Fig. 6-3. *The big-block Chevy Super Ram manifold/plenum/ throttle assembly. A compact design with short runners and good inlet shapes that work well at high flow rates.*

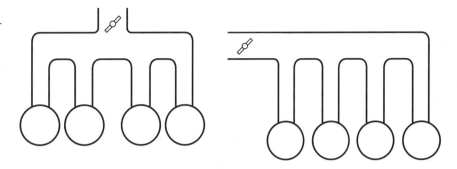

Fig. 6-4. *The symmetrical intake manifold (top) has a higher probability of equal flow to each cylinder than the more compact non-symmetrical design.*

The length of the runner has a strong effect on the amount of air that actually gets into the chamber during the intake valve cycle when the engine is not under boost. Due to its complexity, this phenomenon is best studied separately from turbo design. Here, it is sufficient to say that higher-speed engines will tend toward shorter intake runners. Low-speed and mid-range torque generally shows gains from longer runners. Turbo applications will generally find

Fig. 6-5. *A modest performance EFI manifold created from the classic V-8 intake manifold.*

Fig. 6-6. *Individual intake runners from a plenum are useful design features. A good example of a symmetrical design.*

Fig. 6-7. *A four-injector, single-throttle intake manifold for the Mazda rotary engine. This is a non-symmetrical design.*

best results with long runners, which provide a broad, flat torque curve at low speeds, while the turbo keeps the top end strong. In the fuel injection application where only air is moving inside the runners, the runner design becomes free to go up, down, or sideways.

Symmetry of design is a desirable characteristic, either race or street, as it facilitates equal distribution of airflow to each cylinder.

Fig. 6-8. *Ungainly, perhaps, this is the shape of an ideal air inlet.*

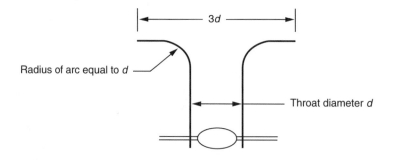

Fig. 6-9. *An intake plenum should be several times larger than a cylinder's displacement. This Ford GTP car satisfies that requirement well.*

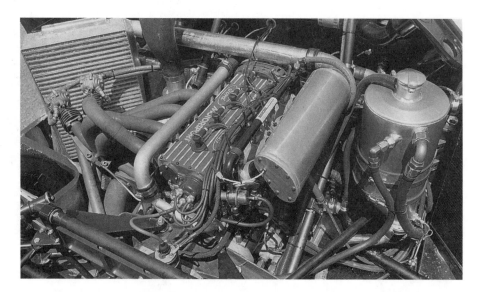

Plenum   Virtually all fuel injection manifolds will have a plenum. The plenum volume should be a function of engine displacement—in general, 50–70%. One of the critical design points in the manifold is the plenum-to-runner intersection. This is the point at which a bell-mouth-shaped inlet to the runner must be carefully made.

Fig. 6-10. *The shape of the intersection between plenum and intake runner must approach the ideal air inlet shape.*

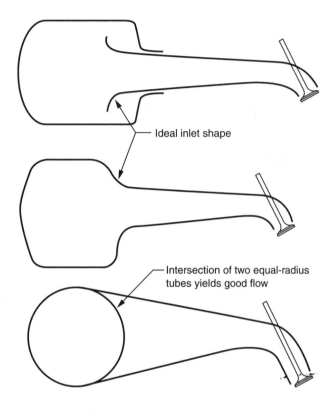

Ideal inlet shape

Intersection of two equal-radius tubes yields good flow

Fig. 6-11. *This Porsche Indy engine clearly illustrates plenum size requirements.*

Injector Location

Only two basic rules apply to the location of an injector. First, it must be aimed as straight down the center of a port as possible. Second, it should discharge at a point where air velocity is at or near its highest.

Occasionally a system will have such a large airflow or rev range that a single injector cannot provide enough fuel. In such circumstances, at least a secondary fuel injector will be required, and sometimes even a third. Alignment of the secondary injector is not as critical as the primary, because the secondary is generally not used until the system has achieved a relatively high rate of airflow. In street applications, it is still desirable to point the secondary injector downstream. Race applications, however, have occasionally aimed the secondary back upstream. Although data are scarce, this may offer slightly better atomization and is worthy of consideration.

Fig. 6-12. A standard injector. The injector angle with respect to the inlet port should be as shallow as possible. Consider 20° the maximum.

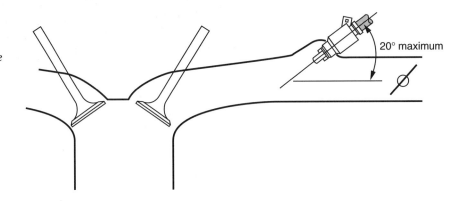

Fig. 6-13. An upstream injector

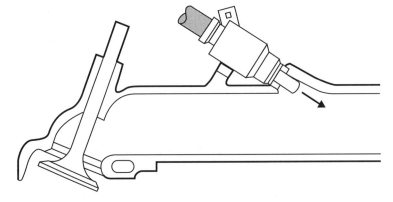

Throttle Bodies

The throttle body is usually one of the serious airflow restrictions in the turbocharger system. Simply making the throttle bigger will alleviate the problem, but low-speed driveability can become an on/off, jumpy proposition. A big throttle plate open a small amount can let in a lot of air, and smooth low-speed throttle response will suffer. A maximum air velocity of approximately 300 ft/sec will keep flow losses acceptable.

Air velocity can be calculated by

$$Velocity = \frac{airflow\ rate}{area\ of\ section}$$

Example:
Let cfm = 500 and throttle throat ID = 2.5 inches.

Fig. 6-14. EFI throttle bodies on a Chevy small-block manifold. With one throttle plate per cylinder, this is one of the lowest-restriction throttling layouts.

Then

$$V = \frac{500 \; \frac{ft^3}{min}}{\pi \left(\frac{2.5}{2}\right)^2 in^2} \times \frac{\frac{1}{60} \frac{min}{sec}}{\frac{1}{144} \frac{ft^2}{in.^2}} = 245 \; \frac{ft}{sec}$$

If 300 ft/sec is exceeded and the single throttle plate is not accompanied by a progressive linkage, it would be time to consider a two-plate progressive throttle body.

For race applications where one throttle plate per runner is employed, it is quite adequate to sum the throttle plate areas and calculate accordingly, or simply to use one cylinder and one throttle. The 300 ft/sec figure should still offer a suitable guideline.

The beautiful race hardware utilizing slide-valve throttles should generally be avoided, because the area times pressure usually yields forces of large magnitude. Special bearings and linkages can make the slide valve workable. In general, life is vastly simplified with the standard old twist-shaft throttle plate.

Fig. 6-15. *The progressive throttle linkage is a simple concept and effective at producing smooth operation at low engine speeds.*

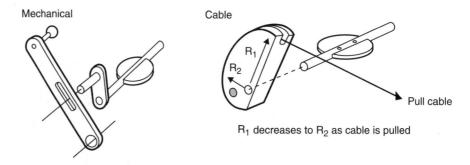

Fig. 6-16. *Neuspeed's large VW throttle body is a progressive unit with obvious value for custom turbo applications.*

Progressive Throttle Bodies

The attraction of a two- (or multiple-) plate progressive throttle body can be strong. The application needs careful analysis, since the progressive is not always of the benefit it may seem. The best place to use the progressive is with large engines that accelerate well at low speeds with little throttle opening. Generally, avoid the progressive on small engines that require a lot of throttle just to make them move.

CARBURETED MANIFOLD

Although seriously on the decline, and with good reason, a few more carbureted turbo systems will certainly be built. Such a huge number of intake manifolds are in production today that selecting a good one amounts to little more than a literature search. In general, manifolds employing one throat per cylinder will yield the most performance. Those with less will usually offer slightly better low-speed driveability.

These are, of course, all of the blow-through style. A discussion on collectors or plenums for blow-through carburetor applications would be much the same as the discussion relative to the fuel injection plenums. Follow the same principles, and you will be on the right track.

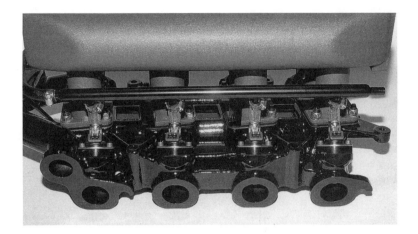

Fig. 6-17. *An example of a carbureted intake manifold converted to EFI on the Maserati Bora.*

AND FURTHERMORE . . .

Will a turbo work with my stock carburetor or stock fuel injection?
- stock carb: no
- stock fuel injection: no, not quite

No fuel injection in use today will automatically provide fuel for the increased airflow created by the turbo. However, stock electronic fuel injection systems work so well in all nonboost modes that it is advisable to retain the system and keep it absolutely stock, for ease of repair.

What constitutes a proper intake manifold?

Streamlining, above all. Uniform port shapes, smooth section changes, and insulation from heat. Symmetry and runner length are important.

Fig. 6-18. *The strong benefits of a good intake manifold design for turbo applications have prompted many people to create interesting and complex designs, such as the one made for this Mitsubishi 3-liter V-6 with twin turbos and intercoolers.*

7

ELECTRONIC FUEL INJECTION

$\mathbf{T}$he atomization of fuel into the air charge is extremely significant to the functioning of the internal combustion engine. If any single aspect of engine performance can be labeled "most important," fuel control is a strong candidate for the honor. Electronic fuel injection, in particular, can do that job better than any other form of fuel injection or fuel mixing device. Principles, applications, and modification of EFI will be dealt with in the discussion that follows. Neither cis ("continuous injection system"), a type of fuel injection that uses pneumatic and hydraulic controls, nor throttle-body fuel injection is discussed in this book. EFI has proven its superiority all the way from economy shoeboxes to Indy champ cars. It has been a long time since a major road race winner was equipped with a fuel system other than EFI. Surely, then, any serious turbo will be accompanied by EFI. Nothing else even comes close. Start with the best there is, and you won't wind up stuck or cornered later on.

Fig. 7-1. *The modern engine-management system.*

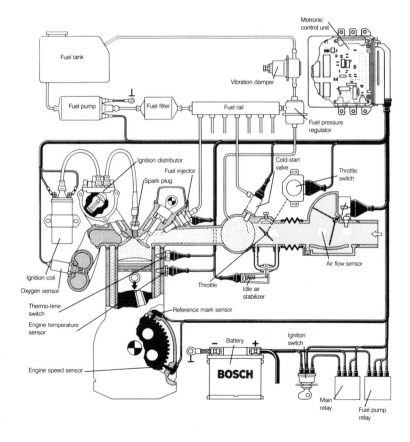

Fig. 7-2. *An adaptation of the Electromotive TEC II EFI to an ultra-modern engine in the Acura Integra.*

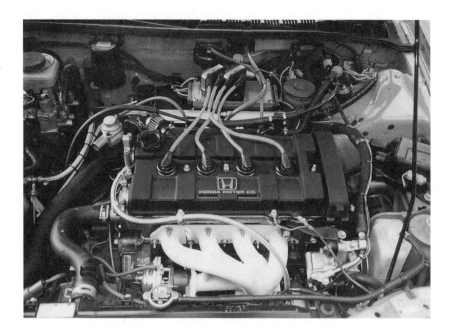

Principle of EFI

An EFI system is composed of electrically actuated fuel valves that open by a voltage signal, permitting fuel to flow. The air/fuel ratio is controlled by the amount of time the injectors are held open per combustion cycle. This is called pulse duration. The EFI computer gathers data from a group of sensors that tell it how fast the engine is running and the load at that instant. With that data, the computer starts looking through its stored information to find how long it should hold the injectors open to satisfy the fuel requirements dictated by those load conditions. When that information is found, it is pulled out of the memory and relayed to the injectors as a voltage pulse of a specific duration. These durations are measured in thousandths of a second, or milliseconds (msec). When that cycle is complete, the programming of the computer tells it to go do it all over again but to be alert for new conditions. All this data acquisition, analysis, and distribution takes about 15% of the computer's attention. The remainder of the time it just sits. Too bad it can't be reconciling your checkbook in its off hours. The sensors the computer relies on to keep it informed are an integral part of EFI and are analogous to the eyes and ears of the system:

Air-mass/airflow sensor. An EFI system configured with an air-mass or airflow sensor is called a "mass flow" EFI system. The sensor attempts to measure the number of air molecules flowing through the system at any instant. If this number is divided by the speed of the engine, it gives an accurate reflection of the amount of fuel needed per combustion putt in the engine.

Air temperature sensor. Air density changes as a function of temperature. Therefore, the computer must know to change the pulse durations slightly if the air temperature sensor detects a change in the air temperature.

Barometric sensor. Air density also changes with altitude. An atmospheric pressure sensor—a barometer—provides the computer a varying signal with changes in altitude.

Coolant temperature sensor. The amount of fuel the engine needs is inversely proportional to engine temperature. The coolant temperature sensor reflects the engine's operating temperature. With a cold engine, a huge amount of fuel is required just to get enough to vaporize, so it can burn. The hotter the engine, the easier vaporization becomes, and the less fuel required.

Manifold vacuum/pressure sensor. Not all EFI systems will be equipped with a manifold pressure sensor. Those that are, are properly called "speed density" EFI systems. When the manifold absolute pressure (MAP) sensor is used, an air-mass sensor or airflow meter is not necessary. The manifold vacuum or manifold pressure at any given instant is a good reflection of the engine load at that time. Hence, the MAP sensor provides the computer with another bit of operating condition data.

Oxygen sensor. The oxygen sensor measures the amount of oxygen left over from the combustion process. It is mounted in the exhaust manifold and thus becomes the after-the-fact watchdog for the computer. If the sensor detects too much oxygen, the computer will know by referring to its stored information that it is time to lengthen the injection pulses slightly, thus adding fuel and using some of the excess oxygen. By monitoring the leftover oxygen, the computer can continuously home the pulse durations in on the air/fuel ratio it was programmed to give. The oxygen sensor's purpose in life is to keep the air/fuel ratio in the ranges needed by the three-way catalytic converter. It is not a power or economy device.

Tachometer circuit. The pulsing of the injectors every combustion cycle must, of course, always be referenced to the engine speed. The tach circuit does this by monitoring the low-voltage pulses to the coil.

Throttle position sensor. The actual output of an engine is largely dependent upon throttle position. Full throttle is obviously asking for everything the engine has, and fuel flow must rise to the occasion. Therefore, throttle position becomes a significant bit of data for the computer. A further data input that the throttle-position sensor offers is the rate of change of the throttle position. This function becomes the equivalent of an accelerator pump in a carburetor. The accelerator pump offers a sudden rich condition to allow a smoother load transition.

Support pieces for the EFI system are fuel pumps, fuel pressure regulators, fuel lines, air valves, idle controls, and relays.

Fuel Injectors and Pulse Duration

A good working knowledge of EFI must include an understanding of how injector sizes vary with differing requirements of cylinder size, power output, and operating range of manifold pressure. First it is necessary to understand the intrinsic nature of the timed injector and the available time in which it must work. The available time is limited to the time required for one complete engine cycle. In a four-stroke-cycle engine, available injector time is the time required to complete two revolutions of the engine. As the speed of the engine increases, available injector time decreases. Thus the injector inherently takes up a greater and greater portion of the available time as the engine speeds up. Eventually, the point arrives at which engine cycle time is equal to the time the injector needs to deliver the required amount of fuel. This point is the 100% duty cycle point.

Two types of EFI systems are available: sequential and nonsequential. Sequential, which is the most common, pulses an injector in the same order as the firing order of the engine. In so doing, sequential pulses each injector every other revolution; that is, once per engine cycle. The nonsequential style usually pulses all the injectors at the same time and on every revolution. Sequential

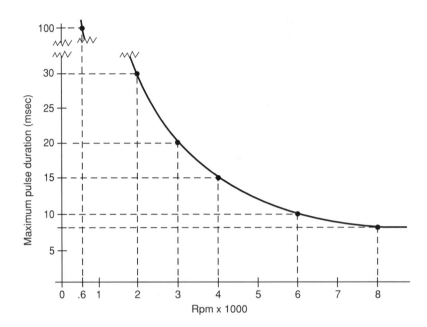

Fig. 7-3. *Maximum fuel injection pulse time available per revolution is a function of engine rpm.*

EFI therefore has a pulse duration twice as long as nonsequential, but nonsequential pulses twice per engine cycle, thereby closely approximating delivery of sequential EFI. A clever variation on sequential injection is the ability to adjust exactly when the pulse occurs relative to the opening of the intake valve.

The two convenient points to remember are at 600 rpm and 6000 rpm. These two points take 100 msec and 10 msec, respectively, per revolution, or 200 msec and 20 msec for complete engine cycles. Again, it is important to remember that 20 msec total time available, whether it is in two pulses of nonsequential EFI or one pulse of sequential EFI. The fundamental idea behind all this analysis stuff is that the injector must be big enough to deliver all the fuel the cylinder requires in 20 msec at 6000 rpm (or even less if the engine runs faster).

Modifying Stock EFI Systems

Within the scope of low-boost-pressure (under 7 psi) turbo systems added to normally aspirated engines, adequate fuel deliveries can be achieved with modification to the stock EFI equipment. The basic requirement of knowing that the fuel delivered through the injector nozzle is the right amount for the conditions still exists and must be satisfied. Increasing fuel flow through the EFI system is limited to one of three choices:

- lengthening injector pulse duration
- increasing nozzle size
- increasing fuel pressure

LENGTHENING INJECTOR PULSE DURATION. Prior to any attempt to increase fuel flow by longer pulse duration, it is necessary to determine the time of an engine revolution at redline (peak horsepower) and the maximum duration of an injector pulse. This will allow us to calculate whether additional time is available to lengthen pulse duration. Injector pulse duration can be determined by an oscilloscope or pulse duration meter. This measurement must be taken while the car is moving at full throttle near the torque peak, which is approximately two-thirds of redline rpm.

As rpm increases from about 3000 rpm and injectors are open a larger percentage of each revolution, sequential EFI reverts to nonsequential. The distinction between the two types can therefore be ignored in calculating additional fuel flow as long as pulse duration is checked above 4000 rpm. Then it is accurate to analyze available pulse increase based on one pulse per revolution.

The time required for one revolution at engine redline determines whether time is available for longer EFI pulses. This can be obtained from figure 7-3 or by calculation:

$$Time\ of\ one\ revolution\ =\ \frac{60\ \frac{sec}{min}}{redline\ rpm}$$

Example:
Let redline rpm = 5500.
Then

$$Time\ of\ one\ revolution\ =\ \frac{60\ \frac{sec}{min}}{5500\ rpm}\ =\ 0.0109\ =\ 10.9\ msec$$

Once the time of one revolution at the redline is known and redline pulse duration has been measured, the available increase can be calculated.
In msec,

$$Available\ increase\ =\ time\ of\ one\ revolution\ -\ redline\ pulse\ duration$$

As a percentage,

$$Available\ increase\ =\ \frac{time\ of\ one\ revolution}{redline\ pulse\ duration}\ -\ 1$$

Example 1:
Let redline rpm = 5500 and redline pulse duration = 6.2 msec.
Then

$$Available\ increase\ =\ 10.9\ msec\ -\ 6.2\ msec\ =\ 4.7\ msec$$

As a percentage,

$$Available\ increase\ =\ \frac{10.9}{6.2}\ -\ 1\ =\ 0.758\ =\ 75.8\%$$

Example 2:
Let redline rpm = 7500 and redline pulse duration = 8.0 msec.

$$Time\ of\ one\ revolution\ =\ \frac{60\ \frac{sec}{min}}{7500\ rpm}\ =\ 0.08\ =\ 8.0\ msec$$

$$Available\ increase\ =\ 8.0\ msec\ -\ 8.0\ msec\ =\ 0$$

In this example, redline pulse duration takes up all the available time at the redline rpm; therefore, no increase is available.

If investigation shows an increase in injector pulse duration is available, then the methods of extending those pulses can be examined:

Sensor signal alteration. Pulse durations can be extended by increasing the resistance in the coolant temperature sensor circuit. The amount of resistance is determined by trial and error. The resistance must be added in increments and only when under boost. This requires a messy series of potentiometers and switches and will always prove less than acceptable.

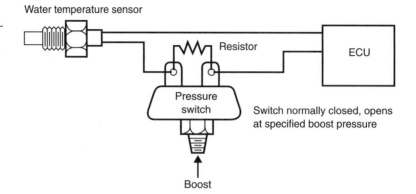

Fig. 7-4. The coolant-temperature-signal-change-based fuel system. Note: This is not a workable fuel system.

Reprogrammed computer chip. Too many problems exist to expect a chip change to offer a means of supplying additional fuel flow. This method is tough to work out on flapper-door-style flowmeters, for example. It will not work on a speed density system unless the MAP sensor is designed to operate at pressures above atmospheric. The tuner with the knowledge to decode an OEM computer program and the equipment to reprogram the system can do the job. These guys are real sharp and real scarce. All in all, this is a tough job to carry out.

Pulse signal interceptor. Currently, the only viable means of extending an injector pulse is to intercept it, modify it based on manifold pressure conditions, and send it on to the injector in place of the original pulse. Good technology and lots of experience are required for success with this approach. Such devices exist in limited applications.

INCREASING NOZZLE SIZE. A change in nozzle size creates a situation wherein, if left alone, the EFI will deliver more fuel all the time under all conditions. This is not acceptable; thus, a means of returning fuel flow to its original level at low speeds is necessary. It is possible to do this either by modifying the air-flow meter's signal to the ECU or, with flapper-door-style flowmeters, by increasing the return spring tension. The latter done inside the flowmeter and is

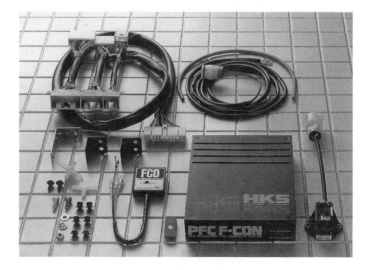

Fig. 7-5. The HKS piggyback computer is designed to operate a factory turbo car at higher-than-stock boost pressures.

Fig. 7-6. The F-CON computer alters the EFI signal based on the magnitude of the boost-pressure signal.

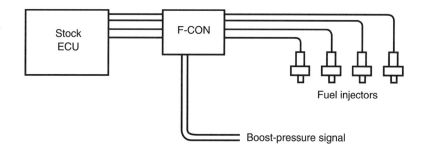

Fuel injectors

Boost-pressure signal

Fig. 7-7. Rising-rate regulator installed in a fuel system

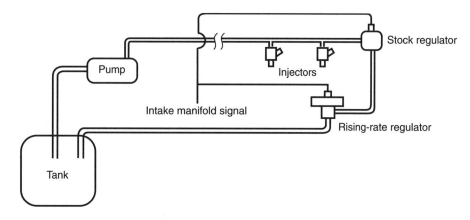

relatively easy. Injector nozzles up to 50% bigger can usually be retuned to good low-speed operation by either method.

Increasing fuel pressure or adding injectors is only practical up to about 9–10 psi (boost pressure), after which larger injectors become necessary. Although OEM ECUs are difficult to reprogram, aftermarket units, which come with software and instructions, are a cinch. With such units, increasing injec-

Fig. 7-8. The rising-rate fuel pressure regulator, invented by Ron Nash in the mid-'70s, raises fuel pressure rapidly as boost increases.

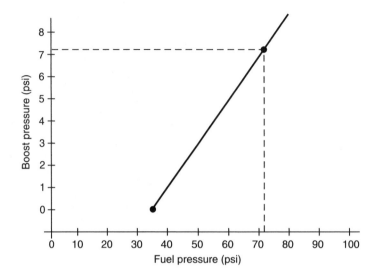

Fig. 7-9. *The rising-rate regulator can deliver significantly higher fuel pressures as a function of boost pressure.*

tor size becomes the most potent method of supplying additional fuel. When boost pressure exceeding 9–10 psi is planned, a change of injectors is necessary.

INCREASING FUEL PRESSURE. Increasing system fuel pressure as a function of boost pressure is a viable method of increasing fuel flow to accommodate boost pressures up to about 9 psi. Fuel flow changes through a nozzle are proportional to the square root of the pressure change across the nozzle. A boost-pressure-powered fuel pressure regulator can be made to drive the fuel pressure up rapidly to keep pace with rising boost pressure. This type of mechanism is able to use the original injectors but is limited to fuel pressure available through the stock pump. Bosch or other high-pressure EFI fuel pumps can be substituted or used as supplementary pumps. These pumps generally offer fuel pressure up to 130 psi, which give the fuel pressure regulator adequate pressure to work with. Proportioning fuel pressure to boost pressure maintains the timed nature of EFI, keeping fuel delivery proper relative to the air-mass rate of flow.

Extra Injectors

Some systems attempt to increase power by adding one or two injectors overall, rather than per cylinder. These injectors are customarily placed in the air tube entering the throttle body and can be pulsed by a small control box based on an rpm and boost-pressure signal. As is the case with increasing fuel pressure, adding injectors is practical only up to about 9 psi. This is not an ideal system, and, if used, care must be exercised in locating the injectors, to achieve

Fig. 7-10. *One or two additional injectors for the entire system can provide fuel for low-boost applications but should not be considered for serious power.*

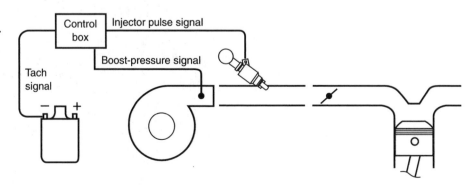

Fig. 7-11. *The inline-six Nissan manifold as equipped with six staged injectors. Original injectors are to the left; secondaries are further outboard, to the right.*

Fig. 7-12. *The "add-on injector" fuel supply will indeed add a useful dose of fuel. The add-on is pulsed with engine speed; duration is controlled by boost pressure.*

Fig. 7-13. *Four staged secondaries can be programmed to operate when under boost.*

equal distribution of fuel to the cylinders in a manifold designed to flow air only. The injectors must also be sized to deliver the fuel required for the desired airflow rates. Ideally, one extra injector per cylinder is required for serious power. Otherwise, consider this a low-boost-power mechanism.

The preceding paragraphs cover the methods by which EFI may be modified to operate under boost. Prior to selecting a method that suits your requirements, make sure your measurements and calculations are correct. Don't get off on any dopey tangents like turning on cold-start spray nozzles, or any other equally inane schemes, without suitable investigation proving that the scheme meets all the requirements of a properly conceived fuel system.

Calculating Injector Size

The EFI fuel injector has a rating of fuel flow per unit time. A huge variety of sizes exist. An equally huge number of units of volume or mass flow are used to rate injector flow capacity. The following will convert cc/min to lb/hr:

$$\frac{cubic\ centimeters}{minute} = \frac{pounds}{hour} \times 10.5$$

The calculations required to come up with a properly sized injector for a given application are not rigorous. No rocket science here. One simple calculation and the job is done:

$$Pounds\ of\ fuel\ per\ hour\ per\ injector = \frac{expected\ bhp \times 0.55}{number\ of\ injectors}$$

The .55 figure is actually the maximum load brake specific fuel consumption (bsfc) of a typical turbocharged engine. In general, the number of injectors is the same as the number of cylinders. Clearly, one should choose the next larger size than the calculated value, to offer some margin for future improvements.

Testing Injectors

An injector can be measured for its flow capability by applying a suitable voltage (usually 9, but check the manual) to the injector and 36 psi (stock fuel pres-

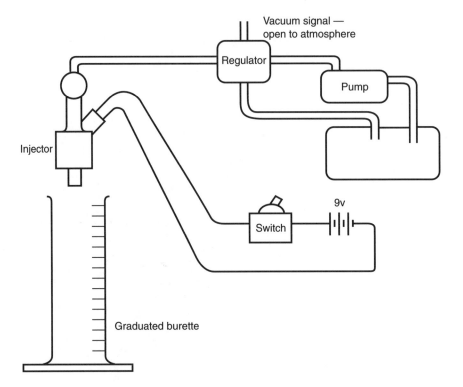

Fig. 7-14. *A simple fuel injector flow-test rig*

sure for most cars and standard pressure for measuring injector flow) to the fuel. Let the fuel run into a graduated burette for one minute. The result is the flow capability measured in cc/min. A couple of 1.5-volt dry cells will hold the injector open just fine.

Fuel Pump Requirements

The fuel requirements of any engine system must be backed up by a fuel supply system. The fuel supply system is the fuel pump, fuel pressure regulator, and fuel lines. The fuel supply system must be able to meet the challenge with a reasonable margin of extra capability. This margin requires a balance between the pump's flow capability and its pressure capability. An odd feature of all pumps is the fact that they produce their greatest flow at their least pressure. The maximum pressure rating of a pump is when your thumb is on the outlet of the pump, not letting anything out. In other words, no flow. On the other side of the coin, the maximum flow of the pump occurs when it is free to pump with no restriction (no thumb). The EFI fuel pump is a positive-displacement pump driven by a dc motor. As the work the pump is asked to do increases, the motor slows down. As the motor slows down, the volume of fuel being pumped falls off. To operate EFI systems, we must have fuel pressures of 40+ psi. Therefore we must know, calculate, or measure the fuel flow rates at these pressures. Any

Fig. 7-15. Turbo fuel systems, especially those controlled by a rising-rate regulator, require high-pressure/high-flow fuel pumps. This Bosch pump will supply 130 psi at flow rates supporting 500 bhp.

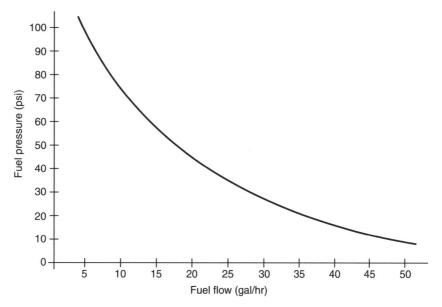

Fig. 7-16. Typical fuel pump flow versus fuel pressure. Fuel pumps deliver less flow with increasing pressure. The engine's requirements must always stay below the curve.

given pump will have a flow-versus-pressure curve. These can be hard to come by, but it is not a real challenge to measure a particular pump's capability.

Perhaps the simplest method of determining a pump's capability (particularly if it is already there) is an actual field test, to see if it maintains maximum required fuel pressure to the engine redline. If it does, fine. If not, however, this test provides no data about what is needed.

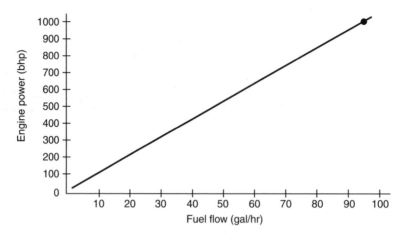

Fig. 7-17. *Approximate fuel pump flow requirements versus engine bhp.*

The standard method for measuring an EFI pump's flow capacity at a given pressure is to connect it to an EFI pressure regulator and measure the volume exiting the fuel return line. This is the volume of fuel that can be taken from the fuel system at that pressure without the fuel pressure's dropping off. With the fuel pressure regulator's vacuum reference open to the atmosphere, fuel pressure will be 36 psi. This is the pressure used on the chart to determine flow capacity. It is equally easy to simulate fuel flows when operating under boost. Feed a pressure signal to the fuel pressure regulator equal to the boost desired and again measure flow out the regulator return line. This can be done with shop air and an adjustable air pressure regulator. Fuel pressure will be equal to boost pressure plus 36 psi. From calculations of the injector sizes required under maximum load, the total flow required is known. That total is injector capacity times the number of injectors. The number of cc's per minute divided by 1000 is the number of liters per minute. If the point on the chart representing your requirements of flow capacity versus fuel pressure lies beneath the line, all is well. If the point lies above the line, two or more pumps operating in parallel are required.

Fig. 7-18. *Fuel pumps in parallel should have separate, dedicated fuel pickups.*

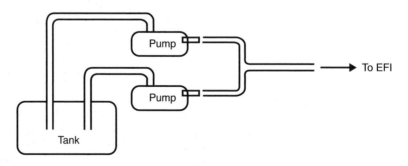

Fig. 7-19. *An effective example of converting a four-barrel carbureted manifold to an EFI system. A throttle body replaces the carb; fuel injector bosses are installed at the ends of the ports.*

Aftermarket EFI Systems

Perhaps not yet recognized for what they really are and for their vast tuning potential, aftermarket EFI systems will prove the greatest boon for hot rodders since the small-block Chevy. This is the equipment that can make a docile lamb and high-economy cruiser out of a twin-turbo Keith Black 600 cid hemi V-8. Aftermarket EFI indeed offers the opportunity to create the 1000 bhp daily commuter automobile. The singular aspect of EFI that permits this is its fine degree of tuning available over huge intake manifold pressure ranges. By comparison, the finest carburetor in the world has four fuel-flow circuits that can be tuned over the range in which it is asked to operate. Over this same range, EFI offers literally hundreds of fuel flow circuits—one for virtually every hundred-rpm band and every inch of manifold pressure. It's equivalent to having 500 main jet circuits in a carb, each one ideally set up for a certain engine load and rpm.

Several aftermarket companies have introduced EFI systems in the last couple of years. Air Sensors, in Seattle, seem to have been the pioneers with

Fig.7-20. *Electromotive, of Chantilly, Va., manufactures this high-quality, high-performance engine-management system.*

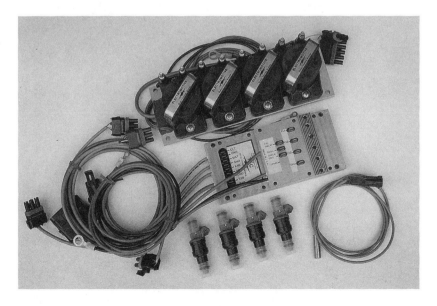

Fig. 7-21. The Australian Haltech EFI has proven durable and versatile for specialty tuners.

their units. More recent developments, like the Haltech, offer a completely programmable EFI. Electromotive, in Virginia, and Digital Fuel Injection, of Detroit, offer similar hardware plus the feature of ignition controls.

Hardware for Aftermarket EFI

Setting up a functioning EFI system means creating the air throttling mechanism as well as doing the hydraulics. The problems to be solved are exactly the same as the problems discussed earlier in this chapter, plus a few new twists. The hydraulic aspects are the same. Intake manifolding layout must be considered; see Chapter 6. Throttle valving, along with number and positioning of injectors, is also discussed in that chapter.

Fig. 7-22. The laptop computer is a basic tool for creating and tuning fuel curves of aftermarket fuel injection systems.

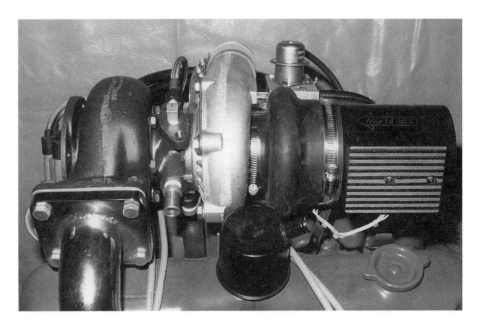

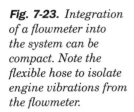

Fig. 7-23. Integration of a flowmeter into the system can be compact. Note the flexible hose to isolate engine vibrations from the flowmeter.

AND FURTHERMORE . . .

Is there any benefit to draw-through throttle designs on fuel injected cars?

A noticeable throttle response improvement between gear shifts can be achieved by placing the throttle in front of the turbo when no intercooler is used. Slamming the throttle shut downstream of a pumping turbo simply causes a greater loss of turbo rpm. This lost speed must be reacquired before boost can again be achieved. A downstream throttle with an intercooler will ultimately prove superior if accompanied by a compressor bypass valve system.

Why are changes needed to existing fuel systems?

Carbureted turbocharger systems do not have any requirement for extra fuel delivery systems. The more air drawn through a carb, the greater the pressure drop at the venturi, and thus the more fuel pushed through the main jet. A properly sized and calibrated carb is necessary, and that is all.

Fuel injection systems are a completely different situation. It is commonly claimed that fuel injection systems will take care of themselves when a turbo is added. This is decidedly not true. A fuel injection system is sized for a given engine. A 2-liter unit will not work on a 4-liter engine. The reason for this is that the airflow meters and fuel injectors are sized for the flow capability of the accompanying engine, and any substantial increase over stock flow rate will bottom out the airflow meter. A 2-liter unit airflow meter subject to an infinite airflow rate might think it's a gorilla 2.2 liter for an instant, but that's about as far as it can stretch. Now add the turbo, and you can easily make a 3-liter engine out of a 2-liter with just 7 psi boost. Obviously, the fuel injection airflow meter is again bottomed out and can't cope with the increased flow. A turbo engine can never be allowed to run lean; therefore, something must be done to meter fuel to accompany the extra air pushed through the system by the turbo.

8 CARBURETION

$\mathbf{A}$t first glance, the idea of a modern turbocharged engine and carburetors all in the same package appears to be a contradiction. A closer inspection reveals that it is indeed a contradiction. Rather than ignore these antique devices, this chapter will attempt to outline the operating principles behind carburetor integration into a turbo system.

The reasons carbs do not completely satisfy the fueling requirements of a turbo engine are basic and clear-cut. Two reasons stand out: the airflow range over which a carb can successfully operate, and the inability of a draw-through carburetor system to function with an intercooler. A carburetor has three items controlling fuel flow: idle jet, main jet, and air corrector jet—and, on occasion, power jets. While these controlling factors will allow satisfactory operation over a range of 20 to 25 psi absolute (5 to 10 psi boost), there is little hope for accurate fuel mixture control to satisfy either peak performance or any emission standards. The physical principles of fluid mechanics simply do not allow it.

Two different setups are possible with carbureted turbo systems. With a draw-through type, the carburetor is positioned in front of the turbo, and all

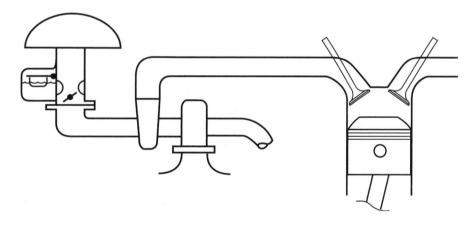

Fig. 8-1. *The basic layout of the draw-through carb system*

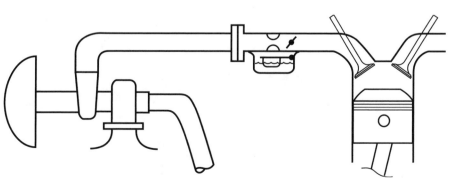

Fig. 8-2. *The blow-through carb layout presents a far superior path for the air/fuel mixture to traverse than does the draw-through setup.*

the air/fuel mixture flows through the entire system. With the blow-through type the layout is reversed, to place the carburetor after the turbo. In the blow-through type, the air/fuel mixture does not flow through the turbo.

The two types have their own areas of merit. The draw-though system is simpler and, because it is a low-pressure system, no change occurs in air density at the carburetor. Further, no compressor bypass valve is required.

That is all that can be said for the draw-through system.

☞ **RULE:** The draw-through system is prone to icing at temperatures under 50°F.

The blow-through system has better throttle response and cold starting, reduced emissions, and permits use of an intercooler.

Weighing the merits, there is virtually no reason to build a draw-through system unless one lives in a year-round hot climate and never intends to produce serious power.

Fig. 8-3. Early carbureted turbos, like this one, generally drew through the carb. These have all been succeeded by the more modern blow-through designs.

Fig. 8-4. This beautiful hardware was created by Lotus for the Esprit and features two blow-through Dellorto side-draft carbs. Note the fuel pressure regulator at the end of the plenum and its boost-pressure sensing line.

Fig. 8-5. Three Mikuni PH44 carbs feed this Nissan Z car engine. Note the antisurge valve below the plenum and its return vent to the air-filter mount.

Layout of a Draw-Through System

The primary concern in the draw-through layout is that the air/fuel mixture be permitted to flow downhill at all times. This condition is not possible due to the compressor inlet scroll, but no other item should be allowed to serve as a low point. Fuel tends to drop out of the mixture and puddle at low points. Puddling will badly upset the cold idle and low-speed response.

A water jacket added to warm the carb mount and bottom of the turbo scroll will alleviate cold fuel puddling. However, the mere thought of purposely adding heat to the intake system should be considered nothing short of revolting. A further addition of heat may be required to prevent carburetor icing when operating under boost. Typically, a correct air/fuel ratio will create about a 45°F temperature drop when the fuel vaporizes in the carburetor. This temperature drop, combined with a cool, damp day, will frequently cause throttles to freeze wide open when operating under boost. A fine circumstance, cured only by adding yet more intake heat.

Sizing the carb for a draw-through system should take into account the basic cfm capability of the engine without considering the turbo. The reason for this is that cfm ratings of carburetors are based on atmospheric pressure drops only, whereas the turbo can violate these conditions by changing vacuum conditions after the throttle plates. Consider that the only way a carb with atmospheric pressure above the throttle plates can flow more air on a given engine is to have lower pressure, created by the turbo, after the throttle plates. In other words, the turbo creates a bigger pressure drop across the carb.

The draw-through carb system has a hidden pitfall in the area of selecting a suitably sized carburetor. This pitfall is created by the odd circumstance that allows one cylinder at a time to breathe through the sum of the carb throats open at that specific time. For example, imagine a dual-throat carb mounted in front of the turbo, all of which is mounted on a four-cylinder engine. Although the carb cfm rating may match the system just fine, we have a situation wherein each cylinder is breathing through the two throats. That equates to putting four dual-throat carbs onto a four-cylinder engine—certainly a situation that would be badly overcarbureted. The disaster comes about from the fact that the one cylinder drawing through two throats yields a very slow air velocity at the carburetor venturi. This sends a weak vacuum signal to the main jet; hence, lousy fuel metering. The situation is somewhat alleviated by having more cylinders, yet the fundamental problem remains. The proper solution to the problem is the selection of a carb with a small primary(s) and vacuum-operated secondaries.

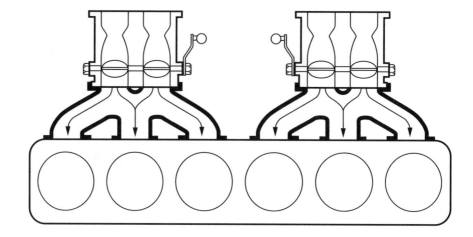

Fig. 8-6. *Do not permit a layout to exist where a single cylinder can be fed by two carb throats simultaneously. This is akin to severe overcarburetion and functions poorly.*

Preparing the draw-through carb for turbo use presents no special problems. Clearly, the jetting will need to be developed on an individual basis. Most situations will call for somewhat larger main jets, accelerator pump delivery, and idle jets than will the normally aspirated engine of the same size. The float needle assembly will usually require considerable expansion in order to keep up with the newfound fuel flow requirements.

Layout of a Blow-Through System

The blow-through system permits an ideal layout for the distribution of fuel to the cylinders. All the classic layouts of carburetor position relative to engine configuration are unaffected by the prospect of blowing pressurized air through the carbs. These layouts worked marvelously in their day as normally aspirated engines and would certainly do so as blow-through turbo applications. Although available space frequently influences the number and type of carbs, one carburetor throat per cylinder should always be the objective.

Several design parameters must be met in laying out a blow-through system:

• Fuel pressure must be controlled as a function of boost pressure.
• All components of the fuel system must withstand the higher fuel pressures.
• A compressor bypass valve is required.

Controlling fuel pressure. The requirement for varying fuel pressure comes about from the fact that the carburetor float bowls will experience a pressure change from roughly atmospheric at idle and cruise to the maximum boost of the turbo. If fuel pressure were a constant 4 psi, say, then when boost pressure exceeded that 4 psi, fuel would be driven backward into the fuel tank. Obviously, the pressure required to get fuel to enter a float bowl occupied by 15 psi of pressure will require fuel pressure of 18 or 20 psi. This 18 or 20 psi, if held constant at all conditions, might work fine under boost but would badly flood all known carbs at idle or cruise. The answer is a fuel pressure regulator that varies fuel pressure as a function of boost.

Fig. 8-7. *The after-market BMW 2002 turbo featured twin blow-through Mikuni/Solex carbs. This design incorporates a water-based intercooler into the plenum.*

Fig. 8-8. *The blow-through system must have a boost-pressure-sensitive fuel pressure regulator.*

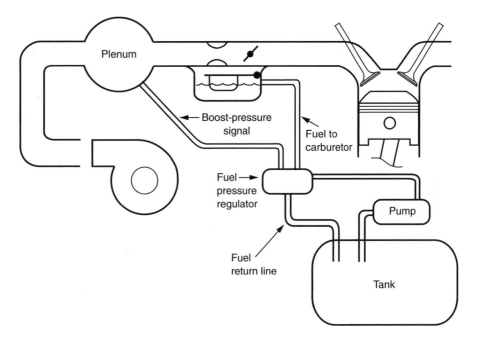

FUEL PUMP REQUIREMENTS. The need to flow large quantities of fuel while operating under boost is obvious. Fuel pumps, pressure ranges, and flow capacities are discussed in Chapter 7.

BYPASS VALVE. The compressor bypass valve, or antisurge valve, is essential to the smooth running of the blow-through system. The particular situation that requires the presence of the valve is when the throttle is suddenly closed after operating under boost. This is nothing more than the process of shifting gears when driving under boost. The problem comes about when the closed throttle creates manifold vacuum. The idle jet discharge orifice is then in a vacuum condition when the idle jet inlet is still pressurized, via the float bowl, from the turbo, which is still trying to pump air. This pressure difference across the idle jet causes a large discharge of fuel out of the jet, producing a sudden rich condition. When the gear change is accomplished and throttle re-applied, engine response deteriorates, due to the sudden air/fuel ratio change to the rich condition. The situation clears up as soon as the system again achieves a constant boost condition, where pressure is the same on both ends of the idle jet circuit.

The bypass valve is designed to dump the pressure upstream of the throttle when the throttle is closed, quickly bringing the system to a stabilized pressure. The valve does this by using the vacuum signal generated in the intake manifold when the throttle is closed to open a valve that lets the pressure rapidly bleed off.

Fig. 8-9. When operating under boost, the entire carb is under pressure. As the throttle is closed, residual pressure in the float and vacuum below the throttle plate will cause considerable flow through the idle jet, upsetting throttle response. The bypass valve rapidly dissipates the float/plenum pressure.

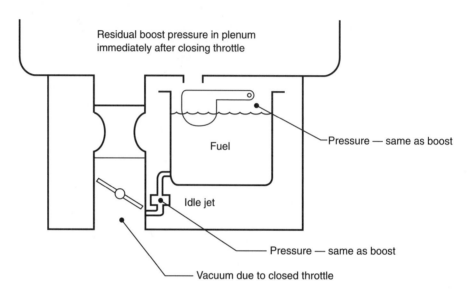

Fig. 8-10. The bypass, or antisurge, valve is necessary in blow-through designs to relieve float-bowl pressure quickly on lifting off the throttle.

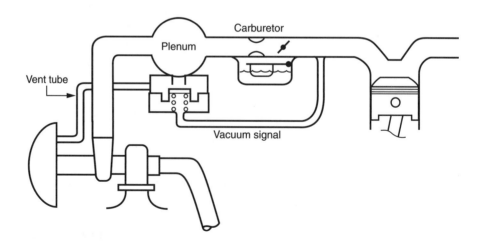

VACUUM AND PRESSURE DISTRIBUTION. Critical to the successful operation of the blow-through carb system is the source of the signals used to control the wastegate and fuel pressure regulator. This condition arises from the absolute need to control the pressure difference across the carburetor float needle. This pressure difference is the difference between the fuel pressure pushing the fuel into the float bowl and the boost pressure that exists in the float bowl at

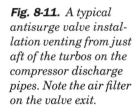

Fig. 8-11. *A typical antisurge valve installation venting from just aft of the turbos on the compressor discharge pipes. Note the air filter on the valve exit.*

any given time. This pressure difference must be held constant under all operational conditions. To accomplish this, it is vital that both control signals be taken from the intake plenum prior to the throttle plates. It is best to take the signals from the same location. To illustrate what can happen if this requirement is not met, imagine hooking both signals to the intake manifold after the throttle plate. This is always the last place to see boost pressure, and it is always the lowest pressure. Pressure losses thru the carb can be as high as 3 or 4 psi. If the wastegate signal then comes from the manifold, the float bowl will see a pressure 3 or 4 psi greater. If fuel pressure is set 5 psi above boost pressure, then the real pressure difference across the float needle will be 1 or 2, certainly not enough to run under boost. If fuel pressure is raised to compensate, the idle setting will be off when the float bowl sees atmospheric pressure. Back at idle, fuel pressure will be 8 or 9 psi, an unstable fuel pressure for a float needle assembly.

PREPARING THE CARBURETOR. Several aspects of the carburetor need inspection and/or preparation for use in a blow-through application.

The blow-through carb must have a solid float. Should the one you choose to use have a brass-sheet float or other style that could collapse under boost pressure, the float must be replaced with a solid unit. A variety of techniques exist to fill a hollow float with lightweight foam. Some of these come in a liquid and harden after being injected into the float. Consult the Yellow Pages, under adhesives.

Inspect the carb thoroughly for lead plugs that cap off intersecting drilled passages. These plugs are prone to dislodge with boost pressure. The plug can be retained by staking it in with a sharp-pointed center punch. Set a ring of punches around the plug such that the base metal of the carb body is raised enough to create interference should the plug try to move. Another method of retaining the plugs is simply to cover them with a high-quality epoxy glue. Be mindful of the fact that larger plugs will fail first, as they inherently have a larger force trying to push them out.

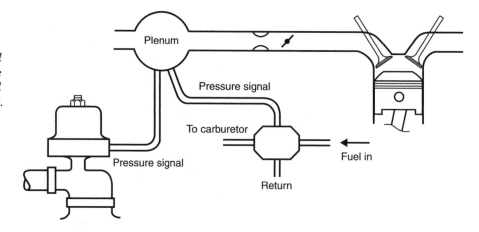

Fig. 8-12. *Signals for the wastegate and fuel pressure regulator need to originate at the same point in the system and before the throttle plate.*

Inspect all the gaskets in the carburetor. Any gasket that appears less than up to the task must be improved. It is possible to retain a gasket with a very light coating of Loctite applied to one side only. Under no circumstances should you use a silicone or similar rubbery-style sealer, as you will be finding it in the fuel jets after the first trip around the block. It is especially important to seal all gaskets or other items on the float bowl lid to avoid losing boost-pressure balance across the main jets. If any pressure leaks whatsoever occur from the float bowl, fuel delivery will grow lean on rising boost pressure.

The throttle shafts on the carb will seep fuel under boost if not sealed against pressure. Most seepage will be in the annoying category and will not affect safety or function. Cosmetics dictate that the shafts receive some form of seal. Probably the easiest and most effective method is to offer a pressure barrier that will tend to force the air/fuel mixture back into the carb throat. This can easily be done by bleeding some boost out of the plenum on the face of the carb, down to small fittings placed into the bosses through which the throttle shafts pass.

Fig. 8-13. *When fuel leakage at the throttle shaft is a problem, boost pressure from above the venturi, which will always be greater than that below the venturi, can be channeled to the shaft pivot bores to blow the mixture back into the throat.*

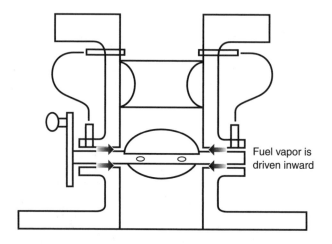

Fuel vapor is driven inward

Cold-start valves of the fuel-dump style, rather than the air-restrictor type, may need to be pressure balanced against a reverse flow when operating under boost. Should this be a problem, it can be dealt with by creating a cap of sorts over the cold-start valve and bleeding pressure from the plenum into this cap. The cap can be bonded onto the carb with a high-quality epoxy cement.

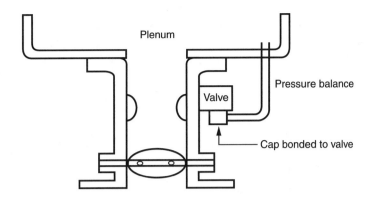

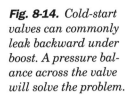

Fig. 8-14. Cold-start valves can commonly leak backward under boost. A pressure balance across the valve will solve the problem.

SUITABLE CARBS FOR BLOW-THROUGH APPLICATION. Almost any carburetor can be prepared for use in a blow-through turbo system. It is clear, however, that some carbs present a serious preparation challenge, while others are just plain easy to use. Manufacturers like Weber, Mikuni, SK, Dellorto, and Holley all make carbs that will, with suitable preparation, function well in a blow-through application. The easiest unit to use is certainly the Mikuni series PHH dual-throat sidedraft. It should be given consideration in applications ranging from V-8s and V-12s to any inline configuration. The Mikuni PHH comes as close to usable right out of the box as is available. It is simple to tune, responsive at low speeds, flows huge amounts of air, and is long-term durable. The new SK carb is virtually its equal, with perhaps even greater fine-tuning capability. In situations where it is not possible to use dual-throat sidedrafts, the Weber IDF downdrafts ought to be given consideration. Although the IDF requires extensive preparation, it is a broad-range, responsive, smooth-running carb. Perhaps the highest-quality carb built in the world today is the Italian Dellorto series. Available in downdraft and sidedraft configurations, these carbs are truly fine pieces of work. Prior to setting your heart on using them, secure your path for parts supply. Holley carbs have been used successfully over the years, and Holley offers a wide variety of sizes and shapes. No manufacturer comes close to Holley in offering special-tuning bits and pieces to tailor a specific application. Motorcraft two-barrel carburetors are versatile and easily adapted to blow-through configuration.

PLENUM DESIGN. The plenum is the component that focuses air for its trip through the carb. Although plenums are simple in concept, a few rules should be observed in plenum design:

* Make the volume of the plenum 110–120% of the engine displacement.
* Straighten out the airflow before the air corrector jet assemblies. Air swirling around an air corrector prevents the jet from functioning.
* Have the shape into the carb throats approach that of an ideal inlet.
* Don't blow air directly across a carb throat.
* Provide for air bleeds to the float bowls.

Fig. 8-15. *The plenum vent ports to the throttle bores must incorporate a bell-mouthed form approaching an ideal air inlet shape.*

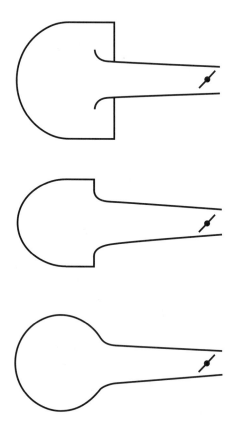

AND FURTHERMORE . . .

Does an air/fuel mixture have trouble staying atomized through an idling turbo at low ambient temperatures?

Draw-through-carb turbo systems inherently have a long, devious route for the air/fuel mixture to travel before reaching the cylinders. If heat is not provided at the carb mount or near the system's low point, fuel will puddle in the bottom of the turbo. In practice, carb preheat allows the engine to idle and run smoothly at low speeds when ambient temperature is less than 80°F. Under boost, such a cyclone exists that puddling is impossible. The problem can be avoided completely by blowing through the carb.

Are blow-through carb systems technically and functionally workable?

Yes. For some heavy-hitting evidence, drive a Lotus Turbo Esprit or a Maserati Bi-Turbo.

Has the controversy of blow-through versus draw-through carb systems been resolved?

Not only yes, but hell yes. Blow-through starts better, idles better, runs smoother at low speed, and produces quicker throttle response and lower emissions. An intercooler can only be used with a blow-through application. The draw-through system is a dead fish.

9 EVENTS IN THE CHAMBER

The real test of a turbo engine and its ability to produce huge amounts of power (without leaving a trail of pungent blue-gray smoke and/or aluminum/iron shrapnel) boils down to what's happening in the combustion chamber. Sparking off a controlled temperature mixture—composed of the right stuff at the right time—is the culmination of all the design effort put into the system. When this event transpires correctly, the fun begins.

Voltage

Igniting the air/fuel mixture in a high-pressure turbocharged engine is tough. The crux of the matter is that air is an electrical insulator. The more air molecules packed into the combustion chamber, the greater the voltage required to drive the spark across the spark plug electrodes. Large amounts of voltage are required at high charge densities. Not only are high voltages required, but all items that carry the high voltage must be insulated with materials of high dielectric strength. This will insure that the voltage really does drive the spark across the plug gap instead of to the valve cover. The tolerance for deterioration in these components is small, again due to the high voltages.

Most ignition systems offered as OEM in the late eighties have sufficient voltage to fire off the mixture at modest boost pressures of 6 to 8 psi. Greater boost pressures will likely require a capacitor discharge ignition supplement to supply consistent ignition. In any system where spark plug life becomes intolerably short, a capacitor discharge unit will be necessary.

Spark Plugs

The choice of a spark plug for a turbo engine application is relatively easy. The heat range of the plug is the key factor to get right. Classifying plugs by their heat range has nothing to do with when or how they manage to get the fire going. "Heat range" means no more or less than how the features of the plug are

Fig. 9-1. The difference between a cold plug and a hot plug is the ease with which heat is transferred out of the center electrode.

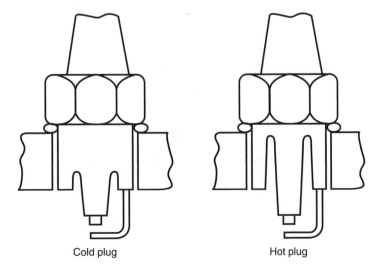

Cold plug   Hot plug

configured to conduct heat away from the electrode. Presume for a moment that it is desirable to have the materials of all spark plugs operate at about the same temperature, regardless of load conditions imposed by the engine. Then the spark plug of a low-speed, low-load, low-compression engine would need to conduct heat away from its electrode slowly, or else the plug would operate too cool. This is called a hot plug. An engine of our liking, clearly, must have plugs that conduct lots of heat away from the electrode. This plug, then, will be referred to as a cold plug. The balance to achieve is to keep the plug hot enough to continuously burn the soot and deposits off yet cool enough to keep the materials from rapid deterioration. A plug that operates at too high a temperature can also serve as an ignition source that actually starts the fire prior to the spark. This is pre-ignition, and it can lead to detonation.

In the actual selection of a plug for a high-pressure turbo engine, the choice should start with a plug about two ranges colder than stock equipment. If the plug deteriorates rapidly or fractures in any way, try a third range colder. Should the plug get dirty and acquire too much resistance to fire, back up one range hotter.

Installation technique will contribute to the plugs' consistency and durability. Certainly all threads and washer seats must be thoroughly cleaned. A proper spark plug lube, like Never-Seize or molysulfide, should be lightly applied to the threads and between the washer and plug. Top this off with tightening the plug to the manufacturer's suggested torque, and you will have done all you can toward good spark plug performance. Torque specs are usually between 10 and 14 ft-lb for aluminum heads and 16 to 18 for iron.

Ignition Timing

Igniting the mixture at the right time is also a challenge. The turbo engine adds one more requirement to the design of an ignition curve. Turbulent turbo mixtures burn faster than normally aspirated mixtures, but the denser mixtures slow the burn. While contrary and confusing, this generally leaves the situation not needing to begin the burn quite so soon. The ignition curve can therefore benefit from a small retard function as boost rises and the mixture becomes both denser and more turbulent. The correct ignition timing under all circumstances is achievable only if the timing curve can be designed right along with the fuel curve. With today's technology, this can be accomplished only with aftermarket engine management systems. At present, the Electromotive and DFI engine management systems can control both ignition and fuel curves.

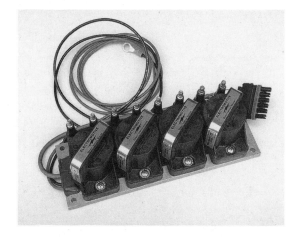

Fig. 9-2. The direct-fire, programmable ignition system from Electromotive is ideal for custom ignition curves required for turbocharged engines.

Electronic Ignition Retard

The boost-pressure-sensitive ignition retard offers a limited degree of adjustability to the ignition system operating under boost. This item can also prove useful in permitting greater ignition advance at low speed and cruise conditions while reducing top-end advance at high boost pressure. The ignition retard can easily be judged just a safety device, but it's not quite so. It also allows a rough tailoring of the high end of the ignition curve to the octane rating of the fuel. A singular disadvantage exists with the pressure-activated retard: it will progressively retard ignition as boost rises, even without the presence of detonation. Therefore, timing is less than optimum at these mid-range points, so that it will be right at maximum boost. This translates to a noticeable loss of mid-range torque. Less torque + less power = less fun.

Fig. 9-3. *The adjustable boost-pressure-actuated ignition retard from MSD.*

Knock Sensor

The pressure-sensitive ignition retard could be called a passive device, in that it does not detect the presence of the event it is there to prevent. It retards the ignition based on boost and retard rate setting only. The knock-sensor ignition retard should be called an active device, however, because it detects the presence of the event and then is charged with the job of eliminating it. The knock sensor does an excellent job of retarding ignition when detonation is detected. This implies that maximum safe power is being developed under the operating conditions at that instant.

For example, add octane, and ignition timing stays forward while power stays up. The knock sensor is an override safety device that is not the least bit concerned with maximum power. If used in an absolutely correct environment, the knock sensor would remain quietly in the background and never be needed. Never, that is, until something went wrong, wrong, wrong. A knock-sensor-controlled ignition curve can display a less-than-fun characteristic. A check on the functioning of the system, as frequently stated in service manuals, is to rap on the cylinder block with a hammer. If the sensor detects the knock and retards the timing, audibly slowing the engine, it is working as designed. Clearly, hammering on the side of the block is not detonation. Why, then, should the retard be activated? Is it possible that a rock bouncing off the block could also retard the timing? How about a failing hydraulic lifter, a water pump bearing, or a broken alternator mount? It is necessary to keep in mind that retarding the ignition raises exhaust gas temperature. This is decidedly a bad thing to do, unless detonation really is present. It is probably stretching the point a bit to

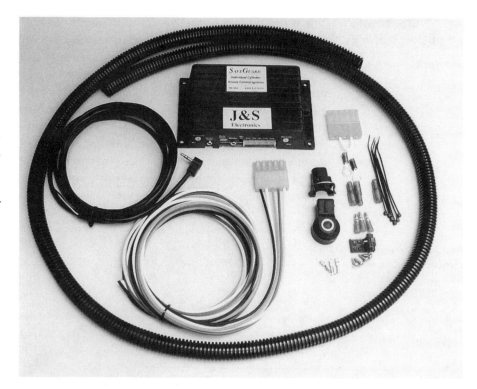

Fig. 9-4. *An active knock-detection system with control of ignition timing is an excellent means of establishing a margin of safety for an engine. These items often add power as well a s safety, by permitting ignition timing to stay closer to the knock threshold than is possible when tuning by ear.*

suggest that a fast trip down a long gravel road might retard ignition to the point of melting an engine.

Mechanical noise of a high-revving engine can cause some knock sensors to activate when no knock is present. This then becomes a rev-based retard, which is not a desirable device.

The development of a knock sensor into a full-fledged computer that does what its software tells it to do is the most optimistic development yet seen. These are in their infancy, but much progress is being made by J&S Electronics. Programming will, wouldn't you know, be the key. Perceived downsides of the knock sensor are not always present. It is, however, necessary to consider these possibilities upon purchase, adjustment, and use of a knock sensor.

Much can be said about the pluses of a knock sensor. The contribution it can make toward peace of mind is not without merit. The vast majority of turbo system installations are not maximum-effort systems; therefore, small power compromises are not crucial. Therein probably lies the distinction of the knock sensor's value in the scheme of things. Overall, the knock sensor is probably the best thing going for control of ignition timing.

Fuels

The quality of the fuel offered up to the burning process is key to the functioning of smooth, powerful turbo engines. High octane, quality refinement, and fast burn rate are the distinguishing characteristics of good turbo fuel. An octane rating is solely a measure of resistance to detonation as tested in a lab test engine. Quality refinement is the production of gasolines without unwanted contaminants, often referred to as "a bad tank of gas." The combustion rate is just the relative rate at which the fuel burns. Combustion rate has a significant effect on detonation characteristics of the fuel and chamber. If the burn rate can be significantly sped up, the little pockets of mixture hidden off in the extremes of the combustion chamber won't have time to overheat and explode.

Absolutely wonderful changes take place as detonation is pushed further out of the picture. A hydrocarbon called toluene presents turbocharging with an intriguing new scope. Toluene is a distillate of oil commonly called methyl benzene. It is a cousin of gasoline. Of some interest is the fact that it is the third component of TNT. That should not imply its power; it is just a curiosity. It does have the remarkable ability to speed up burn rate to such an extent that boost pressures defying imagination can be used. Toluene was the fabled Formula 1 car "rocket fuel" of the mid-eighties. Fourteen hundred horsepower from 90 cid at 75+ psi boost indeed required something out of the ordinary. Think about that for a moment in some humorous circumstances. A Mazda Miata with 1450 bhp comes quickly to mind. Or a NASCAR Winston Cup stock car racer with 5800 bhp. An interesting means of having fun, indeed. Presumably even Richard Petty at his best would have found that a challenge. In the practical use of street fuel, octane rating becomes the most important aspect.

In general, three octane points will offer about 2 psi of boost—assuming, of course that all other factors remain in line. Reformulated gasolines, which include alcohol, are not generally suitable for use with turbos. Octane improvers are readily available and should be considered a viable means of permitting greater boost-pressure levels. Additive quantities vary with brands, so following each manufacturer's recommendations is reasonable. The only downside to octane-improving additives, other than cost and handling, is their dislike for long-term storage after mixing with gasoline. An easy situation to remedy.

Fig. 9-5. Proper gauging tells how well the system is functioning. These combination gauges package nicely and offer a wealth of information.

AND FURTHERMORE . . .

What sort of fuel will I have to use?

You can use the lowest-octane fuel that insures that the detonation threshold will remain at a higher boost level than the setting of the wastegate. In reality, this means the highest-octane fuel currently available. In engines equipped with knock-sensor-controlled ignition timing, power is highly dependent on octane. The greater the octane, the less the knock; consequently, the greater the ignition advance.

Is a special ignition system necessary with the turbocharger?

Stock ignition systems are virtually always adequate for the turbo application. However, three significant gains may be made with a special ignition system:

- increased spark plug life
- smoother running under heavy load by reducing the occasional (too few to feel) misfires
- pressure-activated ignition retard units for greater detonation protection and/or higher boost-pressure levels

Don't buy a special ignition unit for miles-per-gallon reasons. Feet, maybe, but not miles.

10 EXHAUST MANIFOLD

The exhaust manifold plays a key role in all performance aspects of the turbo system. The turbo manifold has many and varied duties to perform. Direct responsibilities include support of the turbo, guidance of exhaust gases to the turbine, keeping exhaust gas pressure pulses moving along intact at a steady pace, and trying hard not to let any heat escape through the manifold walls. To accomplish these chores while glowing cherry red, trying to remain straight, not developing cracks, and hanging in there year after year is not exactly an assignment for boys. An exhaust manifold leads a hard life.

Fig. 10-1. *When designing exhaust manifolding, don't hesitate to copy—just be sure you're copying the best.*

Application

The application, whether competition or high-performance street, will strongly influence material selection, design style, and method of manufacture. Any maximum-effort turbo system will be configured around a tube-style, fabricated manifold. One-off designs, for cost reasons alone, must also be fabricated. A cast manifold is the obvious choice when a large number of parts are to be made.

Design Criteria

HEAT RETENTION. Clearly, performance of the turbine is in part determined by the temperature of the exhaust gases. It is reasonable, then, to expend some effort toward getting the exhaust gas from the combustion chamber to the turbine with the least possible temperature loss. This is fundamentally true, although the strength of materials at elevated temperatures must sometimes be considered and some form of cooling provided. The thermal conductivity of a material is a measure of that material's ability to conduct heat. Since the objective here is to keep the heat inside the manifold, it is reasonable to try to use a material with the poorest ability to transfer heat.

MATERIAL SELECTION.

Stainless steel. Stainless offers an interesting combination of properties. It is low in thermal conductivity, which is certainly desirable. Stainless grade 304 is an excellent choice—easily welded, crack resistant, and relatively easy to work with. All stainless materials have a very high coefficient of thermal expansion; thus, the design, style, and fit of a stainless manifold must account for this unusual property. For example, a stainless header flange drilled perfectly for an exhaust bolt pattern with .3125-inch-diameter bolt holes attached to a cylinder head with .3125-inch-diameter bolts will shear half the bolts on the first warm-up cycle. Larger-than-normal bolt holes are therefore necessary. Stainless steel enjoys long-term corrosion resistance. Because of this and its low heat transfer capability, stainless deserves strong consideration as the material choice for high-performance exhaust manifolds.

Cast iron. Iron alloys offer a designer many options. While not exactly putty in a designer's hands, iron alloys do have the ability to be molded into complex

Fig. 10-2. Top left: A manifold design for twin turbos. Note the wastegate per manifold and no provision for a cross tube. Top right: Typical exhaust manifold casting for a V-8. Note the cross-tube connection entering the manifold from directly below the turbine inlet. Center: A simple, elegant design for the VW GTI engines. Bottom left: Single V-8 turbo design. The lower flange is the cross-tube connection from the opposite bank of cylinders. Bottom right: Big-block Chevy single turbo design with a rear inlet for the cross tube

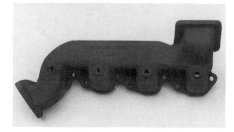

shapes. The limits lie with the ability of the pattern makers. The casting process is the only viable way to make an exhaust manifold with a wide variety of section shapes and wall thicknesses. An experienced or thoughtful designer can take advantage of this characteristic to produce a low-surface-area, thin-walled, smooth, constant-section-passageway manifold.

A wide variety of iron alloys exist, but perhaps the most useful for exhaust manifold design is the alloy called "ductile iron." Ductile iron's characteristics range from good crack resistance and high-temperature shape stability to free machining, all with a relatively high basic strength.

Cast manifolds remain the territory of the volume producer, due to the expense of creating the necessary patterns and tooling.

Mild steel. Although mild steel has no particular characteristics that make it an ideal choice of exhaust manifold materials, it does, indeed, do almost everything well. This material is inexpensive, easy to machine and weld, and readily available in a wide variety of sizes and shapes. Perhaps its poorest characteristic is corrosion resistance. This can be helped significantly by chrome plating. Ask for industrial-quality plating, which is many times thicker than decorative chrome. Perhaps better than chrome are some of the modern ceramic coatings.

Aluminum. Because of aluminum's poor high-temperature strength and high heat-transfer coefficient, rule it out as a suitable material for an automotive exhaust manifold. In some boating applications where exhaust outlet and manifold surface temperatures must be closely controlled, a cast aluminum manifold with water jackets becomes an ideal choice.

Thermal Characteristics

The wall thickness of a particular material will strongly influence the heat transfer, in that the thicker the material, the faster heat will travel through it. This seems contrary to logic at first thought, but consider how fast heat would be drawn out of a high-conductivity, infinitely thick aluminum manifold, as opposed to a very thin piece of stainless surrounded with a nice insulator like air. Heat transfer is directly proportional to surface area. It is therefore reasonable to give considerable thought to keeping the exposed surface area of the exhaust manifold to an absolute minimum. Clearly, the less surface area, the less heat loss. Reducing the amount of ambient air flowing around the exhaust manifold and turbocharger will further reduce heat loss from the system. It is generally not feasible to directly wrap the exhaust manifold with an insulating material, as the manifold material itself will overheat to the point of structural failure.

A further effect on heat transfer out of the exhaust manifold is heat distribution inside the manifold. Hot spots inside the manifold should be avoided, because they can quickly pump a lot of heat out. They are created by sharply angled intersections or by too many exhaust pulses through one segment of the manifold. Keep in mind that the temperature difference between the inside and outside of the manifold is the force that pushes heat through the manifold.

Reversion

Reversal of the exhaust gas flow back into the combustion chamber during valve overlap is called reversion. Creating an aerodynamic barrier that reduces the reverse flow yet does not impede outward-flowing gases can pay dividends in performance.

Style of Manifolding

In general, much greater freedom exists in the choice of manifold styles when the manifold is fabricated. These choices range from the simple log style to the

Fig. 10-3. Durability of an exhaust manifold can be influenced by the basic design. A log-style manifold is subject to more heat abuse and thermal expansion than a separate-tube header. Overlapping heat pulses in the log style create extra hot spots and greater expansion.

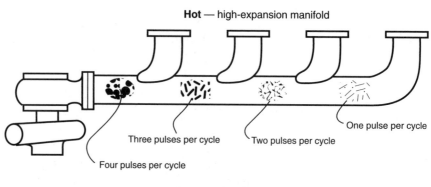

Hot — high-expansion manifold

Four pulses per cycle
Three pulses per cycle
Two pulses per cycle
One pulse per cycle

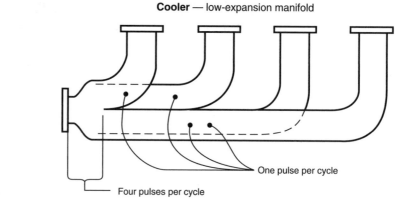

Cooler — low-expansion manifold

One pulse per cycle
Four pulses per cycle

Fig. 10-4. The anti-reversion cone can offer a reduction in exhaust gas reversion during valve overlap. The cone creates a partial barrier to reversal of flow.

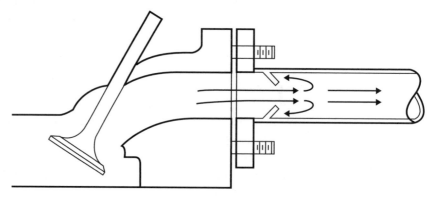

equal-length, multiple-tube, individual-runner style. A great amount of research has been done on the performance benefits of various manifold styles. Most of this research, plus the tremendous efforts put into the recent era of turbocharged Grand Prix cars, strongly indicates that the best manifolding is multiple-tube, individual-runner style.

TUBING SIZES. Almost all applications of a turbo are to an existing engine. Therefore, the choice of tube sizes will usually be dictated by port size and the size of the turbine inlet on the turbocharger. Where a clear-cut choice does not exist, it is best to select the smaller of the sizes available, thus increasing exhaust gas velocity.

☞ **RULE:** When a choice exists as to tube size, always opt for the smaller, to keep gas velocities high.

Fig. 10-5. Four-into-one designs for 4- or 8-cylinder engines

Fig. 10-6. An example of good, compact manifolds. These designs also use weld els.

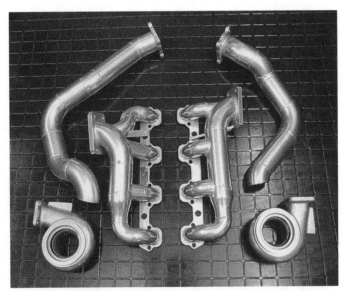

Fig. 10-7. V-12 custom header. The sharp intersections are not ideal for power. Long collector tubes are going to experience large thermal expansion, necessitating flexible braces on the turbos.

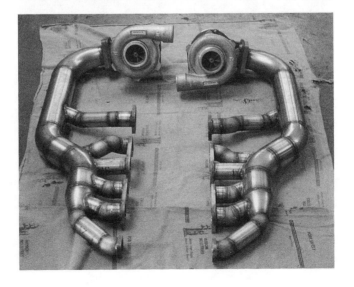

The strength of the manifold will be controlled largely by the wall thickness of the materials. In a fabricated manifold where wall thickness drops below .09 inch, it may be necessary to support the turbo by a brace or small truss assembly. The thermal expansion of the manifold will tend to move the turbo around as the heat cycles up and down. Thus, a mount must have some degree of flexibility while supporting the weight of the turbo. Mandrel-bent tubes are available in a wide variety of sizes to meet the needs of the custom header maker. These are generally high-quality items and can be fabricated into any bundle-of-snakes style turbo manifold one's imagination can conjure up.

A variation of the tube manifold can be constructed based on a cast-steel part called a weld el. Weld els are basically industrial hydraulic equipment, used commonly in oil well and other similar heavy duty applications. These els are available in a variety of sizes and radii, and in either mild steel or stainless. Although heavy and expensive, weld els can be used to form a proper high-strength manifold. Weld els are sized according to pipe nomenclature—that is, inside diameters.

Fig. 10-8. *Jim Feuling's wild twin-turbo Quad 4 featured some of the best headers ever built. Note the particularly smooth collectors.*

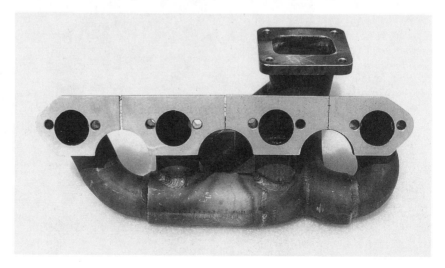

Fig. 10-9. *A weld el manifold. Note cuts in the flange to avoid warpage on thermal expansion.*

Fig. 10-10. *Weld el manifolds as a functional work of art*

Fig. 10-11. *Fitting weld els together to form the triple-turbo Jaguar exhaust manifolds*

Table 10-1. *Weld el selection chart for 90° elbows (inches)*

Nominal pipe size	Bend radius	Outside diameter	Inside diameter	Wall thickness
1/2	1 1/2	.840	.622	.109
3/4	1 1/8	1.050	.824	.113
1	1 1/2	1.315	1.049	.133
1 1/4	1 7/8	1.660	1.380	.140
1 1/2	2 1/4	1.900	1.610	.145
2	3	2.375	2.067	.154
2 1/2	3 3/4	2.875	2.469	.203
3	4 1/2	3.500	3.068	.216

Table 10-2. Weld el se-lection chart for concen-tric and eccentric reducers (inches)

Nominal pipe size	Length	Nominal pipe size	Length
3/4 x 3/8	1 1/2	2 x 3/4	3
3/4 x 1/2	1 1/2	2 x 1	3
1 x 3/8	2	2 x 1 1/4	3
1 x 1/2	2	2 x 1 1/2	3
1 x 3/4	2	2 1/2 x 1	3 1/2
1 1/4x 1/2	2	2 1/2 x 1 1/4	3 1/2
1 1/4 x 3/4	2	2 1/2 x 1 1/2	3 1/2
1 1/4 x 1	2	2 1/2 x 2	3 1/2
1 1/2 x 1/2	2 1/2	3 x 1	3 1/2
1 1/2 x 3/4	2 1/2	3 x 1 1/4	3 1/2
1 1/2 x 1	2 1/2	3 x 1 1/2	3 1/2
1 1/2 x 1 1/4	2 1/2	3 x 2	3 1/2
		3 x 2 1/2	3 1/2

Cast Manifold

The casting process lends itself to simpler designs, due largely to the complica-tions and costs of patterns. These designs usually adopt log-style manifolds—good for production but not quite so good for maximum performance. It is nec-essary to understand that a cast manifold can deliver very good performance, but it is not race car hardware.

Wastegate Integration

Early in the planning of the exhaust manifold design, consideration must be given to location of, and bleed-off to, the wastegate. The principles involved in integrating the wastegate into the system are that bleed-off to the wastegate must occur after all exhaust pulses headed for the turbo have been combined into one tube, and the flow path must be streamlined.

Fig. 10-12. A simple adaptation of a produc-tion exhaust manifold to a turbo application. The turbo-mount boss is fabricated from steel plates and welded into place.

Fig. 10-13. *Integration of the wastegate into the exhaust manifold*

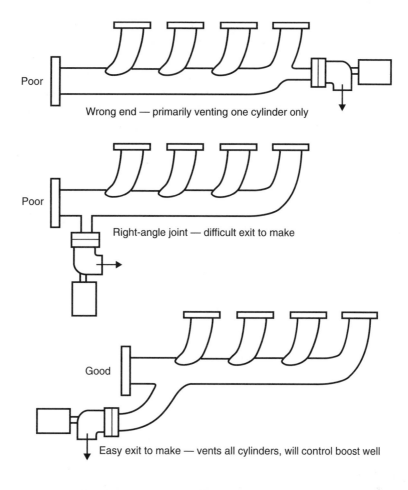

Poor
Wrong end — primarily venting one cylinder only

Poor
Right-angle joint — difficult exit to make

Good
Easy exit to make — vents all cylinders, will control boost well

Fig. 10-14. *The Toyota GTP four-cylinder engine was one of the most successful turbocharged engines ever. Two of the reasons were the smooth header and integration of the wastegate into the turbine housing at an ideal angle.*

Thermal Expansion

Changes in the shape of a manifold as its temperature rises from ambient to operating must be considered during layout. Heat-induced warpage can cause severe problems with constant exhaust gas leaks. Warpage is caused by unequal temperature distribution through the material of the manifold. As an example, the header flange will not reach the same temperature as a segment of the tubing or the collectors; therefore, it will not change length as much. These varying changes in length will induce warpage if they are not accounted for in the design. Each port flange, for example, should be separate from the others.

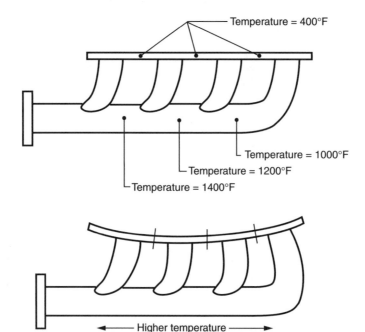

Fig. 10-15. *Temperature-induced warpage: the header is forced to warp due to uneven temperature distribution between the tubes and the flange. The fix is to sever the flange into as many segments as there are ports.*

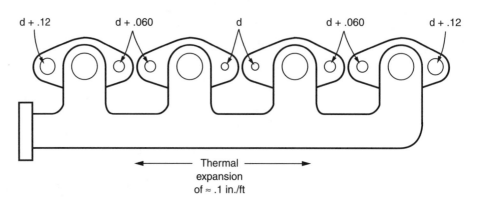

Fig. 10-16. *Thermal expansion can fracture header bolts. This can be avoided by making the bolt holes progressively larger as their distance from the center of the manifold increases.*

Thermal expansion characteristics will require attention to bolt hole sizes, particularly at the cylinder head. Tight, close-tolerance bolt patterns can actually cause fastener failure by placing the fasteners under severe binding when a manifold reaches maximum operating temperature. The solution to this problem is enlarging the bolt hole size as it gets farther away from the center of the manifold. This is essential when stainless steel is the material used. On long engines, like six-cylinder inline, the designer should consider using two manifolds, with interconnections from a tubular flex joint. This type of slip joint is common on aircraft and large industrial engines.

Fasteners Selection of fasteners is a twofold decision. The heat involved in a particular joint determines the choice of material, while the type of joint determines whether a bolt or stud is used.

The idea of holding parts together at the operating temperatures induced by a flat-out turbocharger system is cause for some thought. Almost any mild steel will have its heat treat cooked out of it. Mild steel will eventually oxidize to the point where fasteners are corroded virtually to the base materials. Cadmium plating will burn away at these temperatures. The most reasonable solution to fastener problems is stainless steel. Stainless steel bolts work better at temperatures above 1200°F. Below that, stainless is nice but not cost-effective.

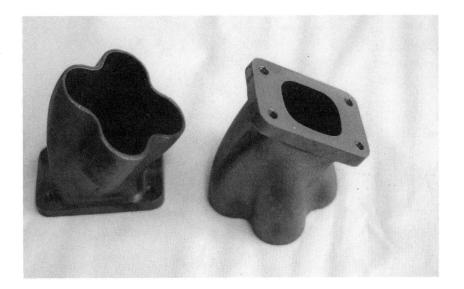

Fig. 10-17. Cast iron collectors suitable for 4- and 8-cylinder headers

Depending on the style of joint, three fasteners are possible: through-bolt, stud, or bolt. Observe the following guidelines:

- A through-bolt with a nut (a con-rod bolt, for example) is always the first choice.
- A stud anchored in a threaded receiver (cylinder head to exhaust manifold, for example) is a decent second choice.
- Last and clearly least is a bolt screwed into a threaded receiver. These joints cannot stay tight unless secured with safety wire. Use only as a last resort.

Large, heavy, flat washers are necessary, as are lockwashers. Forget using any form of spring lockwasher, as the heat treat merely gets cooked out. Interference-style lockwashers, with ramps, ridges, or serrations, are the only lockwashers that are survivors.

Stainless mechanical locknuts are able to keep a positive lock at high temperature. Copper-alloy locknuts cannot cut the temperature; they simply sag.

☞ **RULE:** Bolted turbo joints are trouble. Give them your best shot.

Gaskets Although the function of a gasket seems obvious, the gasket can also be used as somewhat of a thermal barrier. Some joints need gaskets for sealing, while others benefit solely from the reduction of heat transfer. The mating surfaces of two parts operating at about the same temperature don't necessarily need a gasket. The turbo attachment to the manifold is such a joint. A wastegate attachment is quite the opposite, however. It is desirable to reduce heat in the vicinity of the wastegate diaphragm, to improve the diaphragm's life expectancy. A gasket here serves as a useful heat block. This same condition exists at the tailpipe joint to the turbo and the wastegate vent tube to the wastegate.

Gaskets obviously take a serious beating in any exhaust system. The presence of the turbo doesn't help the situation. In certain situations where the quality of the machining permits, the best solution to a gasket problem is to leave the gasket out. This is particularly viable between two cast iron surfaces. Steel flanges upward of 1/2 inch thick will likely be stable enough to seal long-term without the gasket.

Fig. 10-18. Excellent exhaust plumbing details on a single-turbo V-8

When a gasket is obviously required, the metal/fiber/metal laminated type is perhaps the best all-around combination of sealing gasket and insulator for the high-heat environment of the turbo. A simple stainless-steel-sheet gasket or annealed copper gasket is also an excellent choice. The latter two are usually .02–.03 inch thick and can seal well where surfaces are slightly irregular or the joining parts are not stiff enough to operate without the gasket. All else should be considered of only temporary value. In general, all-fiber gaskets should be avoided, as none of the fibrous materials exhibit long-term durability with respect to heat. Money spent on good-quality, metal-based gaskets will save many headaches and exhaust leaks.

Eliminating gaskets is a valid design objective. With thick flanges and careful surface machining, by and large, most gaskets can be eliminated. There is an element of logic to the idea that an absent gasket can't blow.

AND FURTHERMORE . . .

What constitutes a proper exhaust manifold?

An exhaust manifold is a complicated design exercise involving many parameters. The single most important parameter is the material, and cast iron is the best material for typical street applications. Plain steel is the poorest choice, because it oxidizes rapidly at high temperatures, flakes off, and ultimately cracks. Internal streamlining is important, to avoid pumping losses. Another critical design feature is flow velocity. Exhaust gas must not be forced to speed up and slow down, since it will lose considerable energy otherwise available to the turbine. Smooth, constant-velocity flow is ideal. Heat retention is important. The more heat that can be retained inside the manifold, the less the thermal-lag portion of the total turbo lag. A design that allows exhaust gas pulses to arrive at the turbine at regularly spaced intervals is ideal but difficult to achieve.

Fig. 10-19. *Note the "doubling back" of the exhaust manifold on this 1986 YBB engine fitted with a turbo. This placement has permitted an unusually compact layout while maintaining a smooth 4-into-1 design.*

Fig. 10-20. *One of the early Toyota GTP engines with beautiful plumbing in all respects. This layout merits study. Note the wastegate tubes venting from the exhaust manifold just before the turbine housing, and the relatively small header tubes. Note also the thermal expansion joints just above the wastegate, where the exhaust tubes fit into the legs of the Y coupling without being welded.*

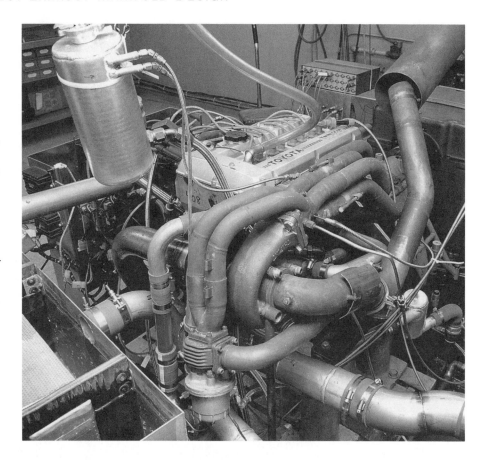

Do the joints interfacing the turbo have any reliability problems?

Gaskets between exhaust manifolds and turbos are often unreliable due to the extreme heat. The most practical solution to this problem is precision flat surfaces that seal without gaskets.

11 EXHAUST SYSTEMS

The modern turbocharged automobile has brought new meaning to the term "free-flow exhaust system," with its connotation of low back pressure. The modern exhaust system also invariably has a catalytic converter, with its implication of high back pressure. At first glance, these two items are somewhat at odds with each other. At last glance, the situation is a bit better than generally believed. If the turbo could step up and dictate terms for design of exhaust systems, it would categorically state: *None!* If the feds could step up and dictate the design of exhaust systems (which they can, have, and will continue to do), they would state that the best tailpipe is one that nothing comes out of. Somewhere between these two dissimilar requirements lies a real good exhaust system for street use that will keep both parties happy. Well, relatively happy.

Fig. 11-1. The best exhaust for a turbo is the least exhaust.

For our purposes, we shall call the exhaust system everything after the turbo. Virtually all turbos require special tailpipes. Stock, non-turbo tailpipes don't cut it. Seldom do aftermarket tailpipes prove satisfactory either. An exhaust system is an accumulation of optimized, carefully thought out features. The objective that must be met in correlating these design features is the creation of a clean-running, acceptable-noise-level, lowest-possible-back-pressure tailpipe.

☞ **RULE:** Back pressure in an exhaust system is evil.

Fig. 11-2. *Turbos do not like back pressure; the lower the better. Note the separate exhaust pipes for the wastegates.*

Design Considerations

TURBO-TO-TAILPIPE JOINT. This part of the exhaust system is subject to temperatures ranging up to 1500°F, a factor that dictates much of the configuration of the components. This is perhaps the most highly stressed section of the exhaust system. Therefore, strength is of prime importance. Strength starts with the thickness of the turbine outlet flange. This flange can arguably be as thick as 1/2 inch and still call for additional ribs or braces.

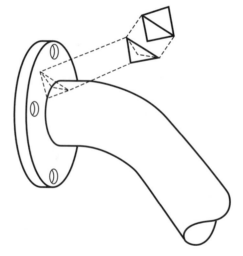

Fig. 11-3. *Strengthening ribs between each fastener will greatly increase the durability of a flange-to-pipe joint.*

As flanges do not stay flat during welding, the mating surface to the turbine must be surfaced prior to installation. Welding is generally harmful to the base metal. A weakened condition thus exists at the flange/tube weld. An easy way around this weak point is to weld the tube inside the flange and only intermittently on the outside, making the weak segments discontinuous.

BASIC TUBE SIZE. It is easy to get overeager on fitting large-diameter pipes into an exhaust system. "The larger the better" is not the case. As indicated in Chapter 5, there is an exhaust gas velocity that ought not to be exceeded. I am going to suggest that for exhaust calculations, this velocity is approximately 250 ft/sec. The considerable expansion of exhaust gas due to the temperature increase also requires a significant increase in the desired volume of the tailpipe. The tubes for the hot gas on the exhaust side should therefore be larger than the tubes for the cooler intake side. Base the calculation on the same conditions as for intake tubes, but use a maximum velocity of 250 ft/sec rather than 450 ft/sec. To size a tailpipe, you can adhere to this exhaust gas velocity or to the simple guideline of selecting a tube diameter approximately 10% larger than the turbine outlet diameter. Figure 11-4, exhaust tube size versus bhp, offers a good guide to choosing an adequate tailpipe size.

Fig. 11-4. Approximate exhaust pipe flow area for specific power output

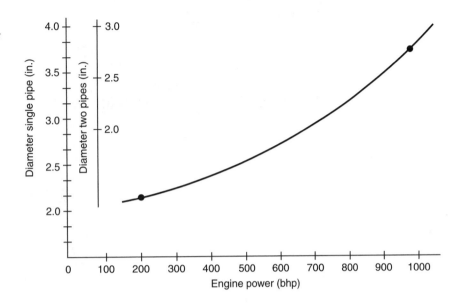

Fig. 11-5. Turbine outlet flange connections should not be welded a full 360° on the external joint.

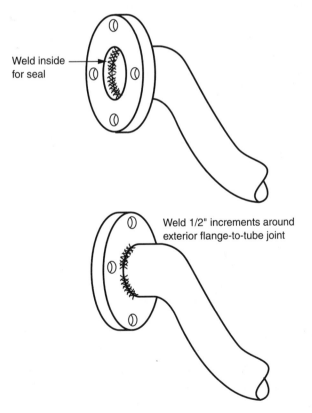

Weld inside for seal

Weld 1/2" increments around exterior flange-to-tube joint

CONVERTER POSITION. The position of the catalytic converter is locked in by law. The converter must stay in the original position. Do yourself a favor and leave it alone. Modern matrix-style converters are not very restrictive. Most units will contribute less than 2 psi to the total back pressure in the tailpipe. That is acceptable.

When adding a catalytic converter to a system not previously so equipped, place the converter as close to the turbo as possible, to help the converter reach operating temperature quickly.

Fig. 11-6. A good example of fitting exhaust tubing in the available space while maintaining adequate tube size and mandrel bends. This also shows a good Y connection combining two turbine outlet tubes.

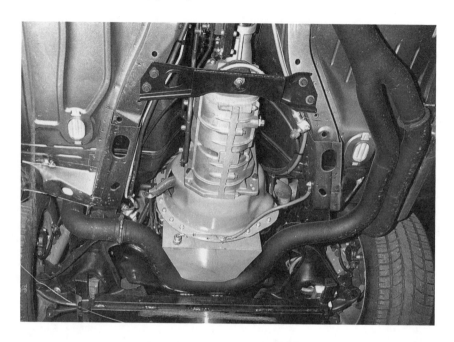

OXYGEN SENSOR POSITION. The oxygen sensor ideally wants to be as close to the combustion chambers as temperature permits. In most circumstances where a turbo is involved, the oxygen sensor should be immediately aft of the turbo.

EXPANSION JOINTS. The wide temperature fluctuations experienced by the tailpipe of a turbo engine cause somewhat greater thermal expansion than would otherwise be the case. Permitting the tailpipe to expand and contract without restraint thus becomes vital, to avoid cracking caused by thermal-expansion-induced binding.

Fig. 11-7. Thermal expansion of the exhaust system must be allowed, to avoid cracking.

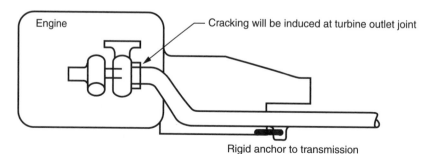

Fig. 11-8. *A joint at the transmission should be flexible.*

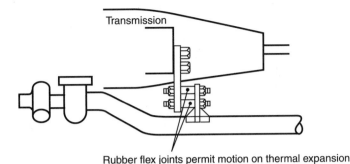

Transmission

Rubber flex joints permit motion on thermal expansion

Fig. 11-9. *The swaged tailpipe joint is the simplest and most versatile of all joints.*

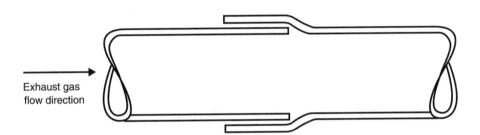

Exhaust gas flow direction

A degree of flex can be built into a tailpipe, with swages used as connectors for the pipe segments. Swages permit easy angular adjustment as well. The pipe clamp can also readily serve as a hanger anchor.

HANGERS. As simple as the idea may be of hanging a tailpipe under a car, you need only look under a Ferrari to get a good feel for the fact that this subject can be taken very seriously. Several problems crop up in properly locating a tailpipe. Vibration, heat, engine rocking motions, thermal expansion, and hanger design are all problems that need to be addressed before one has a durable, unobnoxious tailpipe.

Vibration can usually be damped by frequent hangers and soft spots. Soft spots are flex joints that will not transmit vibration. A swaged joint is an example of a soft spot.

Heat is only a problem if a vulnerable component is within range. In general, it is far better to insulate the item that can get damaged rather than the tailpipe itself. Heat can damage such things as undercoating, fiber materials, and painted surfaces. A bit of time spent looking for such vulnerable things and providing a few shields will prove valuable in the long run. A simple sheet-metal shield will provide a temperature drop of several hundred degrees.

Fig. 11-10. *Swages, either singly or in multiples, can be used as flex joints.*

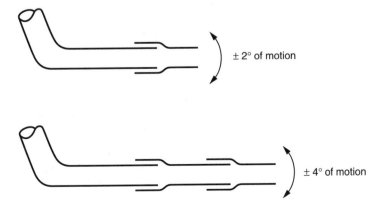

± 2° of motion

± 4° of motion

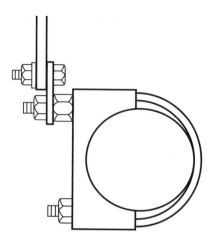

Fig. 11-11. *Simple hanger with clamp*

MUFFLER STYLES, SIZES, AND NUMBER. Generally speaking, the muffler will be the largest single restriction in the exhaust system. Unfortunately, the requirements of low back pressure and silencing are usually at odds with each other. Reasonable compromise can be reached most often with several large mufflers. The need to keep large flow areas through all sections of the exhaust system can frequently be met by installing mufflers in parallel. Inspect the flow area available in each case and be certain the sum of the cross-sectional areas exceeds the basic tube area. It will pay dividends to make the muffler flow areas about 25% greater than the basic tube, as the drag coefficient inside the muffler is usually pretty shabby.

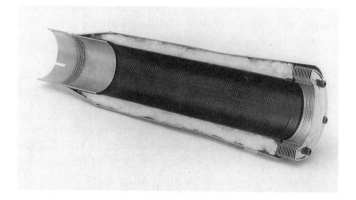

Fig. 11-12. *The clever yet effective low-restriction muffler design from Super-Trap.*

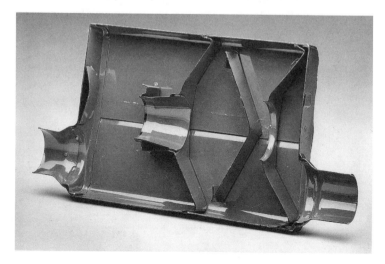

Fig. 11-13. *The Flow-master muffler offers low exhaust gas restriction with adequate noise suppression.*

The choice of muffler styles is limited to straight-through glass-pack types or the relatively popular "turbo" mufflers. Generally, straight-through units offer better flow capability, while baffle-style turbo mufflers provide superior silencing. Glass- or steel-pack units have the reputation of burning the silencing material out at an early age. Oddly enough, the turbo dramatically extends the life expectancy of these mufflers, as it takes out a great deal of heat that would otherwise do damage.

Two types of cores are popular in the glass-pack units: drilled and louvered. Drilled cores have a much cleaner, thus less restrictive, flow path. If drilled-core units prove scarce, louvered-core mufflers work better when flowed backward.

Fig. 11-14. Top: Parallel glass-pack mufflers flow well and offer low restriction. Bottom: This muffler layout may offer an advantage in tight spaces.

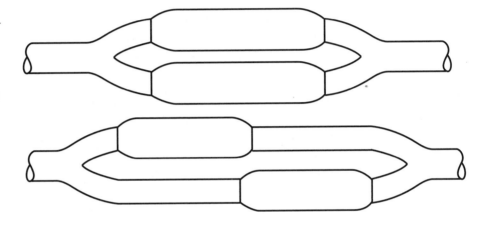

Fig. 11-15. Glass-pack mufflers are made in two different styles, drilled-core and louvered-core. Drilled-core are superior.

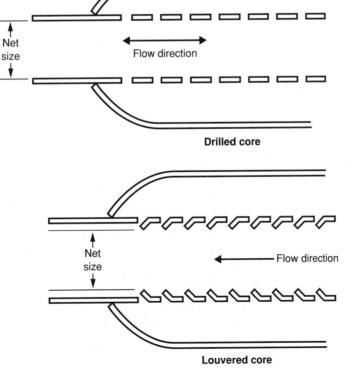

Net size

Flow direction

Drilled core

Net size

Flow direction

Louvered core

Fear of excessive noise with straight-through mufflers is usually valid. This is not the case with a turbo engine, as the turbo alone can be considered approximately one-third of a muffler.

WASTEGATE INTEGRATION. The wastegate, discussed more extensively in Chapter 12, presents no special requirements with respect to silencing but does create an opportunity that can benefit performance. In any catalytic-converter-equipped car, the wastegate discharge must be put back into the tailpipe before the converter, because all the exhaust gas must pass through the converter. Where no converter is required, the opportunity exists to make a completely separate tailpipe solely for the wastegate. A simple muffler may prove necessary to keep noise within limits when the system is at maximum boost. The value in creating a separate tailpipe here is that it effectively increases the exhaust system's total flow area. In general, a wastegate will be more positive in response and somewhat more effective in controlling boost pressure when accompanied by its own tailpipe.

The wastegate vent tube or tailpipe will suffer unusually large fluctuations in operating temperature. This situation exists because the wastegate is closed most of the time, and the vent tube will thus be cold, since no exhaust flow is

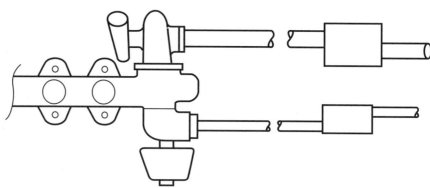

Fig. 11-16. A separate tailpipe for the wastegate is best.

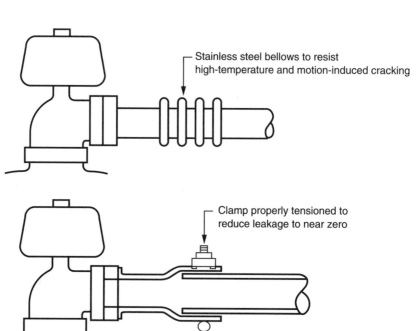

Fig. 11-17. The wastegate vent tube suffers the most from thermal expansion; length changes must be accommodated. Note direction of swage for best seal when not operating under boost, due to normal back pressure in the tailpipe.

Stainless steel bellows to resist high-temperature and motion-induced cracking

Clamp properly tensioned to reduce leakage to near zero

present. As soon as the wastegate opens, the entire vent tube experiences a rapid rise in temperature. This fluctuation will occur every time the wastegate opens. This requires the vent tube design to be such that it can expand and contract without putting itself in a crack-inducing bind. Expansion joints can take the shape of swaged or bellowed connections. Bellows, to prove long-term durable, must be stainless steel and of sturdy construction. The material should be a minimum of .03 inch thick. A bellows must be supported so as to eliminate vibration, or it will fail due to metal fatigue.

MATERIALS AND FINISHES. Mild steel is an entirely adequate material for exhaust system construction. Stainless steel, while distinctly superior, presents the problem of obtaining all the system components from this material. Stainless tubes welded to mild steel mufflers accomplishes little for long-term durability.

Fig. 11-18. This wastegate on a Honda CRX is mounted remotely from the exhaust manifold for packaging reasons.

FASTENERS AND GASKETS. Bolted-together joints are surely the most troublesome parts of any exhaust system. If properly configured, the fasteners and gaskets that hold the joints together can go a long way toward insuring that these joints remain in service without trouble. Creating the correct setup is largely a matter of several do's and don'ts, listed in Chapter 10.

FLANGES. A flange has the twofold responsibility of keeping the gasket securely clamped at all times and insuring that the tailpipe tube receives adequate support. These requirements are easily met by using flanges 3/8 inch thick or greater. A small flange, such as for a wastegate, can survive as thin as 5/16 inch. In general, the thicker the flange, the longer it and its gasket will stay there.

Tailpipe Tips

Since the only visible segment of the entire exhaust system is the last few inches, it is tempting to let style do a number on efficiency. Style is almost always nice, but not when it costs power. Make sure the exhaust flow area is maintained through the tips. Thoughts of tip designs that "extract" exhaust gases might be alluring, but wait until they show up on Formula 1 race cars before getting too enthused about their merit. Most fancy tip offerings will prove less than satisfactory.

Fig. 11-19. *Nice cosmetic exhaust detailing from Borla. The outer tube is the basic pipe size.*

Special Requirements for Front-Wheel-Drive Cars

A front-wheel driver is most often a transverse engine layout. This presents a new problem to the designer, in that the tailpipe is required to flex up and down when the engine moves relative to its mounts when transmitting torque. It is not feasible to bend a tailpipe and expect it to survive more than one fast lap around the block. The flex joint takes on a whole new meaning with the front-drive transverse-engine vehicle. Don't put yourself into the position of building pipe after pipe with the strength to stay in one piece and trying to get one to live. The problem is to design in enough flexibility of joints so that the engine can move virtually anywhere and not overstress the tailpipe. Anticipate 10° of flexibility and provide for it.

AND FURTHERMORE . . .

Do the joints interfacing the turbo have any reliability problems?

Almost always. Stock systems are designed for flow rates produced by stock engines. To try to pump 50% more flow (approximately 7 psi boost) through an exhaust will raise tailpipe pressure to an unacceptably high level.

12 BOOST CONTROLS

The need for effective and positive boost controls in a turbocharger system is brought about by the turbo's characteristic of increasing its rate of airflow faster than the ability of the engine to accept that flow. If unchecked, the turbo can quickly produce damagingly high boost pressures that lead to engine knock. The methods and details by which boost pressures are held in check are key elements in the success of any turbo system design.

Boost-control devices vary in style and effectiveness, from the angle of the driver's right foot to the sophisticated variable area turbine nozzles. The following discussion will outline the schemes and their merits for keeping boost production under reasonable limits.

Restrictor

Boost can be controlled by creating a restriction for either intake flow or exhaust flow. On the intake side, simply drawing through or pumping through a calibrated (by trial and error) orifice at the compressor inlet or outlet, respectively, can limit the flow so boost won't get out of hand. A slightly more clever device varies flow area as boost rises, so nonboosted operation is wide open. Intake charge temperatures will rise with this control, because the boost made will be from less air let in; thus the pressure ratio and temperature are greater.

The restrictor will also work on the exhaust side. Again, the calibrated orifice will limit the flow, as the turbo is free to make huge amounts of boost, only

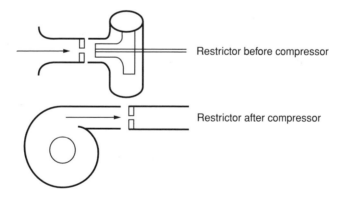

Fig. 12-1. Boost can be controlled by a compressor inlet or outlet restrictor. While effective, this increases heat and is a bad idea.

Restrictor before compressor

Restrictor after compressor

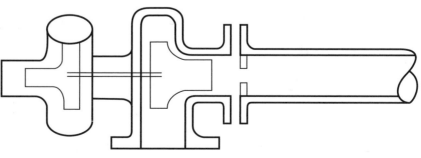

Fig. 12-2. A tailpipe restrictor can control boost, but heat goes up. Effective, but also a bad idea.

to scrap the flow at the orifice. This restrictor can take the form of a large washer at the turbine outlet or even a muffler that hates performance. Any restriction to exhaust flow will drive combustion chamber temperatures up, because exhaust back pressure, and thus reversion, will be greater.

The fundamental notion of adding a turbocharger to increase flow through an engine and then adding a restrictor to control that flow must, in the final analysis, be considered a dopey scheme. No Formula 1 cars have flow restrictors.

Vent Valve

A rather sophisticated radiator cap can be used as a boost-control device. Generally, these types of controls will prove inaccurate and often noisy. While far superior to any form of restrictor, these valves probably have their greatest value as safety controls in the event of a wastegate failure. They can commonly be found on production turbo cars as overboost safety devices. The vent valve has no business being a primary boost-control device. Furthermore, it cannot be used on a draw-through carb system, as it would be required to vent a fuel/air mixture.

Fig. 12-3. *Boost pressure can be vented after work is done to create it. Effective, but a bad idea.*

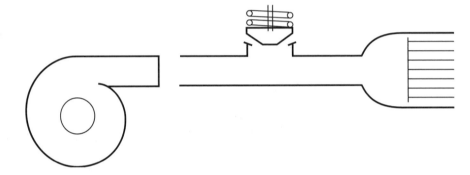

Wastegate

The wastegate derives its name from the fact that it functions by wasting a portion of the exhaust energy. By wasting, or bypassing, a controlled amount of exhaust gas energy around the turbine, the actual speed of the turbine, hence the boost, can be controlled. Imagine the wastegate, then, to be nothing more than an exhaust bypass valve that allows only enough exhaust gas flow to the turbine to produce the desired boost.

Fig. 12-4. *The wastegate. This is the way to control boost with the classic turbocharger.*

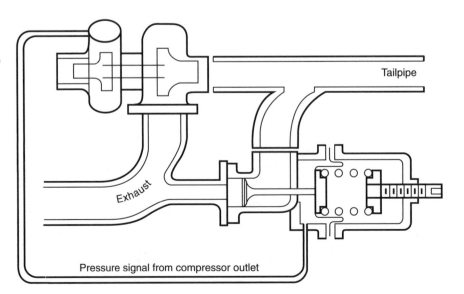

Tailpipe

Exhaust

Pressure signal from compressor outlet

Fig. 12-5. *Two excellent examples of wastegates from HKS*

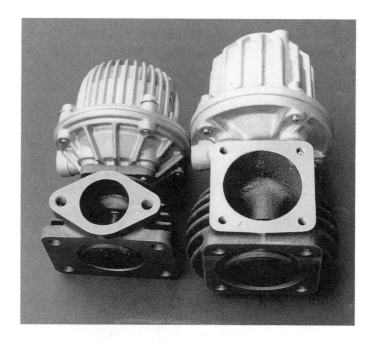

Fig. 12-6. *Adapters to place a wastegate between the turbo and the manifold*

Although the wastegate is currently the best choice for the job of boost control, it is not a perfect concept. That it functions by wasting energy is obviously a flaw. A second flaw is the need for the wastegate valve to start opening quite early in the boost rise time, so it will reach a position to stabilize boost when boost reaches the desired maximum. In other words, a wastegate set at 10 psi will usually start to open at about 5 psi and clearly waste a bunch of energy that could otherwise be used to speed the turbo up. Trying to gain turbine rpm while the wastegate valve is open is, in part, chasing one's tail.

The thousand-horsepower Formula 1 cars used wastegates, and so does every proper turbo system in the world. Until the VATN-controlled turbo becomes widely available at a reasonable cost, the wastegate is the best boost control.

Selecting the Wastegate

Two styles of wastegate currently exist: integral and remote. Integral implies that the wastegate is built into the turbocharger itself. The remote can be placed wherever one feels the need. Or, at least, in a more ideal place.

The decision as to which style to employ is one of balance between economics and performance. The nod on economics goes to the integral style. The per-

Fig. 12-7. *The integral wastegate is inexpensive and easy.*

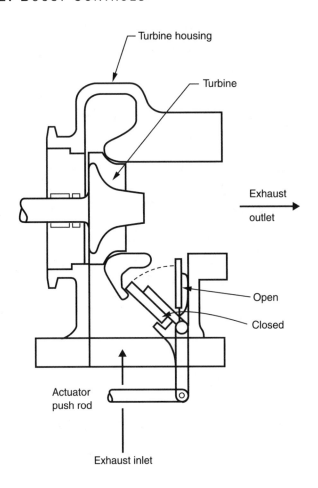

Turbine housing

Turbine

Exhaust outlet

Open

Closed

Actuator push rod

Exhaust inlet

Fig. 12-8. *The remote wastegate is the best of the boost-control solutions.*

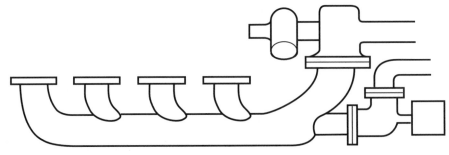

formance advantage, while small, is usually with the remote wastegate. Show me an integral wastegate on a race car.

Integrating the Wastegate into the System

One of the key items in integrating the wastegate into the system is the location of the exhaust gas bleed-off from the exhaust manifold. This feature is critical, because it determines such things as load balance between cylinders, accurate and quick response of the gate, and, in part, turbine inlet pressure. The bleed-off must vent from a location where the pulses from all cylinders have been collected. This virtually always means the manifold, close to the turbine mounting flange. Symmetry and easy flow paths are ideals for laying out a wastegate system.

It is vital that exhaust gases be given an easy job of changing direction from the route toward the turbine to the bypass through the wastegate. If flow has any difficulty whatsoever changing direction to exit through the wastegate, the ability to control boost in the higher rev ranges may simply disappear.

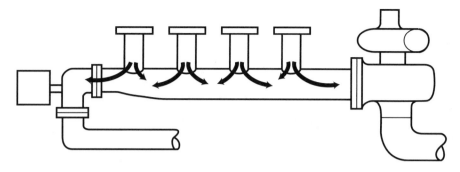

Fig. 12-9. *The wastegate that does not vent from all cylinders uniformly is a bad idea. Nor should it cause reversal of flow from the turbo, as here.*

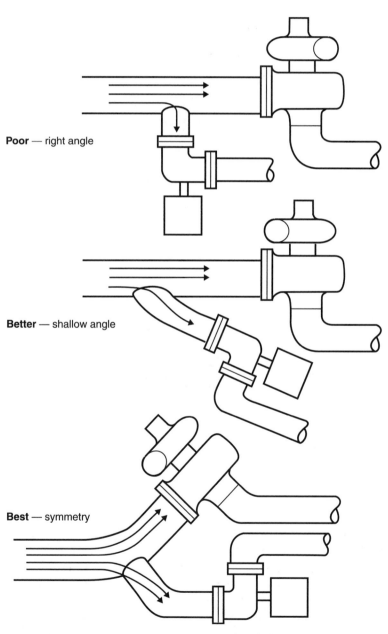

Fig. 12-10. *Bleed angles into wastegates are important, to allow exhaust gas to flow easily out of the system.*

Poor — right angle

Better — shallow angle

Best — symmetry

Exhaust gas return from the wastegate to the tailpipe after the turbine should receive the same forethought as gas entering the wastegate. The principle here is to avoid interfering with exhaust gas flow exiting the turbine. Interference will raise exhaust back pressure, thus reducing power. An integral wastegate will usually channel bypassed exhaust gas back into the system immediately aft of the turbine wheel. This is acceptable for economic reasons but is not in the best interest of power. A few integral wastegate designs, like some models of the Japanese IHI, have provided a separate exhaust pipe for the bypassed gases. When this separate pipe is available, it should be taken advantage of and routed some distance down the tailpipe before being dumped back into the main exhaust system. A minimum distance would be 18 inches.

As discussed in Chapter 11, the ideal circumstance for bypassed gases from the wastegate is a completely separate tailpipe. This offers the most positive wastegate response, lowest back pressure, and no interference with flow

Fig. 12-11. *Integral wastegates usually dump vented gases immediately behind the turbine and create high turbulence, reducing overall flow.*

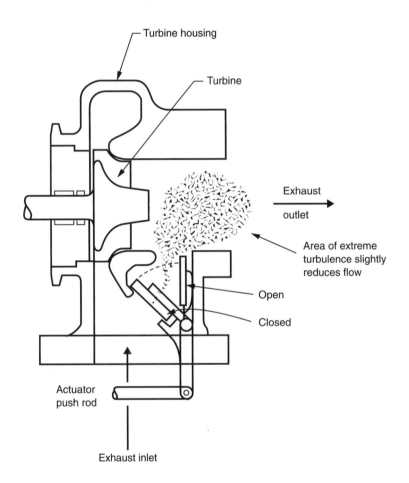

Fig. 12-12. *Integral wastegates that keep vented gas away from primary exhaust gas permit superior power output.*

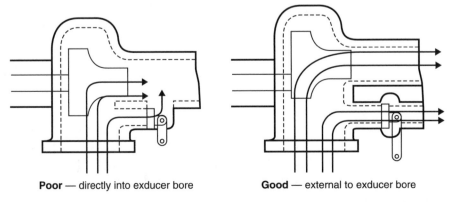

Poor — directly into exducer bore   **Good** — external to exducer bore

through the turbine. Perhaps not cheap or easy, but a maximum-effort turbo system will have a separate tailpipe for the wastegate, with suitable consideration given to thermal expansion of the tube without any cracking of the joint between tube and tailpipe

Fig. 12-13. *A variation on the integral wastegate, but with a separate vent path*

Wastegate Actuator Signal

Boost pressure applied to the wastegate diaphragm is referred to as the actuator signal. The source of this signal can influence wastegate response, ultimate boost pressure, and, under certain circumstances, even fuel flow rates. It is therefore important to consider where this actuator signal should come from. It is vital to know and understand that the wastegate will control the pressure at the point where the actuator signal is taken from the system. If the signal is taken at the compressor outlet, that is the point in the system that will experience boost pressure dictated by the basic setting of the wastegate. Likewise, if the signal is taken from the exhaust pipe (don't laugh), pressure in the tailpipe at that point will, again, be dictated by the basic setting of the wastegate. It is known that pressure distribution through the engine/turbo system varies due to such flow-restricting devices as intercoolers, throttles, sometimes venturis, and just plain plumbing problems. Obviously, then, pressure through the entire system will vary based on the location of the actuator signal source. So, where to put the signal source?

Essentially, three choices exist for sourcing the signal: the compressor outlet, a plenum entering the throttle bodies, and the intake manifold. Each of these has merit and problems.

The signal originating at the compressor outlet offers the best control over the wastegate with regard to its response and ability to consistently control boost to a given value.

The bad side is that torque-curve rise will suffer slightly, as this source will create the earliest possible wastegate cracking point. This early cracking point will offer some relief thermally, because the entire system will virtually never see more boost than the basic setting of the wastegate. This can be important in avoiding a quick heat soaking of the intercooler.

Fig. 12-14. *Flexible wastegate vent tubes allow for extreme expansion and contraction caused by large temperature fluctuations through the wastegate.*

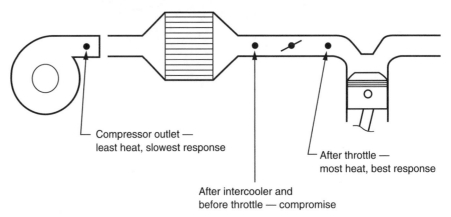

Fig. 12-15. *The wastegate signal source can affect the system with respect to heat load and turbine response.*

Compressor outlet —
least heat, slowest response

After throttle —
most heat, best response

After intercooler and
before throttle — compromise

The intake plenum signal source will slightly improve boost response, since the turbo is free to make all the boost it can until the pressure reaches the signal source and is transmitted to the wastegate. The fact that the turbo is free to make a brief spike of boost will cause the intercooler to be hit by a greater slug of temperature. Greater temperature is always to be considered a negative. For a blow-through carburetor system, where the wastegate and fuel pressure regulator must see the same signal simultaneously, the plenum signal source is best.

Sourcing the signal from the intake manifold should be considered only when turbo response is of the highest importance and the short blast of extra heat can be tolerated or ignored.

All things considered, heat should be the controlling factor. Unless unusual circumstances dictate, hook the wastegate signal to the compressor outlet and call it a day.

Design Features of the Wastegate

A variety of design features influence the function and capability of the wastegate. Most wastegates on the market today have a good balance of features versus cost, but a close analysis of these features may show one unit to be superior to another for a specific application.

COMMON DIRECTION. One general characteristic all wastegates must have is a common direction for the pressures applied to the valve and diaphragm. Exhaust gas pressure applied to the wastegate valve absolutely must push in the same direction as boost pressure applied to the diaphragm.

Fig. 12-16. *Design considerations of a wastegate*

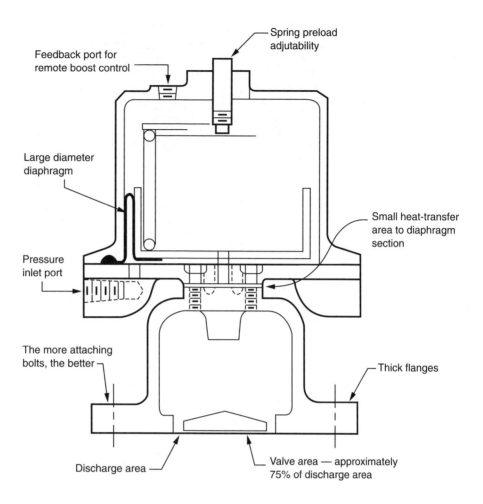

Spring preload adjutability

Feedback port for remote boost control

Large diameter diaphragm

Small heat-transfer area to diaphragm section

Pressure inlet port

The more attaching bolts, the better

Thick flanges

Discharge area

Valve area — approximately 75% of discharge area

STABILITY AND CONSISTENCY. The stability with which a wastegate controls boost pressure, and the wastegate's day-to-day consistency, are generally rrelated to the ratio of the areas of the diaphragm and valve. All other things equal, the greater the ratio, the better the wastegate.

HEAT ISOLATION. Heat isolation is critical to the life expectancy of the wastegate. Heat isolation is, in part, where you choose to put the thing, but it is also very much a function of the path available for heat to get from the very hot valve area up to the diaphragm area. The idea is, of course, to keep the heat away from the fragile diaphragm. Heat travels through heavy sections of metal quickly; thus, the less material area between the two, the better. Aluminum conducts heat superbly, whereas stainless steel is lousy at it. Therefore, a stainless steel wastegate should treat the diaphragm to an easier life.

CRACKING PRESSURE. The cracking pressure of the wastegate is the pressure at which the valve first lifts off its seat. This pressure is usually one-half to one-third of the stabilizing (maximum boost) pressure. A high cracking pressure is important, because a fair amount of energy intended for the turbine will be vented out the wastegate as soon as it cracks, yet the turbo is not up to maximum boost. Thus the turbo's ability to gain boost after the cracking point is reached is slightly diminished.

ADJUSTABILITY. Adjustability is a nice feature to have in any wastegate. This is usually accomplished by a screw that changes the preload of the valve spring. The nature of spring rates, free lengths, and compressed lengths usually dic-

Fig. 12-17. *This clever design by Turbonetics avoids the cracking pressure issue by using a throttle-plate wastegate valve.*

tates a range of adjustment of the basic wastegate limited to about ± 2 psi without changing the spring itself. Virtually all gate manufacturers offer a variety of springs for different boost pressures. Generally, remote wastegates offer an adjustment feature; integral units do not.

MOUNTING FLANGE. Mounting flange styles can be an important consideration when selecting a suitable gate. Rigid, strong, clamped-up flanges are long-term reliable. All else is somewhat less.

Fooling the Wastegate

Turning up the boost is becoming the favorite pastime of serious power enthusiasts. It is simple to think in terms of making more power by just turning the boost screw. Alas, this is not the answer. The premise under which one must operate if one desires to turn up the boost is to remove some heat from the intake charge, make sure the air/fuel ratio stays correct, and, when possible, add octane. Then, and only then, is one entitled to turn up the boost to a new level that adds back to the system the same amount of heat that was taken out by improving the system's efficiency.

For example, a more efficient intercooler that can remove another 45°F from the intake charge will permit the boost to be raised about 3 psi—provided, of course, that the air/fuel ratio remains constant. Arbitrarily turning up the boost without any precautions whatsoever essentially states that you think the designers were conservative bordering on foolish. We are generally agreed that accountants and lawyers determine tolerable boost pressures, but suppose for a moment that the engineer with a graduate degree in thermodynamics was actually the man responsible. Then we are in trouble if we arbitrarily turn up the boost. Take your pick. Chances and logic suggest we would be advised to take some heat out before we turn up the boost. With this bit of soapboxing complete, here are the schemes by which boost can be turned up:

ALTERED SPRING. A simple modification for a permanent change of boost level is to alter the spring in the wastegate actuator. This can be done in three different ways: shim the original spring to a higher preload, replace the original spring with a stiffer one, or add a supplementary spring to aid the original. Estimating the stiffness of the spring required for a specific boost gain is a bit of a lengthy calculation. Perhaps trial and error is easier if you are not keen on calculation. A relatively easy approach to selecting a supplementary spring is

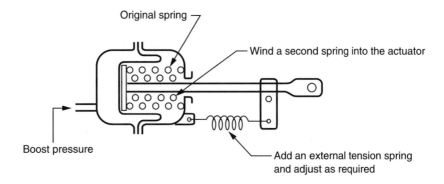

Fig. 12-18. *A simple integral wastegate modification for increased boost*

Original spring

Wind a second spring into the actuator

Boost pressure

Add an external tension spring and adjust as required

to choose one of approximately the same length as the original but about half as stiff. This will result in a boost setting about one-third higher than stock.

DIAL-A-BOOST. Another easy form of variable boost control is the concept of dial-a-boost. This device is nothing more than a controlled leak in the actuator signal line. If, for example, a 2 psi leak can be created in the signal line, it would take 9 psi of boost to open a 7 psi wastegate. An adjustable leak can be created by using a pressure regulator as the leak adjustment. Turn the knob, vary the leak, and presto: dial-a-boost.

TWO-LEVEL BOOST SWITCH. Dial-a-boost with a variation can become a two-boost-level, high-and-low switch. Dial-a-boost works by creating a leak, and the leak can be turned on and off by a solenoid controlled by a switch from the cockpit. This same scheme could be expanded to any number of boost levels deemed necessary. The logic of two or three boost levels is not tough, but the logic of ten different ones would escape me.

BLEED ORIFICE. Perhaps the simplest means yet devised of upping boost is the simple bleed orifice that lets out part of the signal the wastegate actuator receives. Start with a bleed hole of approximately .06 inch. Merely adjust the size up until the desired boost is achieved. A restrictor orifice may be required in the signal line, as turbo systems generate such huge volumes of air that a bleed hole of .06 inch is usually meaningless without somehow reducing the overall

Fig. 12-19. *The basic concept of the remote boost-change device.*

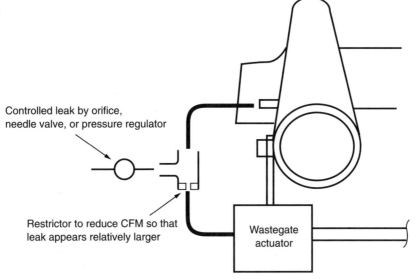

Controlled leak by orifice, needle valve, or pressure regulator

Restrictor to reduce CFM so that leak appears relatively larger

Wastegate actuator

flow available to the actuator. It is best to keep the cfm restrictor hole to about .06 inch also.

ELECTRONIC/PNEUMATIC WASTEGATE CONTROLLER. The electronic controls recently available for the wastegate offer an additional benefit. Not only do they provide several different boost pressures at the push of a button, they also keep the wastegate valve closed until desired boost pressure is reached. This is accomplished by blocking the pressure signal to the wastegate, preventing it from cracking open 5 or 6 psi before maximum boost. Boost rise from midrange to maximum is significantly faster. While difficult to perceive in first gear, the benefits are obvious and substantial from third gear up.

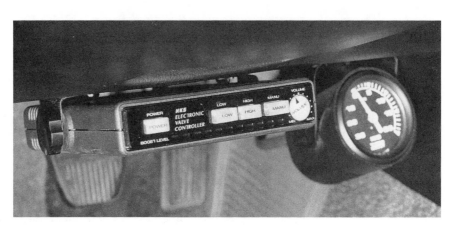

Fig. 12-20. *The HKS Electronic Valve Controller is a multilevel boost-change device that also produces faster boost rise by blocking the signal to the wastegate until near-maximum boost is achieved.*

Override Safety Device

It is hard to argue against some form of emergency boost control that will take over should the wastegate experience a failure. Don't think for an instant, however, that if this happens, the engine is destined to melt down. When a wastegate begins to fail, it does not take a rocket scientist to see the higher readings on a boost gauge and deduce that something is amiss. Nor does it take Mario Andretti to tell that the vehicle is accelerating a bit faster and that perhaps a change has occurred in something that merits a closer look. Fundamentally, if one blows an engine because of a failed wastegate, one ought to turn in one's driver's license. Nevertheless, it is easy to have an override safety, keep your foot in it, and just not worry about a thing.

Several schemes function satisfactorily as safety devices. In OEM turbo systems, these vary from pop-off radiator-style vent valves to electronic fuel cutoffs or ignition cuts. If one has done one's homework and wishes to raise the boost of an OEM system, the factory overboost safety device must be defeated, but it is still a good idea to install a new one to account for the higher boost level. The individual approach to blocking these devices is likely a search of the factory manual or consulting someone in the aftermarket who has done such tinkering.

If you are designing your own turbo system, it is also advisable to create an override safety device. A boost-pressure-sensitive switch can cut the 12-volt pulse to a coil, igniter, or fuel pump. Merely identify the proper wires, insert a pressure-actuated switch set 1–2 psi above the wastegate setting, and supply it with a boost signal. Killing the fuel supply is probably the better of the two choices. These devices can cause a jerking on and off if the foot is kept in it (as boost repeatedly comes down to a safe level, closing the circuit, which causes boost to rise again), but safety they do offer. This approach is not, of course,

Fig. 12-21. Overboost protection can be achieved by cutting power to the coil or fuel pump.

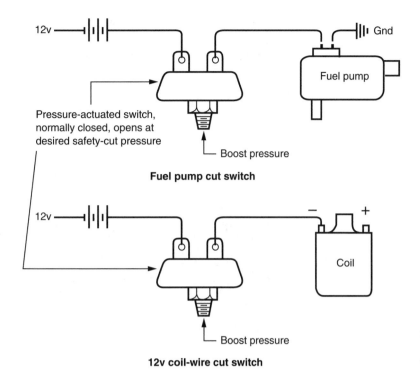

Pressure-actuated switch, normally closed, opens at desired safety-cut pressure

└─ Boost pressure

Fuel pump cut switch

└─ Boost pressure

12v coil-wire cut switch

quick enough for carbureted engines and is therefore limited to those that are EFI-equipped.

AND FURTHERMORE . . .

Why is a wastegate important?

A gasoline-application turbo system must have a boost-control mechanism to prevent the possibility of too much boost causing damaging detonation. The wastegate is the standard-configuration turbo's only technically correct boost control. The only other viable alternative is the VATN turbocharger, which controls turbine speed, and thus boost, by vane position (see Chapter 16). This type of turbocharger has far greater technical merit than standard turbos with wastegates.

How should a wastegate integrate into the system?

A wastegate has two plumbing requirements: where it vents from and where it vents to. The wastegate should draw from the same area of the exhaust manifold as the turbo. The vent from the wastegate should ideally have a separate exhaust pipe and muffler. This causes the least disruption to the flow through the turbo and tailpipe. The vent tube back into the tailpipe ought to be located well down the pipe from the turbo, a minimum of 18 inches. For these reasons, the remote wastegate is always superior to the integral type. Serious turbo people, like Porsche, haven't yet succumbed to the cost savings of an integral wastegate. Furthermore, no race cars have integral wastegates, and I doubt they ever will. It's fun to see ads for turbo kits touting one of the least desirable features of a turbo system: the integral wastegate.

Are there any beneficial safety devices?

Overrev and overboost back-up safety devices are good features. A detonation indicator is useful for the hearing impaired. A closed-loop detonation detection and correction system is a valuable safety addition.

13 PREPARING THE ENGINE

Surely one of the delightful benefits of turbocharging is the fact that a turbo can combine forces with a "good, stock" engine and produce terrific results. That does not imply that careful preparation of the engine would not offer returns commensurate with the effort expended. To do the job right means preparing the engine only to the extent that performance objectives require. Any engine built anywhere by anybody (OEM, that is) will withstand the rigors of a properly set up 5 psi of boost. Therefore, "doing the job right" at a performance objective of 5 psi means you need a "good, stock" engine. One should not, however, expect the "good, stock" engine to survive the performance regimes of 50 psi Formula 1 turbo engines. Further, one should not waste elaborate preparation on an engine only to run wimpy boost pressures. Balancing performance objectives with engine preparation is the subject pursued in this chapter.

Deciding on Specific Objectives

Desired power translates to a boost pressure range required to achieve that power. Engine preparation needed to permit those boost pressures can be reduced to a group of generalities. Certainly, many engines have specific requirements and weaknesses. A literature search for any given engine will usually turn up a wealth of information, probably far more than needed.

Compression Ratio

In outlining engine performance desired, the first decision is the compression ratio. Compression ratio affects a large number of performance and driveability factors. Throttle response, economy, bhp per psi of boost, and that intangible, sweet running condition associated with engines eager for action are some of the performance factors determined in large part by the compression ratio.

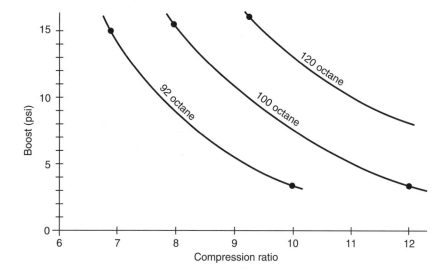

Fig. 13-1. Approximate boost-pressure allowables for varying fuel octanes and engine compression ratios

Do not be hasty to lower compression ratios just because most OEMs like to do so. The proper compression ratio for the job is determined by lengthy thermodynamic calculation and comprehensive testing. All that good technology has its place, but usable numbers can be generated by some experience and will hold for most general applications. The two largest influences on compression ratio are boost pressure desired and intercooler efficiency. Fuel octane certainly plays a big part, but we are usually limited to using commercially available pump gasoline.

☞ **RULE:** A turbo engine must never be reduced to a low-compression slug.

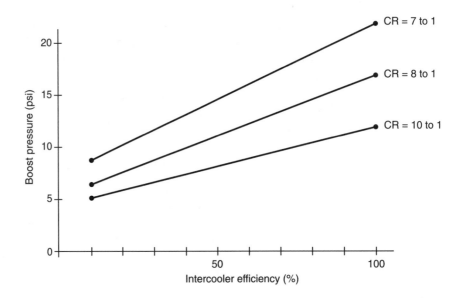

Fig. 13-2. *Approximate boost-pressure variation as a function of compression ratio and intercooler efficiency*

CALCULATING A COMPRESSION RATIO CHANGE. To calculate a compression ratio, we must know the displacement volume and clearance volume (see glossary)

$$Compression\ ratio\ = \frac{displacement\ volume + clearance\ volume}{clearance\ volume}$$

or

$$CR\ = \frac{V_d + V_{cv}}{V_{cv}}$$

where

V_d = displacement volume
V_{cv} = clearance volume

Some minor manipulation of the equation will put it into a form that allows easy calculation of clearance volumes for specific compression ratios.

$$Clearance\ volume\ = \frac{one\text{-}cylinder\ displacement}{compression\ ratio - 1}$$

Example:
400 cid V-8 with CR of 11.0 to 1

$$Clearance\ volume\ = \frac{\frac{400}{8}}{11.0 - 1} = 5.0\ in.^3$$

Fig. 13-3. *Defining the compression ratio*

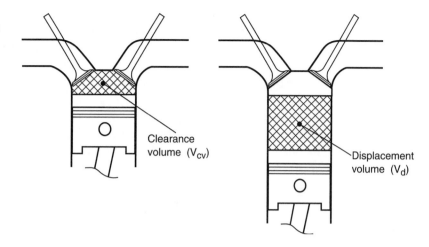

Clearance volume (V_{cv})

Displacement volume (V_d)

To change the CR to 8.5 to 1, the new clearance volume will be

$$Clearance\ volume = \frac{\frac{400}{8}}{8.5-1} = 6.67\ in.^3$$

Clearly then, to get from the 11.0 to 1 compression ratio to the 8.5 to 1 ratio, 6.67 – 5.0, or 1.67 cubic inches, must be added to the combustion chamber volume. How one adds this volume can vary, but the math remains that easy.

CHANGING A COMPRESSION RATIO. A variety of methods exist to change a compression ratio. Almost all are unacceptable. The crux of the matter is upsetting the "squish volume" around the rim of the chamber. A chamber is designed so that the charge is pushed toward its center as the piston achieves top dead center. This is perhaps the strongest deterrent to detonation designed into the system, as it tends to either eliminate end gas or keep charge turbulence high. This squish volume is a rim about .3 to .4 inch wide around the chamber, and approximately .04 thick—a big, washer-shaped volume between piston and head. Consider "squish volume" sacred and do not tamper. It is possible to err so badly in removing the squish that a resulting 7-to-1 compression ratio may ping worse than a 9-to-1 with proper squish. Clearly then, choices for reducing compression ratio are limited to opening up selected parts of the head side of the chamber, installing a new piston with a dish in the center, or remachining the original piston to create a dish. It is perhaps a little risky to undertake remachining a combustion chamber, because the thickness of the material is usually unknown. Furthermore, chamber shapes are closely controlled features of most modern engines. If the chamber must be recut, ultrasonic inspection can determine the material thickness. Commercial inspection service companies frequently offer this service. An entirely new piston, with the required dish that maintains the squish volume, is a proper approach. Machining a dish into the original piston is sound, provided the top thickness is adequate. A reasonable rule would require the top thickness to be at least 6% of the bore. Approaches to lowering the compression ratio that do not work are thicker head gaskets and shorter connecting rods.

Preparing the Cylinder Head

Cylinder head preparation is once again a function of the engine's purpose. A good street turbo engine is usually quite comfortable with a completely stock cylinder head. On the other hand, a full-fledged turbo racing engine will require complete preparation consistent with the type of racing intended.

If the opportunity to prepare a street head presents itself, attention should center largely around assuring that the head is in excellent condition. Flatness of the head gasket surface is of obvious importance. A minimum truing cut would be advisable. All holes should be chamfered and all threads chased with a sharp tap. Every edge and every corner should be deburred. Inspect for casting flash and casting process roughness and remove accordingly. The combustion chambers should be deburred and all edges radiused or blended into the surrounding material. All unengaged spark plug threads should be removed. The purpose is, of course, to eliminate hot spots that could serve as potential ignition sources. The valves themselves should receive similar attention. The quality of the valve seating surface must be first class. Here is the place to spend a little extra money and insure good sealing against the higher pressures induced by the turbo. Quality work on the valve seats will also conduct slightly more heat out of the valves.

Intake and exhaust ports should receive preparation consistent with the objectives of the engine. With a mild street engine/turbo system, a cleanup and matching of ports is logical. Competitive situations are different. Airflow rates through turbo engine ports far exceed those through atmo ports; therefore, imperfections cause considerably greater drag. Turbo heads used for competitive events consequently merit a higher degree of port preparation.

Inspect the manifold mating faces for flatness, and remachine as required. Seldom is there any requirement to improve sealing at the intake manifold gasket. A boost pressure of 14.7 psi (on the inside pushing out) is virtually the same as the pushing "in" with a manifold vacuum of 30 inches (brought about by backing off the throttle at high rpm). Vacuum and pressure are, to a limited degree, the same thing—they're just pushing in different directions.

Preparing the Cylinder Block

Seldom will a cylinder block need special attention just because a turbo enters the scene. A good stock block will serve most applications well. But somewhere between higher performance, longer durability, and plain old pride of workmanship exists a logical reason to give thought to cylinder block preparation.

Vat the block in hot solvent for convenience of handling, deburr everything, and retap all threads. Decks must be flat. Insure that the decks are equidistant from, and parallel to, the crank centerline. Crank bores must be concentric and round. It is extremely important that cylinder bores be round. Vat the block again when all the above is done, to make sure it really is clean.

If one characteristic of a cylinder block could lend a hand to the turbo application, it would be rigidity of the deck surface.

Head Gasket Improvement

The thought of trying to improve a head gasket should not imply that the head gasket is a weak link. A new stock head gasket, mated to flat surfaces and accompanied by properly torqued head studs, is a good joint. Head gaskets in general do not tend to "blow." Rather, one could say that detonation will blow anything, and the head gasket is often the first thing standing in line. Almost always, the most effective cure for blown head gaskets is control of detonation.

Clearly, however, maximum-effort engines must be equipped with maximum-effort head gaskets. Several methods exist for substantially improving a stock head gasket. The fundamental idea is to offer some form of motion barrier that will help the gasket stay put if it is subjected to a few detonation blasts. This barrier usually takes the form of an interlock or mechanical barrier, as shown in figures 13-5, 6, and 7.

Fig. 13-4. *Performance head gaskets. **Top:** The steel wire ring provides maximum combustion sealability but may brinell aluminum heads. **Bottom, left:** The pre-flattened steel wire ring has the strength of steel wire sealing with minimum brinelling of aluminum heads. **Bottom, right:** The copper wire ring will not brinell aluminum heads and offers superior heat dissipation from combustion hot spots.*

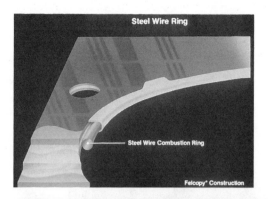

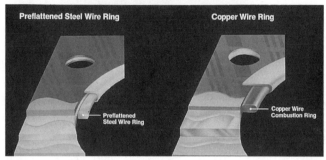

Fig. 13-5. *Head gasket improvement by a groove without an O-ring*

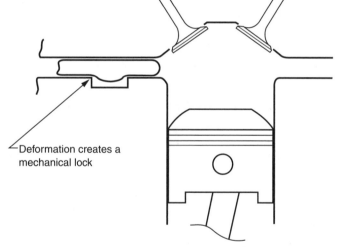

Deformation creates a mechanical lock

Fig. 13-6. *Head gasket strengthened by an O-ring*

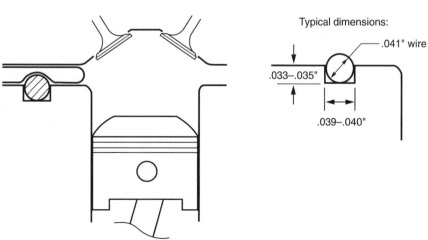

Typical dimensions:

.041" wire

.033–.035"

.039–.040"

Fig. 13-7. *Head gasket strengthened by a double O-ring*

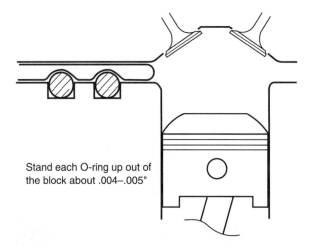

Stand each O-ring up out of the block about .004–.005"

Improving Head Clamp-up

An improved head-bolt system can permit greater clamping loads between head and block. The first serious improvement should be to replace bolts with high-strength studs. A properly anchored stud, with its shank bottomed out in the block, will always prove a superior fastener system to a bolt tightened into the block.

☞ **RULE:** A head *bolt* is an accountant's decision. A head *stud* is an engineer's decision.

It is reasonable to install head studs of the next size up and gain the additional clamp-up force available from higher torque values. Serious forethought should be given to upper-cylinder distortion caused by larger fasteners with higher torque-ups.

Torquing the Head Fasteners

The purpose of tightening a bolt, or a nut on a stud, is to put tension into the shaft of the bolt or stud. The extent to which torque gets converted to tension is almost solely dependent on the friction between the threads of the stud and the threaded hole and the friction between the washer and nut. To achieve

Fig. 13-8. *Studs will always hold a head on better than bolts.*

maximum tension in the shaft for a given torque, friction must be reduced to a minimum. This is accomplished by making sure the threads are in perfect condition and the bottom side of the nut is smooth. This limits the number of times a bolt or stud is used, because it becomes scored, gouged, or otherwise damaged. Three times is probably stretching it.

A second and most important means of reducing friction is a proper lubricant on the threads and between the bottom of the nut or bolt head and the top of the washer. Molysulfide lubricants are best. Light oil will do in a pinch. Consult the shop manual or fastener suppliers for torque values. Unless otherwise specified, these values are for clean, dry threads. When using molysulfide, all specified torque values must be reduced by 10% because of molysulfide's extreme lubricating qualities. Light oil requires torque values to be reduced by about 5%. Lubricating these surfaces is of such extreme importance that if forgotten, one must redo the job before start-up.

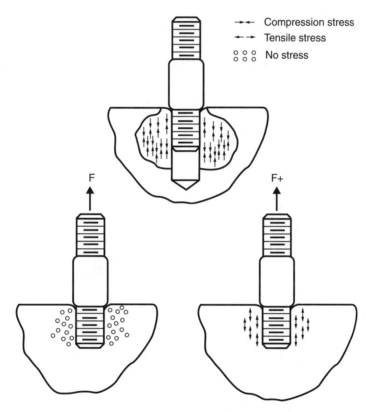

Fig. 13-9. **Top:** *When a stud is torqued up, the shank bottoms out on the chamfer. The stud's threads pull on the shank, inducing compressive stress in the surrounding base metal.* **Bottom:** *An upward force applied to the stud pulls the compressive stress back to zero before inducing tensile stress, resulting in lower net tensile stress.*

Turbo Pistons

The piston is the weak link in a turbo engine. When turbo system functions go astray, it is the poor piston that usually gets beat up. Heat and heat-induced detonation are the two things that do the most damage to the piston. These two enemies can best be resisted by high-temperature-strength material, the mechanical design of the piston, and heat removal.

PISTON MATERIALS. Forged aluminum, cast aluminum hypereutectic, and T6 heat-treated hypereutectic alloys are common choices in piston materials. Forged aluminum is, in some cases, considerably stronger than the cast material. It is not, however, without its own peculiar problems. Forged alloys are similar in strength to T6 hypereutectic alloys, with the hypereutectic having the advantage in the ring land area, where great strength is most important.

Fig. 13-10. *A good turbo piston will have thick, strong ring lands.*

Forgings do have the downside characteristic of needing slightly greater wall clearance. Large wall clearances can destroy a piston in small increments during the engine warm-up cycle. If too great a clearance is used, life expectancy can about equal that of an overloaded cast piston. Some of the more modern forgings have conquered the wall clearance problem and make excellent pistons. The problem is, of course, knowing exactly what you have.

Hypereutectic alloy pistons are cast aluminum alloy with a high percentage of silicon. Their most useful characteristics are lower thermal expansion and reduced heat transfer. The jury is still sequestered, but it will probably reach a favorable decision. Clearly, these pistons merit investigation prior to choosing the best part for your engine application.

The decision should actually be based on three things: percent increase in the rpm limit, boost pressure, and the presence of an effective intercooler. Keep in mind that inertial loads in pistons skyrocket with increasing revs, more boost makes more heat, and good intercoolers take out heat. It's all a judgment call. Unless circumstances are highly unusual, street cars with stock redlines will prove more successful with cast pistons. Forgings should be reserved for the high revvers, while T6 hypereutectic alloys can cover almost all requirements.

☞ **RULE:** Do not rush to the forged piston store every time a turbo engine needs preparation.

MECHANICAL DESIGN. A specially designed turbo piston will be somewhat more robust overall than a piston destined for lesser duty. The area of most concern is the thickness of the ring lands. Ring land area is the focus of most of the pounding that knock gives a piston. The thickness of these lands must be a minimum of twice that employed on pistons for atmo engines. Often the details of a turbo piston will include better heat escape routes from the piston crown to the sidewalls.

HEAT REMOVAL. One way to increase the strength of the piston is to reduce its operating temperature. Two methods seem viable in accomplishing this: ceramic coating on the piston top and/or oil spray on the bottom. With ceramic barriers, it is acceptable for charge temperatures to rise slightly as a consequence of less heat entering the piston. Bear in mind that charge heat is the cause of detonation. Oil spray on the bottom of the piston has proven workable

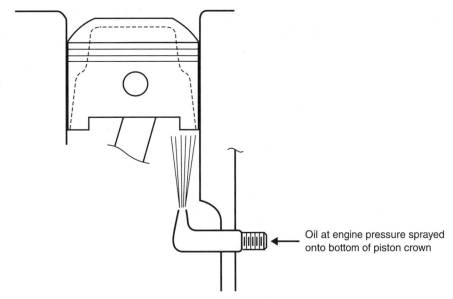

Fig. 13-11. *Oil spray onto the bottom of the piston reduces the piston's operating temperature, increasing its strength.*

Oil at engine pressure sprayed onto bottom of piston crown

on vehicles as varied as M-B diesels and early '80s Grand Prix cars. Although not an easy installation, oil spray should be given the nod first. It should be accompanied by an increased-capacity oil pump, or at least by a stiffened oil pump relief- valve spring. Nozzle diameters will need some experimentation, but .03 inch should be a good place to start.

The rush to ceramic coat everything that sees fire in the engine is, in this writer's opinion, a bit premature. Keeping heat out of the piston is generally desirable. Conducting heat out of the chamber is equally desirable. I feel quite capable of arguing both sides eloquently. Two things are clear: First, if the detonation characteristics of the combustion chamber can stand more heat left in the chamber by ceramic coatings, then raise the compression. Second, when Formula 1 engines use ceramic coatings and we are permitted to know that, we should, too. Until that time, ceramic coat the exhaust port from the valve to the manifold face and get on with other details.

Balancing the Assembly

The turbo has little regard for mechanical smoothness. The fact remains that any engine destined for high-performance preparation gets a complete and thorough balancing, or the end user is simply not serious.

Camshafts

Make no mistake in the fact that turbo performance cams are very different from atmospheric performance cams. The characteristics of long duration and high overlap for atmo cams are unwelcome in a turbo system. The street turbo, which is generally small, operates with exhaust manifold pressure somewhat higher than intake boost pressure. This situation, when presented with long-duration, high-overlap cams, creates a huge amount of reversion. Thus the "turbo cam" tends to become a low-duration, very limited overlap cam.

☞ **RULE:** It is hard to find a turbo cam that works better than the stock item.

Related Systems

The selection of such items as valve gear, connecting rods, bearings, and rod bolts is independent of the turbo. These items should be selected based on expected rpm limits. In general, stock equipment will prove adequate for virtually any turbo system that keeps rpm limits within the original manufacturer's recommendations.

Fig. 13-12. Overlap in the turbo cam should be held to a minimum.

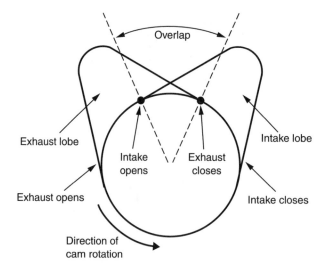

And Furthermore . . .

What is the best compression ratio for a turbocharged engine?

There is no such thing as the best or ideal compression ratio. The simple fundamentals are

- the lower the compression ratio, the easier it is to produce a lot of boost with no detonation
- the higher the compression ratio, the greater the fuel efficiency and nonboosted response

Suppressing detonation is more difficult with a high compression ratio. For all practical purposes, one is forced to use the compression ratio of the standard engine. Serious efforts with intercooling make this both possible and practical.

Is it necessary to change the cam?

No, decidedly not. Stock cams usually work excellently. For the absolute last word in a super-boost (15 psi) performance turbo car, a change of cam will be necessary, but so will several other things. Leave the stock cam alone and you will generally be much happier.

Will I have to modify the cylinder head or rework the valve train?

No on both counts.

Will I have to use a special head gasket?

Head gasket strength varies tremendously from engine to engine. It is necessary that the stock head gasket be in stock condition. If it is in proper order and the head bolts are properly torqued, boost pressure will seldom dislodge the gasket. Special head gaskets and O-rings are often cures to the wrong problem. They are only poor excuses for not dealing properly with detonation. If detonation is the problem, cure it, and a stock head gasket will usually perform well.

14 TESTING THE SYSTEM

Nothing can bring about a better understanding of the relationship of the turbo to the engine than a comprehensive test and evaluation of all the system's parameters. What to check, how to do it, the tools required, what it all means, and how to evaluate the numbers will be discussed in the following paragraphs.

Equipment and Tools

Most of the measurements are of temperature and pressure and will involve a variety of gauges. There are no expensive pieces of equipment here except a really good air/fuel ratio meter. The local hardware store will have a variety of pressure gauges, but temperature measuring equipment usually requires a specialty house.

Air Filter Flow Loss Evaluation

Air filter flow losses can gang up on an otherwise healthy engine and produce undesirable side effects. The simple idea that a restrictive air filter can cost power because it won't let air in is quite easy to grasp. The presence of the turbo, however, complicates this simple situation. As far as the turbo is concerned, after air has been through the filter, it is ambient. This situation is particularly significant because all calculations of temperature changes, pressure losses or gains, and efficiencies are based on what the turbo sees as ambient conditions. For example, suppose boost pressure is set at 10 psi and the mythical zero-loss air filter is upstream. Using the formula for pressure ratio from Chapter 3,

$$Pressure\ ratio = \frac{14.7 + 10}{14.7} = 1.68$$

Now insert an air filter that causes a 2 psi loss at the same maximum load conditions:

$$Pressure\ ratio = \frac{14.7 + 10}{14.7 - 2} = 1.94$$

Fig. 14-1. A vacuum gauge is used to determine flow losses in the air inlet system. Gauge 1 indicates pressure loss through the air filter. Gauge 1 minus gauge 2 indicates pressure loss through the mass flowmeter.

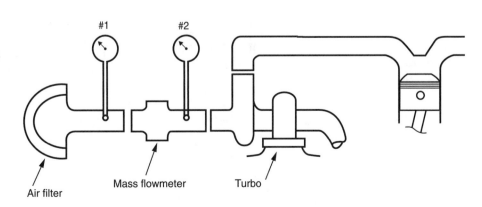

#1   #2

Air filter   Mass flowmeter   Turbo

So here the odd circumstance exists that flow is down, boost remains the same, and the pressure ratio is higher. Any time the pressure ratio goes up, heat goes up. Net result is that power is down and heat is up. Sounds almost like a Roots blower. This may seem like science or some such, but it's not really. The idea that the turbo is told to make the same amount of boost out of less air logically means it must work a bit harder to do so. The harder it has to work, the more heat it makes. We've all experienced similar situations.

To measure flow losses through the intake system upstream of the turbo, insert a vacuum gauge just in front of the compressor inlet. Then

$$Air\ filter\ flow\ loss\ =\ \frac{Standard\ barometric\ pressure}{Standard\ barometric\ pressure - loss\ through\ filter}$$

Standard barometric pressure is 29.97 in. hg. In practice, 30 can be used as an approximation for 29.97.

Should the gauge read 3 inches of vacuum under maximum load conditions, the percent loss can be judged to be

$$Air\ filter\ flow\ loss\ =\ \frac{30}{30-3} - 1 = 11\%$$

Obviously a zero loss is elusive, but the effort to create a low-restriction intake system will be rewarded with more power and less heat. All the same arguments apply to keeping the air filter element clean.

Compressor Inlet Temperature

Thermodynamics is not everyone's cup of tea, but the equations are simple, and a fifteen-dollar calculator can solve them. The value in crunching the numbers is to determine whether the turbo is the correct size. The air temperature entering the compressor is vital information, because it is the number from which all others are calculated. Do not assume this temperature is ambient. If the air inlet is outside the engine compartment, compressor inlet temperature may be the same as ambient. If it is in the engine compartment, too often the inlet air is diluted by air that has passed through the radiator or looped around the exhaust manifold. Measure compressor inlet air temperature with a gauge positioned as in figure 14-2.

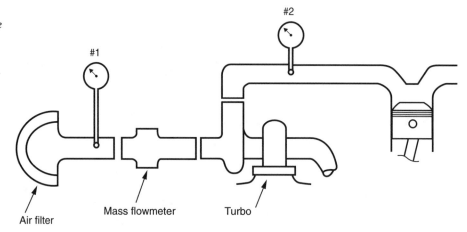

Fig. 14-2. *Temperature gauging the intake for determining temperature rise through the turbo. Gauge 1 indicates ambient air temperature available to the turbo. Gauge 2 minus gauge 1 indicates temperature rise across the turbo.*

#1 #2

Air filter   Mass flowmeter   Turbo

Compressor Outlet Conditions

Two quantities must be known at the outlet side of the turbo: pressure and temperature. Compressor outlet pressure is the true boost produced by the turbo. All measurements of the flow as it gets closer to the engine will be referenced to this pressure for flow loss or efficiency calculations. For example, this pressure minus the pressure entering the intake manifold will measure flow loss characteristics of the intercooler and associated plumbing.

Compressor outlet temperature is the other factor required in calculating the turbo size to fit the engine. It is used twice in the equation for IC efficiencies, so measure it carefully. Once pressure and temperature at the compressor outlet are known, the real pressure ratio can be calculated, provided no intercooler is present. With an intercooler, pressure ratio calculation should wait until the intercooler outlet conditions are known.

The most significant calculations to be made here are spot checks of the turbo's efficiency range. The tools for these measurements are not adequate to determine the entire compressor map. Nevertheless, one can develop a feel for whether the turbo is operating in the efficiency range that will get the job done. These calculations are somewhat laborious, but there is no other way, short of calling on a thermodynamics buddy.

At least two spots should be checked: somewhere around torque peak and at maximum rpm—both, of course, at maximum boost. The check involves calculating the efficiency at which the compressor is operating and comparing those numbers to the efficiency predicted by the compressor flow maps.

Compressor efficiency (E_c) is calculated using the following formula:

$$E_c = \frac{(PR^{0.28} \times T_{abs}) - T_{abs}}{Temperature\ rise}$$

where

PR = pressure ratio

T_{abs} = compressor inlet temperature on the absolute scale (see glossary)

Because this is a thermodynamic formula of general applicability, it is necessary to insert the relevant temperature rise in the denominator (from Chapter 5):

$$Temperature\ rise = T_{co} - T_a$$

The exponent 0.28 in the numerator is determined by the gas constant, a number that indicates the extent to which a gas heats up when compressed. The x^y key on the fifteen-dollar calculator will allow us to find the value of $PR^{0.28}$.

Example:

Let engine displacement = 200 cid, boost = 10 psi, and compressor inlet temperature = 90°F (= 90° + 460° = 550° absolute). At or near torque peak (4500 rpm), let outlet temperature = 210°F; at maximum load (6500 rpm), let outlet temperature = 235°F.

Using the formula for pressure ratio from Chapter 3,

$$Pressure\ ratio = \frac{14.7 + 10}{14.7} = 1.68$$

Calculation of E_c at or near the torque peak:
Using the formula for temperature rise from Chapter 5,

$$Temperature\ rise = 210°F - 90°F = 120°F$$

Then

$$E_c = \frac{(1.68^{0.28} \times 550°) - 550°}{120°} = 0.72 = 72\%$$

Using the formula for airflow from Chapter 3,

$$Airflow\ rate\ =\ \frac{200 \times 0.5 \times 4500 \times 0.85}{1728}\ =\ 221\ cfm$$

Calculation of E_c at maximum rpm:
Using the formula for temperature rise from Chapter 5,

$$Temperature\ rise\ =\ 235°F - 90°F = 145°F$$

Then

$$E_c\ =\ \frac{(1.68^{0.28} \times 550°) - 550°}{145°}\ =\ 0.59\ =\ 59\%$$

Using the formula for airflow from Chapter 3,

$$Airflow\ rate\ =\ \frac{200 \times 0.5 \times 6500 \times 0.85}{1728}\ =\ 320\ cfm$$

These calculations give the pressure ratio and airflow for two points that can be plotted on the compressor flow map, with pressure ratio the vertical axis and airflow the horizontal axis (see Chapters 3 or 17). Compare the efficiency predicted by the curve on the flow map to the calculated values. If the predicted efficiency is two or three points higher or lower than the calculated values, all is well. If the numbers calculated are four or five points higher than the map, we are in wonderful shape. If they are more than four or five points lower, performance has been compromised, and it's back to the drawing board

Ambient Temperature in Front of the Intercooler

Accurate determination of the IC's real capability is in part based on determination of the temperature of the air that cools the cores. Although this factor is not used directly in calculations involving the turbo system, it is of interest in really getting into checking the merit of one core design versus another with respect to heat transfer coefficients.

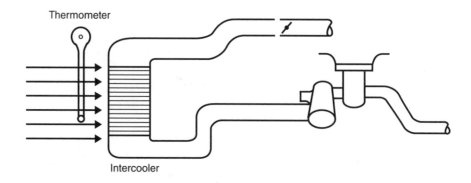

Thermometer

Intercooler

Fig. 14-3. Ambient temperature measurement, necessary for determining intercooler efficiency

Intercooler Outlet Conditions

Temperature and pressure must be measured again at the intercooler outlet. These numbers are significant, because they are the conditions the engine will experience. This naively assumes that not much will happen in the tube from the intercooler back to the engine. With these data, we have enough information to determine the intercooler's efficiency and the power loss due to boost pressure loss.

Intake Manifold Pressure

Should any significant events occur in the charge's trip from the IC to the intake manifold, they will show up in the intake manifold pressure relative to IC outlet conditions. It is relatively common to have a throttle plate far too small

Fig. 14-4. *The five points of interest for temperature and pressure measurement*

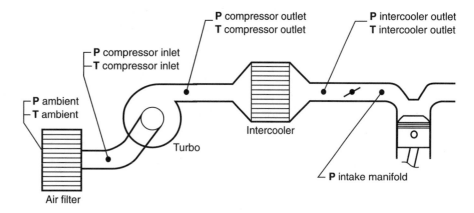

for the job, and here is the way to find it. If more than 1 psi difference exists between the IC outlet and the intake manifold, it will probably prove revealing to check the pressure right in front of the throttle plate versus that in the manifold. This will determine if the loss is in the return tube or if the throttle plate is the problem.

The boost gauge in the instrument panel is set up to read intake manifold pressure. This is the amount of pressure you have left of the original pressure created by the turbo less all losses incurred on the way to the intake manifold. Try to keep the total loss under 2 psi—or, better yet, 10% of the boost pressure.

Fig. 14-5. *Measuring pressure loss across the throttle body. Gauge 1 minus gauge 2 indicates boost-pressure loss across the throttle plate.*

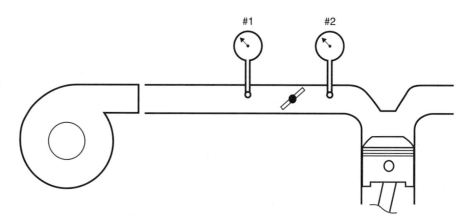

Turbine Inlet Pressure

Exhaust manifold pressure can better be described as Turbine Inlet Pressure. This TIP is an evil thing. In the final analysis, I suspect TIP will be called the *only* evil thing brought to bear by the turbo. The reason TIP is an undesirable quantity is the fact that it is almost always greater than the intake manifold pressure (IMP?) generated by the turbo. When this occurs, a certain portion of the burned exhaust gas is pushed back into the combustion chamber during the cam overlap period. This situation is detrimental to several things, all explained elsewhere in this book.

It is this writer's opinion that a good street turbo system will show the ratio of TIP to IMP to be approximately 2. If a ratio of greater than 2 exists, the turbo is too small and is choking the system down and not permitting much power gain. If the ratio is less than 2, often the boost threshold will be higher than desirable for commuter car use. This situation is offset by the fact that as the ratio comes down, power goes up. In fact, one of the design parameters of a race turbo system is that the TIP/IMP ratio be less than 1. When this crossover point is reached, where intake pressure becomes greater than exhaust pressure, a turbo can begin to make serious power. This is one of the reasons the '87 Formula 1 racers could generate over 1000 bhp from 90 cubic inches. It may come about one day that we can have our cake and more cake again when variable area turbine nozzle turbos are commonplace. They will permit low boost thresholds while allowing boost to exceed TIP once boost has stabilized at its maximum setting.

Measuring turbine inlet pressure requires a bit more effort than other pressure measurements, as exhaust gases are obviously very hot.

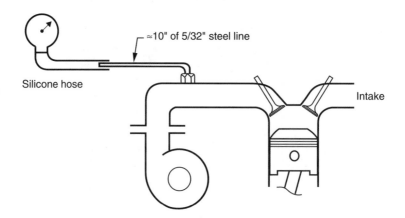

Fig. 14-6. *Measuring turbine inlet pressure. The steel line will reduce exhaust gas temperature to silicone hose allowables.*

Tailpipe Back Pressure

Where do you suppose the fairy tale started that tailpipe back pressure was needed to prevent burned exhaust valves? Someone ought to quickly inform all those racers out there that they are in serious trouble. Tailpipe back pressure can be just as evil as TIP, but at least it is easy to do something about. Potential gains are more power and less heat in the system—exactly the right things to achieve.

In measuring tailpipe back pressure, it is also necessary to measure restriction distribution, as indicated in figure 14-7. In so doing, one can determine what contribution to the total back pressure is created by the pipe, catalytic converter, and muffler.

Tailpipe back pressure is partly responsible for the magnitude of the turbine inlet pressure. Any decrease in tailpipe pressure that can be brought about will be reflected in a nice decrease in TIP.

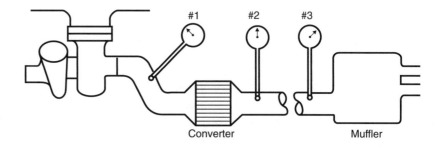

Fig. 14-7. *Determining tailpipe restriction distribution. Gauge #1 indicates total tailpipe back pressure. #2 indicates back pressure caused by the pipe and muffler. #3 indicates back pressure caused by the muffler. #1 minus #2 is pressure loss across the converter. #2 minus #3 is pressure loss through the pipe.*

Air/Fuel Ratio

Knowing the air/fuel ratio is somewhat like knowing your checkbook balance. It tells you what you've got and where you stand, but not what you can do about it. A wide variety of pieces have recently been introduced to the market for measuring afr.

The neat little oxygen-sensor-based units on the market will give you a good guide, if not exact numbers, but real accuracy has yet to come cheap. For serious tuners, the Horiba and Motec meters are perhaps top of the line. Check the source listings at the end of the book and gather the information to make a reasonable decision.

Measurement of the numbers is nothing more than equipment and time. Evaluation of those numbers is where a bit of experience helps out. When testing, two significant numbers will be required: cruise afr and full-throttle afr. Cruise afr will likely be in the range of 14.0 to 15.0 to 1. Full throttle is where the fun is and should be close to 12.5 or 13.0 to 1.

For the home tuner, the oxygen sensor that fits into the tailpipe near the heat source will do a good job. It can be considered a permanent installation and checked as often as desired.

Fig. 14-8. Left: The excellent air/fuel ratio meter from Horiba. While expensive, it offers lab-test-quality results, and its sensor can be mounted at the end of the tailpipe. Right: Although not a lab test instrument, a diode-readout mixture indicator is an excellent low-cost tuning guide.

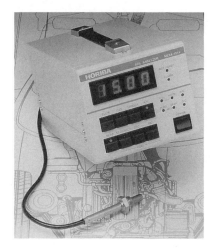

15 TROUBLE

When investigating running problems on a turbocharged engine, you need to remember that there are two categories of problems that can arise. The first category includes those types of problems that can happen to any engine, whether turbocharged or not. Turbo engines can still have problems with spark plugs, plug wires, coils, ignition control boxes, EFI computers, timing chains, water pumps, fan belts, alternators, throwout bearings, cam bearings, and . . . the picture is obvious. With regard to these problems, a turbo engine is no different from a normally aspirated engine. Today's attitude toward service and repair of the turbocharged performance car generally leads to the somewhat ridiculous/comical response of, "Whatever the problem, it's that damn turbo's fault." Fixes for general engine problems can be sought elsewhere and are not within the scope of this book.

The second category is the malfunction of a component in the turbocharger system, or a problem caused by a malfunctioning turbo system. This chapter offers a guide to isolating and recognizing these problems. Also, at the end of the chapter, you'll find a troubleshooting guide which offers a lot of information. Study it carefully and eliminate the simple things first.

Inspecting the Engine for Turbo-Induced Damage

When you encounter any problem that even remotely hints at possible engine damage, it is best to check it out pronto. Get proof that the engine is undamaged, or focus on fixing it. Worrisome signs are rough running at idle, loss of power, or bluish-gray or white smoke issuing from the tailpipe. Excessive puffing of oil vapor from the valve cover or crankcase breather is also cause for con-

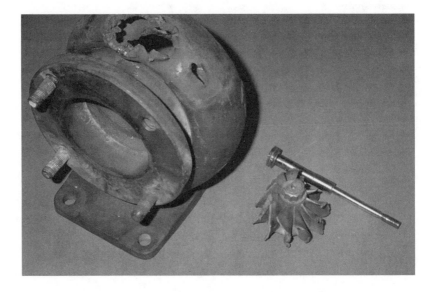

Fig. 15-1. Worst case scenarios are never pretty, and the fallout from a malfunctioning turbo system is no exception.

cern. The proper method of checkout is a leakdown test, which indicates the condition of individual compression rings, intake and exhaust valves, and the head gasket, and the presence of cracks in the block or cylinder head. This is done by pressurizing the combustion chamber and observing the amount of leakage and where the leaks are. The amount of leakage is measured by regulating the compressed air going into the chamber to a convenient number. One hundred psi is the most useful pressure, as the pressure remaining in the chamber is the percentage seal of the chamber. The location of leaks can be determined by listening at the tailpipe for exhaust valve leaks, at the air filter for intake valve leaks, and through the oil filler cap for blow-by past the rings. Damage to the head gasket or cracks that intersect the water jacket will show up as bubbles in the cooling system.

The leakdown must be done on a warm engine, with both valves closed and the piston at top dead center. Judgment of the measured numbers is somewhere in this area:

97–100	Very good
92–96	Serviceable
89–91	OK but impaired
88 or less	Fix it

The leakdown check is superior to the old compression check in a variety of ways. The condition of the battery and starter motor don't matter. Valve lash variance won't matter. Cam timing doesn't count.

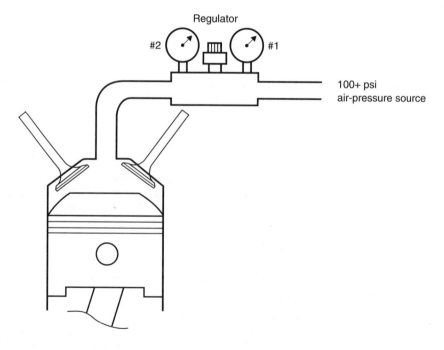

Fig. 15-2. *The leakdown check is the most sophisticated test yet devised for determining the integrity of the combustion chamber. The regulator controls pressure to the cylinder. Gauge 1 indicates that pressure. Gauge 2 indicates pressure remaining in the cylinder after all leakage. With the source regulated to 100 psi, gauge 2 reads the percentage seal of the chamber.*

Cylinder head gasket sealing can easily be checked by a chemical process that identifies traces of exhaust gas products that find their way to the coolant. Check the parts store for the product.

The area around the combustion chamber is just about the limit for turbo-induced engine damage. It is extremely unlikely that any other damage can be even remotely related to the turbo.

Fig. 15-3. *The air/fuel ratio meter is an indispensable testing and troubleshooting tool.*

Inspecting the Turbo System for Malfunction

WILL NOT START. The turbo can cause a starting problem only if the problem is related to an air leak in the system. This is even limited to EFI cars equipped with an air-mass flow sensor and to draw-through carb systems. An air leak in the presence of a mass flow sensor will rob the sensor of some of its signal, creating a lean condition on start-up. It's a similar deal for a draw-through carbureted system. Frequently the flowmeter is responsible for turning the fuel pump on. Thus, a large leak can often appear as a fuel pump failure. A speed density EFI, which employs no air-mass sensor, cannot fail to start due to a turbo problem, as air leaks are of no consequence. A draw-through carb system can have one additional problem: trying to get a rich cold-start mixture through a mass of cold metal. Not too bad in Yuma in August, but Duluth in December will rule out going anywhere. This is not a turbo problem, but a design problem—reason enough not to build a draw-through piece in the first place.

Finding a vacuum leak is a standard troubleshooting procedure. The same technique applies when a turbo is present, except for leakage upstream of the throttle. Leaks upstream must be huge to affect starting. Look for disconnected hoses, big cracks in hoses, tubes dislodged, and items of that magnitude.

POOR IDLE QUALITY. Less significant leaks than those generally associated with hard starting can upset idle quality. Idle air/fuel ratio will always be a critical adjustment. Consult the proper instruments and adjust accordingly. These leaks will likely be downstream of the throttle.

MISFIRES. The turbo can create two conditions in which the engine will misfire: a lean condition and a requirement for higher voltage to spark off the denser mixture in the combustion chamber. The turbo can occasionally cause an EFI-equipped car to suffer a lean spot at or near atmospheric pressure in the intake manifold. This is brought about by the fact that the turbo will actually be pumping pressure up from, say, 15 inches of vacuum to maybe 10 inches. To keep the vehicle from accelerating, the throttle position must be reduced slightly, thus reducing the throttle position sensor's signal to the EFI computer. This reduced signal will slow down the fuel flow for any given airflow, producing a lean condition.

Any misfires at full throttle induced by a lean condition are serious and must be dealt with prior to operating at that boost level again. A lack of fuel raises chamber temperatures dramatically. Heat is the cause of detonation, which is the nemesis of high performance. Don't be too slow to fix any lean conditions.

Lean running conditions can easily be detected by some of the portable oxygen sensors. A requirement for increased voltage to the spark plugs is sometimes encountered and is due to the fact that the air/fuel mixture in the combustion chamber is actually an electrical resistor. The more air and fuel pumped into the chamber by the turbo, the greater the resistance; hence, the greater the voltage required to drive the spark across the plug gap. This problem is readily helped or cured by adding voltage to the system and/or by installing new spark plugs.

POWER LOSS. Troubleshooting power loss should be centered around inspection and optimization of boost pressure, ignition timing, air/fuel ratio, throttle opening, and tailpipe back pressure. Except for throttle angle, which is self-explanatory, these items are all covered elsewhere in this chapter.

EXCESSIVE BOOST PRESSURE. Overboost is worrisome. Since the wastegate is charged with boost-control responsibility, it is certainly the first item to investigate when overboost is encountered. Several facets of the wastegate are subject to failure:

Signal line. The wastegate can malfunction if it fails to receive a proper signal. The signal line can get clogged, or it can develop a leak. Check out both possibilities. Also, check the fittings at both ends of the signal line.

Actuator. Virtually the only part of an actuator subject to failure is the internal diaphragm. On an integral actuator, the simplest test is to blow into the signal port. The signal port should be a complete dead end. Any sign of leakage is evidence of the problem and requires replacing the actuator. This same test can be used on remote wastegates, except that pressure must be applied to the atmospheric side of the diaphragm. The valve side of the diaphragm is almost always designed for a small amount of leakage around the valve stem; thus, testing from the valve side will measure stem guide leak as well as the damaged diaphragm.

Valve. The wastegate valve can become jammed and refuse to open, or become otherwise dislodged. This requires removal and disassembly of the wastegate valve mechanism to determine the cause and the fix.

Flow. The owner of a homemade turbo system must know that the flow capability of the wastegate is up to the demands. This can also afflict kit makers on occasion. Matching these flow requirements is a design problem, not a troubleshooting problem. If all else checks out and the wastegate strokes properly when given a pressure signal, investigate its size relative to the application.

TAILPIPE. The tailpipe can frequently cause an overboost problem. Often, the wastegate depends on an increment of back pressure in the tailpipe to function properly. This is particularly true with integral wastegates. The problem can be further aggravated by the OEM's tendency to use smaller-than-reasonable turbos. These factors can combine to cause overboost when something in the pipe fails and reduces back pressure. Wouldn't it be fun to have a rust hole in the muffler of your expensive turbo car cause an overboost problem that leads to engine failure? No wonder Yankees park their performance cars in winter. It could be argued that some ought to park them regardless.

EXHAUST HOUSING. If a homemade or aftermarket turbo system exhibits overboost but the tailpipe and wastegate are known to be in order, turbine speed may be too high for overall engine/turbo conditions. This means that the turbo exhaust housing is too small, thus overspeeding the turbine and making too much boost. The answer is to increase the A/R ratio of the exhaust housing, slowing the turbine, which in turn reduces the tendency to overboost.

Low or Sluggish Boost

TURBO. Several aspects of the turbo can cause low or sluggish boost response. Most of the causes are applicable to either a misbehaving new setup or an old system with a new problem.

Size. If the turbo is too big, certainly the response will be sluggish. It is possible to get the turbo so large that it does not produce any boost at all, because exhaust gas from the engine is insufficient to power it. Although this is highly unlikely, it is almost equally unlikely that the optimum size turbo was selected on the first try. The fix is generally to reduce the size of the exhaust housing.

Exhaust leaks. Large exhaust gas leaks before the turbine can contribute to sluggish response. Leaks this large will not only be audible, they will be obnoxious. Unless a hole is found that you can stick a pencil through, don't expect the exhaust leak to fix a response problem.

Compressor nut. The compressor retainer nut, if loose, will allow the shaft to spin inside the compressor wheel. Access to the turbine wheel is necessary to anchor the shaft while tightening the compressor retainer nut. These nuts are generally tightened to about 25 in.-lb of torque. This can be approximated by tightening the nut until it touches the compressor wheel and then an additional quarter turn. When tightening a compressor nut, it is important not to permit any side load to reach the turbine shaft. This eliminates the possibility of bending the shaft with the torque wrench.

No air filter. Damage to a compressor wheel can reduce boost. Operating without an air filter will eventually cause the compressor wheel to erode to the point that it can no longer pump air. When the eroding process is occurring, the compressor wheel will lose its efficiency, causing the air temperature to rise, which in turn can lead to detonation problems.

WASTEGATE. A mechanical problem that keeps the wastegate from closing properly will create a large exhaust leak around the turbo, producing sluggish

Fig. 15-4. One way to tighten the compressor retaining nut. Using a T handle will eliminate bending loads in the turbine shaft.

low-speed response. A failed wastegate valve will seldom keep the turbo from producing about the normal amount of boost, but it will take a lot more revs to reach that normal amount. If, for example, the wastegate valve seizes at the position it reaches to control maximum boost, the system must produce enough revs just to overcome the leak before producing any boost.

TAILPIPE. Any failure in the tailpipe that creates a blockage for the exhaust gases will tend to produce a higher boost threshold and/or less maximum boost. Check the pressure in the pipe upstream of any possible blockage. In general, back pressure greater than 10 psi will cause almost a complete loss of boost. Back pressure greater than 2 psi is undesirable under any circumstances, even if not of a magnitude to cause loss of absolute boost pressure.

AIR FILTER. An air filter that is too small or too dirty will keep the system from functioning up to expectations. This condition will also create the bad side-effect of raising intake temperature.

COMPRESSOR INLET HOSES. Almost always, the air filter or airflow meter will be connected to the turbo compressor inlet by flexible hose of some sort. If the filter or flowmeter is restrictive, it is possible for the vacuum thus created to collapse the connecting hoses. Usually the symptom of collapsing hoses is a sudden loss of all boost. The forces on large hoses from small pressure differences can be deceptively large.

MISFIRES. Any misfire while under boost will be caused by a failure to ignite the mixture or by an air/fuel mixture too lean to burn. Failure to ignite the mixture can be a bad plug, wire, coil, or all those stock ignition problems. If the ignition checks out properly, then the problem will be found with the air/fuel ratio.

BOGGING. A distinct type of full-throttle malfunction is an overly rich air/fuel-ratio-induced bog. This is manifested in a loss of power at full throttle, often accompanied by black smoke from the tailpipe.

Another frequent cause of bogging, with similar full-throttle feel, is an overactive ignition retard. A failing knock sensor can induce the same symptoms. A dangerous side effect of retarded ignition is a dramatic rise in exhaust gas temperature. Exhaust manifold and/or turbine damage can result from retarded timing.

DETONATION. The audible metallic pinging sound of detonation is a clear signal that the engine's life is threatened. Every effort must be focused on ridding a system of detonation problems. The wide variety of detonation causes can prove lengthy to troubleshoot, but a turbo engine that pings under boost must be considered a pending serious expense. In general, all detonation problems will stem from one of the six items discussed in the following paragraphs. Their likelihood as the source of the problem is approximately the same as the order in which they are listed.

Octane. A fuel's octane rating is a measure of its resistance to spontaneous combustion, or detonation. The greater the octane, the greater the resistance. Fuel quality is relatively consistent, but it is advisable when quality is suspect to change brands.

Ignition timing. Improper ignition timing is rarely a system failure but, rather, an adjustment error. A check of both static and maximum advance will virtually always uncover any discrepancy in the ignition system. The knock-sensor-controlled ignition timing retard can be subject to many types of failure, one of which is failure to recognize knock and do something about it.

Should a knock-sensor system failure be suspected, consult the service manual for the unit or, in OEM applications, for the vehicle.

Lean air/fuel ratio. A lean running condition will promote detonation, because a lesser quantity of fuel, when vaporized, will absorb less heat. Thus a lean mixture increases heat, the root cause of detonation. A turbo engine offers the freedom to run slightly richer mixtures than with a normally aspirated engine, permitting the extra fuel to act a bit like a liquid intercooler. Call that an OEM intercooler.

Exhaust gas back pressure. A very small turbine, blockage in the exhaust manifold, or some form of restriction in the tailpipe will cause an increase in the system back pressure. Back pressure keeps the burned, hot gas in the combustion chamber. A failure of any sort that increases back pressure seriously aggravates the detonation characteristics of an engine.

Intercooler. An intercooler strongly affects the detonation threshold of the turbo engine. Anything that comes along and compromises the intercooler's efficiency will lower the detonation threshold. Other than removing the obvious newspaper stuck in front of the intercooler, the only periodic service needed is to clean out the internal oil film that accumulates in normal use. The oil film will noticeably decrease the efficiency of the intercooler.

Ambient heat. There are days when nothing works right, and ambient heat certainly contributes to some of these. Higher-boost-pressure turbo systems usually operate somewhere near the detonation threshold and can easily cross over to the dark side when the ambient temperature takes a turn for the worse. David Hobbs, one of the more able and literate racers, once suggested that turbocharged race cars were so sensitive, he could feel a power loss when the sun came out from behind a cloud. Engineering around the seasonal and daily changes of ambient temperature is not within the scope of this book.

AND FURTHERMORE . . .

What is detonation, and why is it so destructive?

Detonation is the spontaneous combustion of the air/fuel mixture ahead of the flame front—combustion by explosion rather than controlled burning. It occurs after the combustion process has started and is usually located in the area last to burn. As the flame front advances across the chamber, the pressure—and thus the temperature—in the remaining unburned mixture rises. If the autoignition temperature is exceeded, this remaining mixture explodes. The audible ping is the explosion's shock wave.

Detonation is extremely destructive. This is a result of temperatures that can reach 18,000°F in the center of the explosion. The pressure spikes caused by the explosion can reach several thousand psi, and pressure rise is rapid enough to be considered an impact load. These temperatures and pressures are almost ten times higher than those accompanying controlled combustion.

No metals in existence today, no forged pistons, and no special head gaskets can withstand sustained detonation. Virtually nothing can withstand sustained detonation. Consider also that at 6000 rpm, fifty explosions can occur in each combustion chamber in one second. Thus:

☞ **RULE:** If you ever hear a ping, you lift your foot.

Trouble and symptoms	Probable causes code numbers	Probable cause description by code number
Engine lacks power	1, 4, 5, 6, 7, 8, 9, 10, 11, 18, 20, 21, 22, 25, 26, 27, 28, 29, 30, 37, 38, 39, 40, 41, 42, 43	1. Dirty air cleaner element 2. Plugged crankcase breathers 3. Air cleaner element missing, leaking, not sealing correctly; loose connections to turbocharger 4. Collapsed or restricted air tube before turbocharger 5. Restricted/damaged crossover pipe, turbocharger to inlet manifold
Black smoke	1, 4, 5, 6, 7, 8, 9, 10, 11, 18, 20, 21, 22, 25, 26, 27, 28, 29, 30, 37, 38, 39, 40, 41, 43	6. Foreign object between air cleaner and turbocharger 7. Foreign object in exhaust system (from engine; check engine) 8. Turbocharger flanges, clamps, or bolts loose 9. Inlet manifold cracked; gaskets loose or missing; connections loose
Blue smoke	1, 2, 4, 6, 8, 9, 17, 19, 20, 21, 22, 32, 33, 34, 37, 45	10. Exhaust manifold cracked, burned; gaskets loose, blown, or missing 11. Restricted exhaust system 12. Oil lag (oil delay to turbocharger at start-up)
Excessive oil consumption	2, 8, 15, 17, 19, 20, 29, 30, 31, 33, 34, 37, 45	13. Insufficient lubrication 14. Lubricating oil contaminated with dirt or other material 15. Improper type lubricating oil used
Excessive oil turbine end	2, 7, 8, 17, 19, 20, 22, 29, 30, 32, 33, 34, 45	16. Restricted oil feed line 17. Restricted oil drain line 18. Turbine housing damaged or restricted
Excessive oil compressor end	1, 2, 4, 5, 6, 8, 19, 20, 21, 29, 30, 33, 34, 45	19. Turbocharger seal leakage 20. Worn journal bearings 21. Excessive dirt buildup in compressor housing 22. Excessive carbon buildup behind turbine wheel
Insufficient lubrication	8, 12, 14, 15, 16, 23, 24, 31, 34, 35, 36, 44, 46	23. Too-fast acceleration at initial start (oil lag) 24. Too little warm-up time 25. Fuel pump malfunction 26. Worn or damaged injectors
Oil in exhaust manifold	2, 7, 17, 18, 19, 20, 22, 29, 30, 33, 34, 45	27. Valve timing 28. Burned valves 29. Worn piston rings 30. Burned pistons
Damaged compressor wheel	3, 4, 6, 8, 12, 15, 16, 20, 21, 23, 24, 31, 34, 35, 36, 44, 46	31. Leaking oil-feed line 32. Excessive engine pre-oil 33. Excessive engine idle 34. Coked or sludged center housing

Damaged turbine wheel	7, 8, 12, 13, 14, 15, 16, 18, 20, 22, 23, 24, 25, 28, 30, 31, 34, 35, 36, 44, 46	35. Oil pump malfunction
		36. Oil filter plugged
		37. Oil-bath-type air cleaner:
		   a. air inlet screen restricted
		   b. oil pull-over
		   c. dirty air cleaner
		   d. oil viscosity low
		   e. oil viscosity high

Drag or bind in rotating assembly	3, 6, 7, 8, 12, 13, 14, 15, 16, 18, 20, 21, 22, 23, 24, 31, 34, 35, 36, 44, 46	38. Actuator damaged or defective 39. Wastegate binding 40. Electronic control module or connector(s) defective 41. Wastegate actuator solenoid or connector defective
Worn bearings, journals, bearing bores	6, 7, 8, 12, 13, 14, 15, 16, 23, 24, 31, 35, 36, 44, 46	42. Egr valve defective 43. Alternator voltage incorrect 44. Engine shut off without adequate cool-down time
Noisy	1, 3, 4, 5, 6, 7, 8, 9, 10, 11, 12, 13, 14, 15, 16, 18, 20, 21, 22, 23, 24, 31, 34, 35, 36, 37, 44, 46	45. Leaking valve guide seals 46. Low oil level
Sludged or coked center housing	2, 11, 13, 14, 15, 17, 18, 24, 31, 35, 36, 44, 46	

16 DEVELOPMENTS IN TURBOCHARGING

Today   High-performance automobiles have no right to abuse our environment. No individual has the right to litter the atmosphere with emissions, any more than he would litter the side of the road with beer cans. Everyone living in this atmosphere must exercise a certain level of responsibility toward keeping it clean. Through turbocharging, the high-performance, emissions-compatible automobile of today has increased performance more than any other class of vehicle from any era. This situation is not coincidental.

The response of the automotive engineering community to federal and state emissions laws has created a set of controls with such exceptional technology that today's powerful street car can achieve more mpg than yesterday's econobox, and today's econobox can often outrun yesterday's supercar. Good technology applied to an urgent problem, with the performance car enthusiast constantly pushing the envelope, has resulted in a fleet of vehicles that perform better, are more economical, last longer, require less maintenance, don't pollute the environment, and are just downright fun to drive. What did technology do to turn this trick? They invented new equipment. They optimized it well and calibrated it within tight limits. They manufactured it under such control that it is hugely durable. No doubt whatsoever exists as to the extreme durability of electronic engine-management systems relative to breaker-point distributors and carburetors. The technology developed to contend with to-

Fig. 16-1. The best-known 0–60 time for a turbocharged VW is somewhere under 3.0 seconds.

day's needs consists primarily of electronic fuel injection, programmed igni-tion-timing control, oxygen-sensor closed-loop feedback, and catalytic converters.

The combination of these four items is the heart of obtaining the superb driveability and economy we need while keeping emissions within necessary limits. These items are all available in the aftermarket. It is technically feasi-ble to use these pieces of equipment, tune them carefully, and create a fully cer-tifiable vehicle within operational requirements. The first place to start is learning the rules. The most stringent rules are those of the California Air Re-sources Board (9528 Telstar Avenue, El Monte, CA 91731; (818) 575-6800). It makes sense to play by the strictest set of rules. These rules are available upon request. Secure them, learn them, and let them be the guidelines under which designs are created.

The Future

These are exciting times for car performance. Engineering, quality, perfor-mance, economy, emissions, and durability are all experiencing great improve-ments. It seems as though we get acquainted with a great new model only to have another come along in swift succession, rendering the first one obsolete. Predicting the path of development that turbo- and engine-related systems will take then becomes both timely and precarious.

If it all happens the way I think it should, much work will be done in three distinct categories: the turbocharger, turbocharger system-related hardware, and the engine proper.

Turbocharger Improvements

Virtually all improvements to the turbo will be aimed at forcing it to leap up to boost-producing speeds in less time. If a turbo could be made instantaneously responsive, the shape of the torque curve of a normally aspirated engine and of a turbo engine would be essentially the same. That is the goal. While it is not yet quite possible to achieve that, progress will come in two primary areas: bearing losses and variable A/R ratio turbine housings.

BEARING LOSSES. Power wasted in the bearings of the turbo is simply the drag loss in shearing the oil film in the bearing as the shaft rotates. This loss is pro-portionately large at low speeds, when little exhaust gas energy is available to drive the turbine, but wanes to minor importance at high speeds. At high speeds, enough exhaust gas energy exists to kick the turbo so fast as to scare most journalists. The actual power lost in the bearing area is, however, enough to mow your lawn. If this power loss could be applied to revving the turbo up quickly from low speeds, the rate of acceleration of the turbine would be con-siderably greater.

Low-friction bearings can come about in three ways: smaller-diameter shafts, ball bearings, or air bearings. Each approach has problems. Smaller-di-ameter shafts create higher bearing loads and aggravate critical vibration fre-quencies. Good engineering will be required to make them work.

Ball bearings hold great promise for low friction. The extreme quality con-trol required of a bearing to operate at turbocharger shaft speeds is not fun for a manufacturing engineer to contemplate. It can be and is being done, and one day will be here for us to use. The willingness of some automakers to spend an extra twenty-five dollars per car for an improvement of the magnitude of low-friction ball bearings in the turbo is a situation that is more likely every day. Performance is now as competitive as any other aspect of the automobile.

Fig. 16-2. This cross section shows details of the two oil-wick-lubricated ball bearings of the Aerocharger.

Air bearings may see use in select applications where cost becomes less a determining factor. The technology of air bearings is well established, but quality control again becomes a huge barrier to volume production. These are the lowest-friction bearings of all and would yield substantial performance gains.

In view of production technology in the world today, I'll vote on ball bearings as the next bearing system for the turbocharger.

VARIABLE A/R RATIO TURBINE HOUSINGS. All other things remaining the same, the smaller the A/R ratio of the turbine housing, the lower the rpm at which the turbo will produce boost. This same low A/R turbine housing will cause increasingly large exhaust gas back pressure as total exhaust flow rises with increasing rpm. Big A/Rs make large amounts of power because of reduced back pressures but are not exactly splendid for low-speed response.

While not yet commonplace, turbochargers are in production with a design feature that permits the turbine housing to act like a small A/R at low speeds

Fig. 16-3. Closing one of the two ports creates a small A/R ratio, improving low-speed response. The gradual opening of the second port at higher speeds creates a larger A/R ratio.

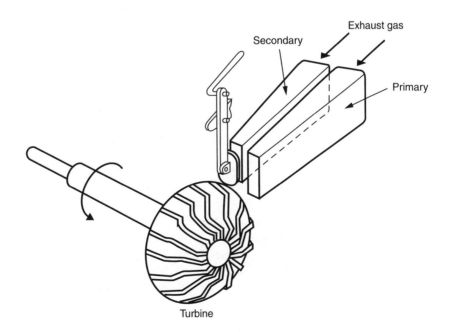

and a large A/R at higher speeds. This feature is generally referred to as the variable A/R turbine housing. It indeed offers the merits of both large and small A/Rs, all in the same package. With this feature, the turbo comes much closer to the instant response we want. It also acquires the ability to produce a torque curve similar to a larger, normally aspirated engine at low engine speeds. Two types of variable A/R units are likely to see some form of popularity. The relatively simple twin scroll idea is an inexpensive mechanism that may prove adequate when judged on its own merit. The other mechanism is the VATN (variable area turbine nozzle). The VATN so far outshines all other possibilities that it will prove to be the winning ticket.

Twin scroll turbine housing. The TST housing derives its name from the geometry of the exhaust gas inlet into the turbine. Two different-sized scrolls are generally used, a primary and a secondary. Typically, the primary is open for low-speed operation, and both for high-speed use. This creates the ability of the TST to be a small A/R housing at low speeds and a large A/R at higher speeds.

TST designs are of merit in that they offer a better combination of low-speed response and high-speed power. It would be difficult to configure the unit to control boost by effectively varying A/R. A wastegate is therefore still necessary to control boost pressure. Simplicity of the twin scroll turbine housing is its big selling point.

Variable area turbine nozzle. The VATN is a whole new deal. The vanes of the VATN pivot to present varying areas to the discharge stream, changing the exhaust gas velocity as it enters the turbine, permitting the speed of the turbine to vary. The merit of the VATN lies in several areas: it acts like a small A/R when asked to do so, a large A/R when required, and it produces a smooth transition through all points between the two extremes. The VATN can create such a huge A/R that turbine speed over the entire range of operation can be controlled by varying the A/R alone. Thus the VATN becomes its own boost control, and no wastegate is required. When no wastegate is present, all exhaust

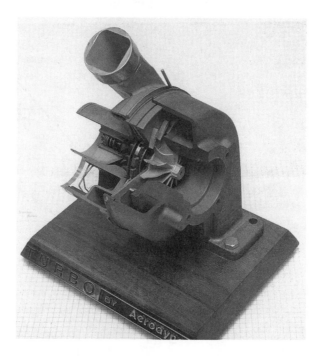

Fig. 16-4. *The fastest-response turbo in the world is the VATN Aerocharger.*

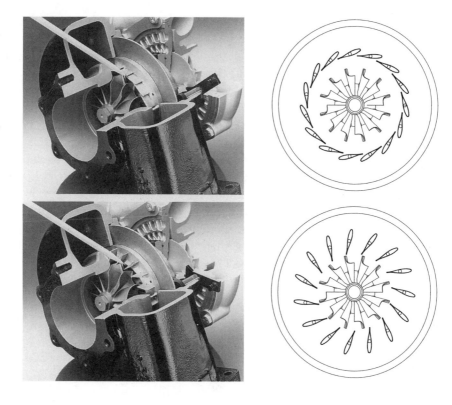

Fig. 16-5. *Details of the VATN. When the nozzles are nearly closed, exhaust gas velocity is high. When they are open, velocity, and therefore back pressure, is lowest.*

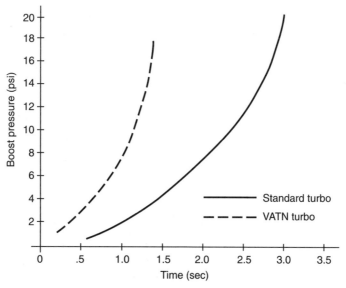

Fig. 16-6. *Response time of the VATN versus standard turbine response. The time required by the VATN is approximately half that of the standard turbo.*

gas energy is available to power the compressor, and "waste" becomes a thing of the past. Turbine performance can take on whole new dimensions. Since turbine speed is always controlled by the VATNs, the A/R ratio is always the largest possible for the boost pressure at that instant. If the A/R were smaller, turbine speed would rise, creating more boost, which would raise turbine speed, which would raise boost again. This situation will always keep exhaust gas back pressure at its lowest for any given boost pressure. This creates the wonderful condition of the exhaust back pressure being less than the boost pressure. When this "crossover" occurs, power production takes on new dimensions. This condition is not generally feasible with conventional turbos without the turbine's being so large that it becomes unresponsive at low speeds.

The success of the VATN is directly attributable to having the vanes in the right position at the right time, which depends on the "intelligence" of the vane controller. Varying load conditions will require the controller to create the correct A/R for exactly that situation. The load condition of steady-state cruise will want the vanes fully open for the least possible back pressure. On application of throttle, the controller must anticipate the pending demand for boost and close the vanes, so as to bring the turbine up to boost-producing speeds as quickly as possible. Once the desired boost level is achieved, the vanes will gradually open as engine speed rises, in order to control turbine speed and thus the boost pressure. Sufficient range of motion for the vanes must exist that the engine redline can be reached before the vanes are fully open. It is clear, then, that the VATN controller is the secret to the extreme benefit of the VATN concept.

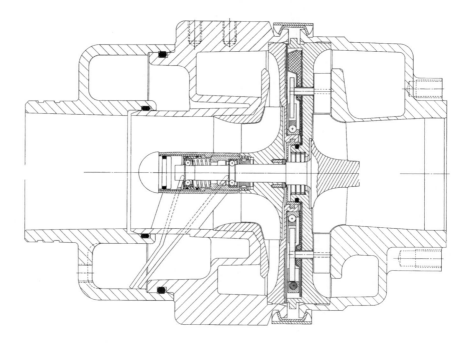

Fig. 16-7. *This cross section shows the complexity of the marvelously crafted and engineered Aerocharger. Complexity is the trade-off for the Aerocharger's extraordinary response.*

SELECTION OF TURBOCHARGER SIZE. Few of today's turbocharged automobiles are equipped with the proper-sized turbo. I remain convinced that the reason for this is the incorrect perception by the marketing types as to the desires of the end user. I contend that the end user wants a powerful automobile, not necessarily one that makes boost at the lowest possible rpm. When, and if, major manufacturers size the turbo for the enthusiast, we will see an increase in power, a decrease in charge temperatures, smoother driveability, and an overall increase in margins of safety—all of which is possible with simple changes in size.

CERAMIC TURBINES. A dramatic reduction in the rotational inertia of the turbo can be brought to bear by the use of ceramic instead of metal for the turbine wheel. While a wonderful idea, yielding a tangible improvement in the turbo's response, the ceramic turbine remains expensive and fragile. This writer believes that other than for brief field tests, the ceramic turbine is a feature for the twenty-first century.

Fig. 16-8. Lighter-
weight ceramics
offer the difference
illustrated by curves
*T25 Ceramic versus
T25 Metal.*

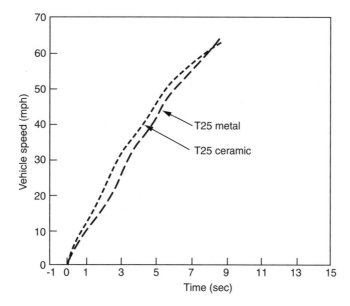

Fig. 16-9. The
ceramic turbine will
need to prove its long-
term durability for its
better response to be an
overall benefit.

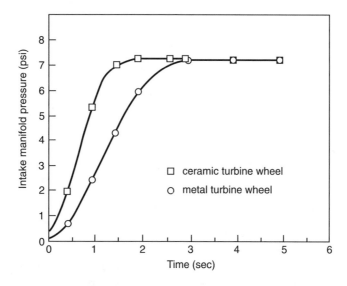

COMPOSITE MATERIALS. Carbon composites have tremendous strength and stiffness-to-weight ratios. The possibility of compressor-wheel inertia reductions brought about by composite materials seems likely. Further reducing the inertia of the lowest-inertia component of the turbo is perhaps worthwhile. But fixing the weak links first has an element of logic, and the compressor wheel is not the weak link.

GENERAL REFINEMENTS. Without the fanfare accorded revolutionary components, most of the items inside the turbo will continue to be improved in both efficiency and durability. Bearing losses will creep downward, rotational inertias will decrease, heat rejection will improve, and turbine and compressor efficiencies will slowly but surely improve. Steady improvements, but no great changes.

Fig. 16-10. Perhaps the turbocharger of the future will take the form of this innovative design, with variable area turbine control and an axial-flow compressor ahead of the radial compressor.

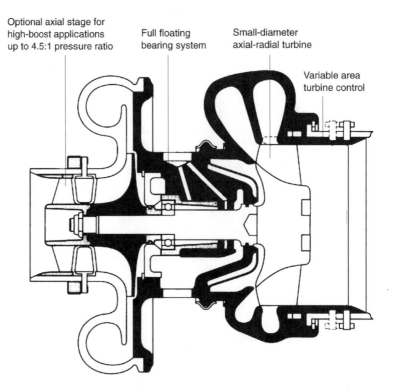

Optional axial stage for high-boost applications up to 4.5:1 pressure ratio

Full floating bearing system

Small-diameter axial-radial turbine

Variable area turbine control

Turbocharger System-Related Hardware

INTERCOOLING. Although the science of intercooling is well known to automobile designers of the world, the next few years should show large improvements in this area. The force behind the improvements will be a change in attitude. When one of the world's great car companies builds a vehicle they call a Super Coupe and places an intercooler in a position such that the only cooling air it can possibly get must first go through the cooling system radiator and the AC condenser, this is evidence of an attitude problem. It is possible that the refrigeration-cycle gas intercooler may one day be practical. New processes and techniques will be required as AC compressors consume more power than better intercoolers can offset. The part-time intercooler, where the air charge is sent directly to the engine at all boost pressures below the threshold of need for intercooling, may one day yield a tangible improvement in response for the entire system.

BOOST CONTROLS. Smarter wastegate controls can produce more responsive turbos as well as flatter torque curves. While ultimate power may be little influenced, a torque curve with one or both ends raised a bit will produce a faster car. Electronic control of the wastegate actuator signal will be the concept that permits these improvements. Conventional wastegates crack open at a point well below the desired boost and then creep to the position required to control boost pressure. This early creep robs the turbine of useful energy with which it could gain speed faster. Having the wastegate open and bypassing substantial energy around the turbine when the turbine is trying to gain speed is basically madness. Electronics will fix that situation. Raising the low end of a torque curve or smoothing a flat spot in it can be accomplished by programming boost signals. A boost-pressure equivalent of an extra passing gear could be programmed as well.

EXHAUST SYSTEM. Virtually all current production exhaust systems are excessively restrictive. Tailpipe-induced back pressure is truly useless. I do believe it possible to produce quiet, low-back-pressure tailpipes as economically as the current bad designs. This would permit the same turbo systems to operate at the same power with less heat, less boost, and a far greater margin of safety.

The inverted-sound-wave silencer is an idea whose time is yet to come. The principle is to record the sound from the engine, electronically invert it, and play it back, superimposed on the original. The hope is that the two sound waves will cancel each other, eliminating the need for a muffler. Back pressure could be way down, so we remain interested.

STAGED AND STAGGERED TURBOS. Many interesting schemes have been created to couple two or more turbos together. The purpose is generally to achieve greater efficiency at extreme boost pressures or to gain low-end response and broad, flat torque curves. Such schemes may be useful in vehicles like the fabulous Porsche 959, but the likelihood of such complexity's reaching the market in significant numbers appears small. The value of a hobbyist's trying to recreate such intricate equipment seems staggering indeed. Complexity and cost of this magnitude, accompanied by all the service and repair problems inherent in that complexity, is mind-boggling. Stick to fundamentals, do them very well, and let performance be the staggering factor.

Engine

A clean-sheet-of-paper engine designed specifically for turbocharging would not be dramatically different. However, many details would change:

- In my view, the positions of the turbo and catalytic converter would be reversed, to improve cold-start emissions. Turbine response would ordinarily suffer in this position, but the VATN turbo would more than restore any lost response.

Fig. 16-11. The Chevy/Ilmor Indy engine was designed from scratch as a turbocharged engine. The camshafts, port sizes, compression ratio, bore/stroke ratio, and rpm operating ranges were all configured to complement the turbocharger.

- Engine speeds would likely be reduced. With the broad-band torque increases offered by the turbo, high rotational speed is no longer necessary to make adequate power. Lower engine speeds would reduce component weights and friction as well.

- With lower engine speeds comes the ability to take advantage of longer-stroke, smaller-bore engines. For reasons buried in the foggy depths of thermodynamics, longer-stroke engines can enjoy greater fuel efficiency.

- Smaller intake and exhaust ports would improve low-rpm torque by creating higher intake-air velocities, permitting better cylinder filling as a result of the increased momentum of a faster-moving column of air. The turbo will take care of torque for the remainder of the rpm range.

- The number of cylinder-head-to-block fasteners should increase. A greater number of smaller studs, perhaps six per cylinder, would be allowed by reduced port areas.

- Heat will be dealt with by at least two changes. First, oil spray onto the bottom of pistons or oil passages through pistons can greatly improve piston strength by reducing operating temperatures. Second, the exhaust port will be insulated to reduce heat transfer to the head and the coolant. This will improve catalyst light-off (response time for the converter to achieve minimum operating temperature from a cold start), reduce radiator sizes, and carry more heat to the turbine for response benefits.

- Electronic controls will play an even greater role in running the turbo engine. Today's engine-management systems will be expanded to control VATNs, boost pressures, and, of course, the relation of spark timing and fuel mixture as they influence engine knock.

17 BRINGING IT ALL TOGETHER

It is easy to get smugly comfortable with the idea that you can design ideal pieces to fit into imaginary spaces in a beautiful and artistic manner. The smugness usually leaves abruptly when you are confronted with the prospect of placing all the items required for a proper turbo system underneath the hood of a modern automobile. The reality of the problem of finding not just space, but the best space and the logical spatial relationship for the components, can humble the cleverest of designers. The first part of this chapter offers guidelines for bringing all the pieces together into a theoretical, coordinated, least-compromise system. Hopefully, this will help you get past the initial fright of looking under the hood. The second part of the chapter deals with the design parameters of installing a turbo system on an actual car, the Acura NSX.

DEFINING A THEORETICAL SYSTEM

The first step is to define the specific performance objectives. Second is defining the system required to meet those performance objectives. Third is creating an outline of the components needed to build that system. A typical outline can take the following form, using a 300–350 cid Chevy V-8 as an example.

Performance objectives:

• 600 bhp @ 6500 rpm

Fig. 17-1. *Gale Banks produced this big-block Chevy twin with a water-based intercooler housed in the cast aluminum plenum atop a Holley carburetor.*

Fig. 17-2. Do not copy any features of this old draw-through on a Capri V-6.

- 650 ft-lb torque @ 3500 rpm
- 20 mpg @ legal cruise speed
- 93 octane fuel

System requirements:

- 300–350 cid engine
- pressure ratio of approximately 2.0
- turbocharger(s)
- wastegate(s)
- intercooling
- programmable electronic fuel injection
- high-voltage ignition
- bypass valves

Specific components:

- Chevrolet 350 cid V-8 (four-bolt mains, forged-steel crankshaft, x.x compression ratio, aluminum cylinder heads)
- turbocharger (brand, water-cooled bearing housing, compressor size, turbine size, exhaust housing style)
- wastegate (brand, basic boost setting, valve size)
- intercooler (air or water style, charge air flow area, heat exchange area

This outline should continue until the components, brands, and sizes are all defined. When the outline is complete, the scope of the task will be clearly spelled out.

General Layout   Once the outline of the job is clear, the actual component positions can be studied and determined. Paper, pencil, some study and sketching will go a long way toward eliminating problem areas.

All aspects of the layout must give full consideration to the need or intention to seek a California Air Resources Board exemption order for the system. A prime factor is the position of the catalytic converter and the oxygen sensor. There is no need to move an oxygen sensor, but traditionally, the turbocharger is placed between the engine and converter. With respect to any certification, you need to consider converter light-off (the point at which it is hot

Fig. 17-3. *Jim Feuling built this marvelous 200 mph Quad 4 system. Note integration of the wastegate after all exhaust pulses are in one tube.*

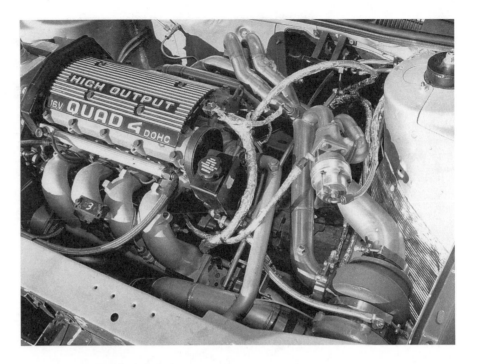

enough to start working) as of foremost importance in order to pass the warm-up cycle emissions test.

The first job is positioning the turbo. The factors contributing to the choice of position are as follows:

- Is exhaust gas entry into the turbo from the engine as direct as possible? This will influence or dictate the manifold or header pipe design. Can a smooth, large-radius-bend exhaust manifold fit in the space dictated by the turbo position?
- Does the position permit space for and easy installation of the turbine outlet pipe and proximity to the catalytic converter? The closer to the converter, the better.
- Does the compressor inlet allow easy entry from the air filter and the outlet easy exit to the intercooler?
- Can the wastegate be properly tied in to the exhaust manifold collector?
- Will heat from the turbine damage any nearby components, and are heat shields necessary?
- Is the turbo high enough for a gravity-powered oil drain to be adequate?
- Does the turbo need support other than the exhaust manifold?
- Does the position allow clearance to objects that could contact components of the turbo system when engine torque forces distortion into engine/drivetrain flex mounts?

Once the best combination (least compromise) of position requirements is determined, the turbo can be anchored by temporary hangers while installing connecting hardware.

The second job is building the defined intercooler and placing it into position. Considerations are as follows:

- Is the spatial volume sufficient for a large enough intercooler?
- Does the general layout of the vehicle require a water-based intercooler or some other unusual feature?

Fig. 17-4. *Good basic plumbing from Porsche, as one would expect. The intercooler can get excellent ambient air from behind the rear wheel and is protected by a heavy wire-mesh screen.*

Fig. 17-5. *The great Ferrari Turbo GTO used one wastegate to control two turbos. Note the integration of anti-surge valves into both compressor outlets. The intercoolers show good internal streamlining and generous core area, but ambient cooling air is sparse.*

- Can the tubes be routed conveniently to and from the intercooler, and do they meet flow requirements?
- Will the cores receive adequate ambient airflow, or will they require air ducts?
- Is the position safe from road hazards?
- Is the intercooler in front of the radiator bulkhead, if front-mounted? Does it block the least amount of airflow to the radiator (if applicable)?

The third job is defining and positioning the air filter. Use the filter manufacturer's recommendation on size versus horsepower. Keep in mind the following:

Fig. 17-6. *Larger air filters are necessary for performance and to help keep thermal loads in check. Note the thermal blanket over the exhaust housing. The compressor inlet flex hoses need to be reasonably stiff to avoid being collapsed by the slight pressure drop through the filter.*

- The filter requires clean air but must be protected from puddle or splash water. However, cool ambient air is not essential if the system is properly intercooled.
- The further the filter is from the vehicle occupants, the quieter it will be.
- A bell-mouth-shaped transition from the filter to the flowmeter or compressor inlet tube is desirable.

Fig. 17-7. *Taking system air from directly above the exhaust manifold is not a good idea, particularly where no intercooler is present. A simple air duct to the front would lower the charge temperature about 50°F.*

The fourth job is the location of a muffler with an adequately large flow path. If the system is rear- or mid-engined, the muffler becomes key to the packaging, due to its relative size. If front-engined, the positioning requirements relax considerably.

The fifth job is creating a connection to the throttle body. This establishes the destination of the tubes exiting the intercoolers. The throttle plate in the throttle body is a relatively high-drag point in the system. For this reason, particular attention must be given to smooth section changes in this area and avoidance of other drag-producing imperfections.

The sixth job is to design and build the exhaust manifolding. Factors to keep in mind include easy oil-line access, clearance to heat-susceptible parts, compressor inlet and outlet paths, turbine outlet space, and turbo section clocking problems due to an integral wastegate (if present). Spark plug and plug wire access need close attention.

Fittings
Where possible, pipe-thread fittings should be chosen for simplicity and sure sealing. The less-than-wonderful aesthetics of pipe threads can easily be masked by sinking fittings up to the last thread.

All intersections of signal-line hoses should be made with brass tees. Signal lines should be silicone-based material, resistant to heat and hydrocarbons.

The locations of all components in the system must receive due consideration. When that has been done and done well, the major hurdle of bringing the components together into a system will have been accomplished.

DEFINING AND TESTING AN ACTUAL SYSTEM

Here we will further examine the design, development, construction, and testing procedures discussed in the previous sections in regards to creating a new twin turbocharger system for an Acura NSX. The validity of the lessons in this book can be determined by comparing the defined objective with the finished product.

Objectives
For economy of operation and to more easily keep engine emissions within EPA/CARB certification limits, the engine has been kept absolutely stock.

The obvious hurdle presented by this project is the high compression ratio of the NSX engine, at 10.2 to 1. This value, in an engine powered by street fuel of 92 or 93 octane, dictates low maximum boost pressure to obtain long-term durability.

Any construction effort of this nature must consider the guidelines for engine system modifications drawn up by the U. S. Environmental Protection Agency and the California Air Resources Board. The decision to apply for an exemption order from CARB for the NSX turbo system for true street-legal status dictates several facets of the design:

- All electronic engine management functions are to remain unaltered.
- The original catalytic converters must remain stock and in the original position.
- Fuel system controls must function only when under boost.
- Actual engine emissions must remain within CARB guidelines for the NSX.

Torque and power of the system should complement the engine's broad-range torque curve and substantial power. Honda/Acura spent considerable

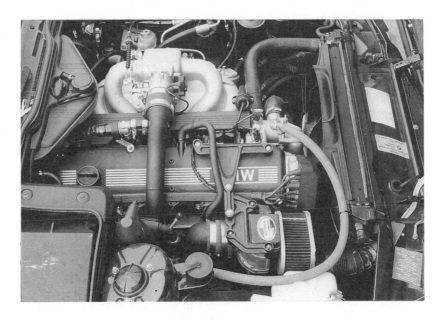

Fig. 17-8. *This modest 5 psi system for the BMW 535i was designed with low maximum boost pressure for long-term durability. In order to get comparable durability, the Acura NSX engine will dictate a similarly modest system because of its high compression ratio.*

money and engineering talent on creating a broad torque curve, largely through use of a clever variable valve-timing mechanism. To preserve the superb driveability offered by the NSX's torque curve, it will be necessary to achieve substantial boost at low engine speeds. This is a characteristic of smaller turbos. However, achieving high-rpm torque increases without huge exhaust gas back pressure losses dictates the need for a larger-than-normal turbocharger. These diametrically opposed requirements can be dealt with in three ways:

- A variable area turbine nozzle turbo, which has the ability to act like a small turbo at low speeds and a large turbo at high speeds, thus potentially satisfying both requirements
- Two turbos, utilizing one for low speed and both for high speed, where a twin scroll turbine is not available in a large enough size
- A standard turbo with the best possible sizing between the two opposing requirements

Ordinarily, the factors discussed in Chapter 3 (vehicle cost and class, system cost, objectives) would influence which of these three options is selected. Lack of pizzazz rules out a system based on a standard turbo. With a twin sequential layout, performance is good, but complexity rivals a space shuttle's main engine.

A complicating factor is that space restrictions in the NSX dictate mounting the turbo low in the chassis, which is inadequate for the gravity oil-drain requirements of a standard turbo. The choice is then between installing sumps and pumps for return oil on a standard turbo or using the self-lubricating Aerocharger. The added attractions of the Aerocharger's fast response and good low-rpm boost make this an easy decision.

The original power rating of the NSX, while substantial, (275 bhp at 8000 rpm), still falls short of the desires of most buyers with $65,000 to spend on a performance automobile. Simple calculation of serious performance-car weight per horsepower suggests that the NSX can step into the high end of the supercar category with the addition of 100 bhp, which will require two Aerochargers, since no single unit is large enough to provide the desired airflow. An increase in base engine output of 36% will then be necessary through the turbo system:

$$\text{Performance gain} = \frac{\text{desired bhp}}{\text{original bhp}} - 1$$

$$= \frac{275 + 100}{275} - 1 = 0.36 = 36\%$$

The perceived value of an add-on system like this is always a balance of power gain versus cost, installation complexity, increased service requirements, and expectation of long-term durability degradation. The relatively low boost required (performance gain times atmospheric pressure, or 0.36 x 14.7=5.2 psi) for the anticipated 100 bhp gain suggests that the other value considerations will fall into line.

As mentioned in Chapter 3, after the field of available compressors is narrowed to two or three that appear, from their flow maps, to be in the right range of pressure ratio and cfm, with efficiency not below 60%, it is necessary to calculate which of the compressors is the more suitable. In this case, two sizes of Aerocharger will be examined: models 101 and 128.

Preinstallation Test Data

Long-term durability of an engine/turbo system is in part keyed to exhaust gas temperature. Although a high temperature is able to really kick a turbine up to speed quickly, performance must be weighed against durability. The size of the turbine will depend partly on exhaust gas temperature. Heat distribution through the exhaust system can be illustrated by the temperatures before and after the catalytic convertors. These measured a remarkably low 1100°F before and 1040°F after.

As described in Chapter 7, a fuel pump's ability to deliver the rate of flow required for the anticipated bhp must be verified, or the unit must be replaced with one of known capability. Here, the fuel pump will be tested by actual trial. If fuel pressure stays constant at maximum load, the pump is adequate.

The pulse duration of a fuel injector required to fuel a maximum-torque pulse is useful information. This pulse duration will be compared to the engine cycle time to determine the method of supplying fuel to operate under boost. With the objective of a 36% torque increase, the fuel supply must be increased by 36% also. If a 36% increase in pulse duration does not exceed engine cycle time, it is possible to achieve the fuel flow increase by electronically extending the pulse durations. If the pulses are too long to permit this, a rising-rate fuel pressure regulator or an entirely reprogrammed fuel curve, using larger injectors, will be necessary. The obvious difficulty of matching Acura's accuracy in fuel system calibration will likely point to the rising-rate regulator for the job. Another reason not to use the extended-pulse method is the inability of the NSX's ecu to interpret above-atmospheric pressure signals from the manifold air-pressure sensor.

Further test data were needed regarding this vehicle's emissions. Emissions were checked on a four-gas analyzer from a cold start and every 10 seconds thereafter until the vehicle was warmed up. Emissions plotted versus time are shown in figure 17-9.

Fuel Injection Analysis

It is necessary to know the time of one revolution, in order to compare it to the pulse duration of the fuel injector at maximum load. This comparison will determine whether the injector can stay open longer to feed the additional air supplied by the turbos.

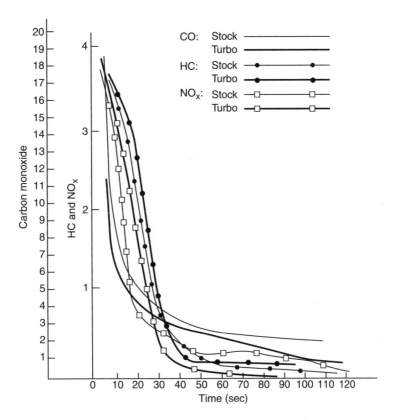

Fig. 17-9. Prior to the expensive emissions laboratory cold-start tests, it was considered advisable to run an inexpensive test on a four-gas analyzer. Results showed cold-start emissions essentially unchanged.

As indicated in Chapter 7, the time of one revolution can be determined either from figure 7-3 or by formula. Using the formula, let rpm = 8000. Then

$$\text{Time of one revolution} = \frac{60\ \dfrac{sec}{min}}{8000\ \dfrac{rev}{min}} = 0.0075 \text{ sec} = 7.5 \text{ msec}$$

The NSX's EFI is sequential, which reverts to nonsequential over approximately 3000 rpm, as discussed in Chapter 7. Therefore, pulse duration should be checked at over 4000 rpm. Actual pulse duration at maximum load was measured at 5.0 msec.

$$\text{Duty cycle} = \frac{\text{stock pulse duration}}{\text{time of one revolution}}$$

$$= \frac{5.0 \text{ msec}}{7.5 \text{ msec}} = 0.67 = 67\%$$

The inverse of the duty cycle minus one is the available increase in fuel flow from extending injector pulse duration. This is .5, or 50%. Therefore, we could hold the injectors open all the time and achieve a 50% increase in fuel flow. This is adequate for the 36% increase in airflow necessary to achieve the 36% performance gain (and, therefore, fuel flow) calculated earlier.

The fuel pressure required to operate at a 36% increase in airflow can be approximated by squaring the sum of one plus the airflow rate increase:

$$(1.36)^2 = 1.85$$

This shows that 85% more fuel pressure than stock will be required:

$$1.85 \times 45 \text{ psi} = 83 \text{ psi}$$

where 45 psi is stock pressure for the NSX.

Preliminary test and calculation have shown that the fuel system can supply sufficient flow for the power desired by either increasing pulse duration or raising fuel pressure as a function of boost pressure. As the latter approach is less expensive, it is the prime candidate unless proven inadequate.

Performance Testing

The Varicom VC200 acceleration computer was used to collect the following data:

0 to 60: 5.7 sec
1/4-mile time: 14.0 sec
1/4-mile speed: 101.0 mph
Estimated bhp: 268

Turbo Selection

Determination of the best compressor for the job is a process of looking at whether the airflow and efficiency numbers are sufficient to push the required amount of air through the system.

The new pressure ratio will generally be close to the performance gain. Therefore, the performance gain of 36% calculated earlier means the pressure ratio must be approximately the same value, or 1.36. This would represent the following airflow requirements:

Using the airflow rate formulas from Chapter 3, with 90% as the volumetric efficiency for a 183-cubic-inch engine,

$$\text{Airflow rate} = \frac{183 \text{ in}^3 \times 8000 \text{ rpm} \times 0.5 \times 0.90}{1728 \frac{\text{in}^3}{\text{ft}^3}} \times 1.36 = 520 \text{ cfm}$$

In a twin-turbo system, this figure would be divided by 2 to obtain the required cfm per turbo:

$$\frac{520}{2} = 260$$

The pressure ratio of 1.36 and the cfm of 260 plotted on the compressor maps being considered will reveal the best combination of peak efficiency, efficiency at maximum load, and low-speed surge characteristics.

The line on the first Aerocharger compressor map (model 101) crosses the maximum-efficiency island at 78%. As engine rpm increases, and thus airflow (cfm) at the same boost pressure, efficiency drops off to an indicated 50% at maximum load.

The second Aerocharger map (model 128) shows efficiencies of 76% peak and approximately 60% at maximum load.

Although the 101 has higher peak efficiency, efficiency at maximum load is of greater significance and is the basis for the decision. Since the second map shows greater efficiency at maximum load, the model 128 is the better choice for this application.

The following calculations at these two points will show the charge air temperature gains through the compressor.

As discussed in Chapter 14, when the air inlet is not in the engine compartment, one can assume compressor inlet temperature is equivalent to ambient. In this case, assume an ambient temperature of 80°F, which will be an abso-

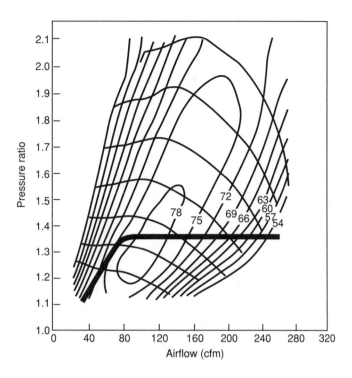

Fig.17-10. *Aerocharger model 101 compressor flow map. The heavy line indicates the path of the boost. Note that at 260 cfm, the line extends out to approximately 50% thermal efficiency. This is too low for an acceptable system.*

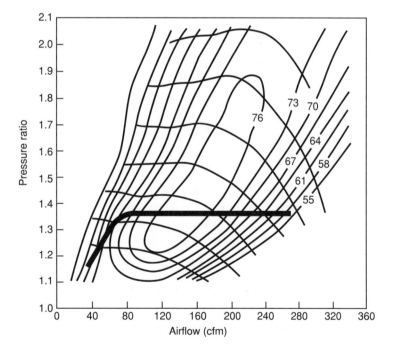

Fig.17-11. *Aerocharger model 128 compressor flow map. The same data plotted on this compressor map show a maximum load efficiency dropping from a peak of 76% to a low of 60%. This is 10% greater than the model 101 at maximum load and is thus a better choice.*

lute temperature of 80° + 460° = 540°.

Using the formula for compressor efficiency from Chapter 14, we can derive the temperature rise at maximum efficiency:

$$E_c = \frac{(PR^{0.28} \times T_{abs}) - T_{abs}}{\text{Temperature rise}}$$

Therefore,

$$\text{Temperature rise at maximum efficiency} = \frac{(PR^{0.28} \times T_{abs}) - T_{abs}}{E_c}$$

Inserting the above values,

$$\text{Temperature rise at maximum efficiency} = \frac{[(1.36)^{0.28} \times 540°] - 540°}{0.76} = 63°$$

Since the size of an absolute degree is the same as that of a Fahrenheit degree, the rise of 63° at maximum efficiency added to the ambient temperature of 80°F equals 143°F

Temperature rise at maximum load can be derived by multiplying the calculated value of 63° by the ratio of the highest efficiency to the lowest efficiency of the system as previously plotted on the flow map:

$$\text{Temperature rise} = 63° \times \frac{0.76}{0.60} = 79°$$

The rise of 79° at maximum load added to the ambient temperature of 80°F equals 159°F.

This calculation predicts a maximum compressor discharge temperature gain of 79°F above compressor inlet temperature.

Intercooling Value

The value of intercooling can be estimated by a ratio of the absolute temperatures before and after cooling. This ratio represents the relative density change. It is adequate to assume an intercooler efficiency of 85% for preliminary calculations. An 85% efficient intercooler will remove 85% of the heat put in by the compressor. Therefore, using the formula from Chapter 5 for temperature removed, the expected temperature exiting the intercooler will be

$$\text{Temperature removed} = 80 - (0.85 \times 79) = 13°F \text{ above ambient}$$

Using the formula for density change from Chapter 5,

$$\text{Density change} = \frac{540 + 79}{540 + 13} - 1 = 0.119 = 11.9\%$$

In view of the high compression ratio (10.2 to 1) of the NSX engine and a charge density gain of 11.9%, the decision to include intercoolers in the system is an easy one.

Layout

Refer to earlier in this chapter for the factors to consider in deciding layout.

TURBO POSITION. The Aerocharger gives a freedom of choice not heretofore available in positioning the turbo. The absence of any oil lines to the self-lubricating Aerocharger removes the requirement for either a gravity drain or a sump-pump-aided oil return.

Although the turbocharger is traditionally placed between engine and converter, the selection of turbochargers with the ability to make considerable boost at low exhaust gas flow suggests that they can be placed after the converters. This position still offers a high degree of response yet permits the converters to get exhaust gas heat undiminished from the engine, to facilitate catalyst light-off.

Some attention to a symmetrical turbo position with respect to the exhaust header will require one header pipe to be longer than the other, but this is not of major significance.

INTERCOOLER DESIGN. Anticipated power output will dictate the internal flow area of the intercoolers. As discussed in Chapter 5, when pressure loss through

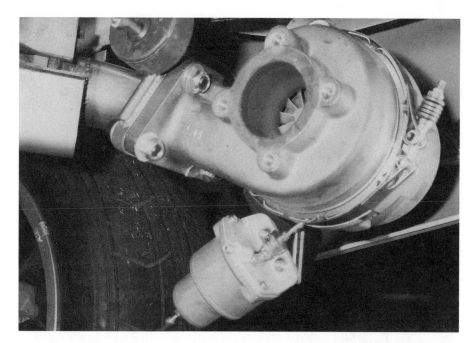

Fig. 17-12. *Positioning the right turbo required temporarily hanging it from fasteners on the heat shield directly above it, then making a mock-up of and building the short tube assembly between the converter and the turbine inlet.*

Fig. 17-13. *The left turbo hangs from the original rubber tailpipe mount. The turbine inlet pipe originates at the center converter. The fiber hose runs forward to the valve-cover breather.*

the cooler is controlled to an acceptable value, temperature drops will always fall in line, with no other requirement than an adequate supply of ambient air.

The suggested value is 6 square inches flow area per 100 bhp. Assuming a desired bhp of 375,

$$375 \text{ bhp} \times \frac{6 \text{ in.}^2}{100 \text{ bhp}} = 23 \text{ in.}^2$$

Using the guidelines discussed in Chapter 5, the core material with 23 square inches of flow area will typically be a core with 46 square inches on the core face exposed to the charge, because about half the face is composed of the air tubes. So a core with a depth of 3 inches will need to be 15 inches wide.

A search for space for a core this size, or two cores half this size, reveals a location aft of the rear wheels with space for cores of 3.5 inches deep by 9 inches wide. Two cores of 31.5 square inches each exceeds the objective. The

Fig. 17-14. *The intercoolers are positioned behind the rear wheels. Heavy mesh screens offer protection from road debris.*

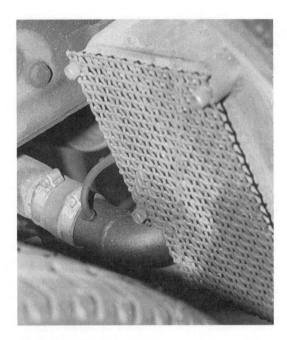

Fig. 17-15. *Plumbing from the intercoolers unites in a single inlet to the throttle body. The mechanism attached to the forward side of the throttle inlet casting is an overboost safety vent valve.*

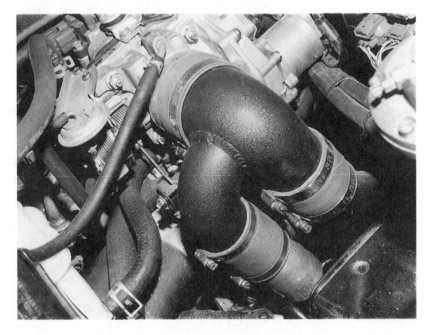

unique location of the intercoolers, behind the rear wheel, offers abundant ambient cooling air. Debris thrown by the tires is a problem to be resolved. Heavy screens of stainless wire mesh that will allow airflow but defeat rock flow are adequate to protect the intercoolers from foreign-particle damage.

EXHAUST SYSTEM. The quality and material of the Borla stainless steel muffler were felt to be consistent with the vehicle's quality. As the turbine exit diameter is 2 inches, the turbine outlet pipe to the muffler need be no greater than 2 inches. A brief discussion with Borla settled the question of the proper muffler volume and style. The design settled on was a drilled-core, straight-through style with two paths from opposite ends of the muffler, one for each

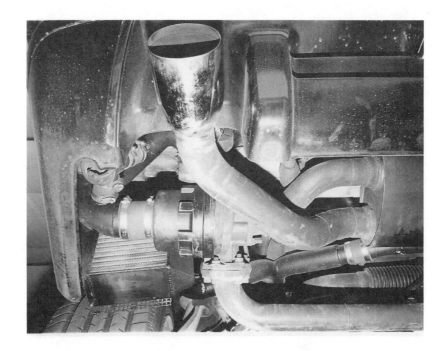

Fig. 17-16. *A two-path Borla muffler, placed between turbine outlets, gives each turbo its own tailpipe.*

turbo. Although the exhaust system is quite compact, silencing proved to be adequate, since the turbos themselves function as approximately one-third of the silencing requirement.

COMPRESSOR BYPASS VALVE. The need for compressor bypass valves to suppress surge noise on lifting off throttle is less necessary with the Aerocharger than with standard turbos. Initial testing showed the noise not entirely suppressed by the Aerocharger; thus, valves were incorporated into the design.

Because bypass valves can offer their own characteristic air venting sound, they were placed at the farthest point in the system from the driver. The available space is directly across the compressor, from outlet to inlet.

The bypass valves are operated by intake manifold vacuum signals. For coherent signals, two dedicated lines were run from the intake manifold to the valves.

Fig. 17-17. *With the compressor discharge tube to the intercooler installed, the bypass valve can be set to vent directly from the discharge tube to the compressor inlet tube.*

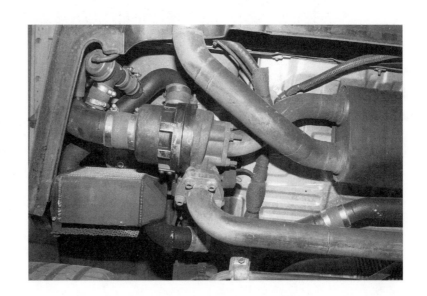

Fig. 17-18. *Because the ECU is not programmed for pressure above atmospheric in the intake manifold, a signal block is necessary to keep the MAP sensor from receiving pressure when the engine is under boost.*

Material Selection

Material selection is critical only with respect to the hot side of the turbo system. Because the layout will not cause thermally induced expansion, stainless steel can be used for the hot side. Stainless grade 304 was chosen for its combination of high-temperature strength and long-term corrosion resistance. It is also readily weldable with the tig process. Mild steel was used for flanges, which need not be stainless.

Tubing used in the cold-side plumbing is all mandrel-bent, thin-walled mild steel, which is easily welded, internally smooth, and can be finished in a wide variety of processes. The ends of the tubes are soft enough to permit flaring, for better hose retention. All hose connections are of high-temperature, hydrocarbon-proof silicone hose material.

The aluminum intercooler cores are welded to cast 363 aluminum alloy caps. All tabs, mounts, and hose bosses are cut from aluminum 6063-T3 (heat-treated) alloy.

Construction Sequence

Construction sequence follows the order given in the list of factors to consider earlier in this chapter.

Fit and Finish

Stainless grade 304 does not require any coatings for long-term durability or appearance. All aluminum and mild-steel components are subject to corrosion and discoloration without protective coatings. Chrome plating was not considered, as it is difficult to keep hose connections from sliding off chromed parts. Powder coatings satisfy all appearance and durability requirements, with the added benefit of a wrinkle-texture finish for improved grip on hose connections. Powder coating of wrinkle black was applied to all parts that do not see temperatures in excess of 300°F. Threaded connections must be protected from the coating; otherwise, the thickness of the coating will prevent assembly or require retapping.

Fasteners The NSX design offers a series of flanged joints. These are best served by through-bolts. (See earlier discussion.) The turbine outlet requires a stud anchored into the cast iron housing with a mechanical locknut.

Gaskets All joints must be examined as to the need for a gasket. If a gasket is required, the choice of style and material must be made. The NSX design offered no circumstances where a gasket could be omitted from a bolted joint. Although it is common to omit a gasket between a turbo and an exhaust manifold with machined flat surfaces, the NSX presented no such opportunity.

As discussed in Chapter 10, the sandwich-type gasket is preferable, but it was not available. The second choice, embossed stainless, is included with the Aerocharger.

Testing The testing process has two primary objectives: tuning the details and checking to see if any major errors in the designer's judgment have occurred.

Tuning the air/fuel ratio is clearly the first necessity. Measurements were made with the Horiba meter. This meter has an electrically heated oxygen sensor that conveniently mounts in the exhaust pipe outlet. Initial bench calibration of the fuel pressure regulator was for 82 psi at 5 psi boost. This number did not prove quite adequate, as a fuel pressure of 92–95 psi was required to achieve the desired 13 to 1 air/fuel ratio. The discrepancy comes from the need to run a richer mixture under boost than the normally aspirated engine runs at full throttle. The regulator was therefore adjusted to provide the higher flow rate.

Checks on the air/fuel mixture were also made at 1 and 3 psi boost to assure that the regulator was keeping the mid-range mixtures correct as well. These pressures measured 55 and 70 psi, respectively. The Horiba indicated that these pressures created a progressive change in air/fuel ratio from 15 to 1 down to 12.3 to 1 as boost increased from 1 to 5 psi.

With the confidence that the air/fuel mixture is in the appropriate range, we were free to test for engine knock. Trust in the ability of the ear to detect detonation did not seem appropriate with an engine as expensive as the NSX's, so a J&S Electronics knock indicator was used as a supplement. Both

Fig. 17-19. *The rising-rate fuel pressure regulator fits easily in the space previously occupied by the air filter box. The regulator has two adjustments. The side adjustment, a needle valve, determines fuel pressure at maximum boost. The spring-loaded center screw sets the point of onset of pressure gain.*

Fig. 17-20. *The lower side of the finished assembly.*

indicated no knock was present in repeated runs to the redline under maximum boost. Testing weather was a hot and sunny 100° August day. The judgment that this was harsher than most operational conditions suggested that the system would be free of detonation virtually anywhere.

With safety of the system established, testing of adherence to the design objectives can begin.

Verifying Turbo Compressor Efficiency

Since a graph of efficiency of the compressor plotted versus airflow and boost pressure is always a curve, it is necessary to determine whether our data points are on the upslope or downslope.

Four items of information are necessary: temperature into and out of the turbo compressor, boost pressure, and engine rpm. Measurements must be made at full throttle yet must also be as near steady-state as possible. To do this, we chose 6000 rpm in third gear and 4000 rpm in fourth gear. By dragging the brakes and not permitting the vehicle to accelerate, some reasonable degree of steady state can be achieved. From the gauges, it appears to take 6 to 8 seconds to reach a steady state. Three trials created the data shown in the following table. The pressure ratio and cfm are calculated as shown earlier in this chapter. One should always make note of the ambient temperature.

Boost (psi)	Rpm	Temperature in (°F)	Temperature out (°F)	Pressure ratio	Calculated cfm
6	4000	99	171	1.41	298
6	6000	99	173	1.41	448
6	4000	101	177	1.41	298
*6	6000	100	177	1.41	448
*6	4000	98	174	1.41	298
6	6000	100	176	1.41	448

Three trials are barely adequate to establish the best and worst conditions, but this is a field test, not Porsche's research laboratory. The data with asterisks, which are median numbers, will be used for analysis. The process is to

Fig. 17-21. *The vacuum/boost gauge is not used frequently and is therefore mounted in the glove box, where it can be referred to if necessary.*

calculate what the compressor maps indicate the temperatures ought to be and compare those numbers with the actual measurements.

The estimate of temperature gains at the initial selection of turbo compressors was 61°F and 83°F. Testing showed all gains to be between 72°F and 77°F.

Temperature inlet measurements in the above table indicate a 2° temperature rise at the point of air pickup by the filters. With the filters positioned inside the rear fenders, air temperature should be ambient. Possibly the temperature sensor was receiving heat radiated from the exhaust housing, or a convection current (misunderstood airflow) was carrying heat from the turbo toward the temperature sensor. Curious, but insignificant.

Turbine Section

The exhaust gas pressure change across the turbines tell us two things: whether turbine size is close to that desired, and the amount of exhaust back pressure created by the muffler and tailpipe.

Turbine inlet pressure is measured by placing a fitting on one of the turbine inlet pipes and attaching a pressure gauge. The expected turbine inlet pressure is usually two to three times greater than the boost pressure generated; therefore, we expected 12 to 18 psi. Surprisingly, 15 psi was the maximum pressure developed before the turbine, with just .5 psi after. Although a slight decrease in inlet pressure would be desirable, it is not enough so to install bigger turbines and produce any less low-speed response. The .5 psi loss through the muffler and exhaust plumbing is entirely satisfactory.

Intercooler Efficiency

Verifying the value of the intercooler will indicate that temperature drops across the coolers are sufficient and that pressure loss remains below 1 psi at maximum load.

Only one pressure-loss check was made at redline rpm; it showed a tick over 1 psi at 7700–7800 rpm. While this was slightly disappointing, the decision was made to keep the intercoolers as is if heat rejection efficiency exceeded 80%.

Temperature probes placed in the compressor outlet and intercooler outlet will collect the necessary data for intercooler efficiency calculation, including ambient temperature.

Testing was conducted by holding steady-state maximum boost at 4000 rpm in fourth gear. Again, 6 to 8 seconds appeared to be needed to stabilize temperatures and the response times of the gauges. Four tests were made to collect the data, as shown in the table. Although the results are reasonably consistent, data collection is not always as one wants it to be. The real efficiency is probably close to the average of the four trials.

Using representative values from the table in the formula for intercooler thermal efficiency from Chapter 5,

$$E_i = \frac{172 - 114}{172 - 101} = 0.82 = 82\%$$

The net result of the intercooling effort is to get the charge temperature to within 12 to 14°F of ambient. Pressure loss of 1 psi suggests that these are not race-quality intercoolers but are excellent for street use.

Test	Ambient temperature (°F)	Turbo outlet temperature (°F)	Intercooler outlet temperature (°F)
1	100	171	112
2	101	173	115
3	101	172	114
4	101	177	115

Emissions Testing

The four-gas-analyzer emissions test was repeated after system installation was complete. No surprises were in store. Hydrocarbons and carbon monoxide showed a slight decrease, all else remaining virtually unchanged. The odd note of air/fuel ratios running about 2% richer at all times was observed. No ready explanation is offered. The conclusion is that the system should not have any difficulty passing the CARB test procedures.

Performance Verification

The Varicom VC200 was again the instrument of measurement for post-turbo performance. Six efforts at establishing some degree of consistency gave the following data:

0 to 60: best, 4.4 sec; average, 4.7 sec
1/4-mile time: best, 12.8 sec; average, 13.0 sec
1/4-mile speed: best, 113.0 mph; average, 111.5 mph
Power: 390 bhp

AND FURTHERMORE . . .

How difficult is it to install a turbocharger system?

The skill required is comparable to that of overhauling a two-barrel carburetor. The time required is at least twice the kit maker's claim. You may be assured that the lowest time claim will be the least comprehensive turbo kit. It takes no time at all not to install a wastegate, for example. Be assured also that the details determine the success of a turbo installation. Anyone can figure out where the exhaust manifold goes, but it takes patience and care to get all the small adjustments made correctly. It is in this respect that the do-it-yourselfer will usually excel in a truly quality job.

Will I need any special tools?

Not likely, although a special tool for torquing the cylinder-head bolts may be required.

What gauging should accompany a turbo?

A vacuum/boost gauge is a virtual necessity. An exhaust gas temperature gauge is a nice addition, particularly on engines with characteristically high exhaust temperatures. Diesel engines are another matter. Their redline is a function of exhaust temperature, and they must have egt gauges.

Will I have to buy anything else to supplement the turbocharger?

Wow, what a loaded question. Every kit maker's system is "complete." If the kit is heavily advertised as "complete," you had better be prepared to bring along your own wastegate, exhaust system, boost gauge, fuel system, and detonation controls. "Comprehensive" is the descriptive term you are looking for, not that tired, overworked term "complete."

Are chromed steel parts necessary?

Chrome does not rust and is durable. Chrome is a nice touch, provided it is consistent with the OEM components. It is, however, too slippery for hose connections. The general rule is, If it doesn't work well, chrome-plate it.

18 INSTALLING A TURBO KIT

It is profoundly unnecessary to know anything about the science and engineering of turbocharging to competently install a well-designed aftermarket turbocharger system. The installer need only be a competent hobbyist mechanic. The experience level is about equivalent to that of changing a clutch or removing and replacing an intake manifold.

A German proverb clearly states the problem of accomplishing such a job: "The devil is in the details." To illustrate the accuracy of this proverb, it is easy to imagine that most people could install an exhaust manifold correctly. Yet a simple air hose not properly attached to a fuel pressure regulator can keep an otherwise faultless system from functioning correctly. Therefore, thoughts about one's competence to install such things should center around how conscientiously one can do the details.

This chapter is a walk-through of the installation of an aftermarket turbo system into a Mazda Miata. The vehicle is stock. The system carries the CARB EO number D-349.

Follow instructions faithfully. When a system has a street-legal exemption order, it is absolutely necessary to follow instructions to the letter to maintain the legal status. Furthermore, the installer should presume the designer knew what he was doing.

There is some logic to the process. Read the instructions and make notes of questions, if any, to pose to the kit maker. It is both easy and natural for instruction writers to gloss over many points of the installation, since they know all the pieces and processes intimately. Service is supposed to begin after the sale. You purchased a kit in good faith and were told that with modest ability, you could properly install it. You will likely need many points of the instruc-

Fig. 18-1. *Clean the engine compartment prior to starting an installation and the experience will be more pleasant.*

tions addressed before and during the installation. It is entirely fair to require the kit maker to give you guidance on the procedure where necessary. Clearly, this form of feedback also improves the writer's ability to create proper instructions.

Familiarize yourself with the parts of the system. Learn the name the writer has given each part. Inventory the parts with respect to the packing list, to be certain all items were included. Call the manufacturer for shortages at the earliest opportunity.

No kit maker should be shipping parts less than spotlessly clean. However, it is a serious error to assume they are clean and ready to install. Any installer worth at least his weight in salt will insure that every part is perfectly clean.

The vehicle subject to the installation need not be in perfect condition. A proper installation on a 90% vehicle will, however, yield only 90% results. While clearly superior to stock, 90% is not the objective of this book or what this writer perceives as the objective of the fellow hard-core enthusiast. If something is mechanically amiss, fix it before the installation.

Prior to starting the installation, fill the fuel tank with gasoline of the octane suggested in the instructions. Do not dilute with lesser octane fuel already in the tank. If necessary, drain the tank. Never use octane boost as a testing aid—it will mask many critical characteristics, such as air/fuel ratios and ignition timing controls.

It is convenient to establish directional references with respect to the instruction writer's viewpoint. If unspecified, consider left and right from the position of the driver.

After the installation has begun, the best procedure is to complete the entire job prior to driving the vehicle. Certainly the job can be broken up into segments, like installing the boost gauge, fuel pump, heat shield, etc. The catch is, one cannot install only the turbo and associated pipes and then set out to see how fast it will go. That will surely prove a disaster.

Always read the statement of warranty prior to starting the installation. If questions of policy exist, this is the best time to discuss them.

The speed with which you accomplish the installation is not of any consequence. A few extra hours mean nothing.

Tools and Equipment

A reasonable selection of hobbyist mechanic's tools is all that's required for a successful installation:

- Metric open/box combination wrenches
- Metric socket set
- SAE open/box wrenches
- Assorted slot and Phillips screwdrivers
- Electric drill and assorted bits
- Ignition timing light
- Sealing compound
- Never-Seize compound
- Loctite #271
- Spray can of cleaning solvent
- Oil filter and oil change
- Teflon tape
- Safety wire
- Clean rags

- Floor jack
- Jack stands (4)
- Factory shop manual

Preliminary Position the car on four jack stands. Check the shop manual for the suggested hard points. Be certain the car is supported by all four stands.

Disconnect the negative battery cable. Consult the manual for any special precautions.

Keep the removed parts organized, especially the nuts and bolts.

Major items to remove:

- Air filter and flowmeter assembly. When removing the electrical connector, do not pull the wires.
- Flowmeter from filter box
- Cross tube to the throttle body
- Intake resonator/silencer box below the throttle
- Exhaust manifold heat shield
- Oxygen sensor from exhaust manifold. Avoid touching the element end of the sensor.
- Exhaust manifold
- Cruise control actuator and mount. (Leave cable attached to linkage and place actuator on valve cover.)
- Valve cover breather tube at left forward corner
- Lower splash pan and black radiator inlet duct
- Exhaust pipe hanger bolt attached to left lower side of transmission
- Fuel filter cover beneath car (on passenger side, about 2 feet forward of differential)
- Bracket beneath flowmeter/air filter box. This bracket will unbolt from front gusset at strut tower

Miscellaneous The water bypass tube located beneath the exhaust manifold must be repositioned slightly to clear the turbo exhaust pipe. Anchor the tab to the second-from-rear exhaust stud by sandwiching the tab between two nuts. This will force any bending to take place aft of the tab. With a suitable pry bar, bend the bypass tube aft toward the firewall. Bend the end of the tube approximately 3/4 inch.

Wrap the heater hose located aft of the exhaust manifold with insulation. Safety-wire the insulation securely in place.

Wrap the brake line at the left side of the frame rail in a similar manner.

Auxiliary Fuel Pump Installation Attach the high-pressure auxiliary fuel pump to the left rear frame rail, approximately 4 inches in front of the shipping anchor, as follows. At the filter, the fuel lines are rerouted to and from the pump.

> **NOTE** ——
> Remove the fuel tank cap to let pressure out—less fuel will be spilled.

Install the banjo hose barb and connecting bolt onto the fuel pump. Use the copper sealing washers. Add the short segment of hose and the p/n 21009 adaptor.

The fuel pump will hang inside the segment of rubber hose. The pump is retained in the hose with a large hose clamp. See Fig. 18-3.

Fig. 18-2. *The auxiliary fuel pump is suspend ed in rubber and placed at the rear of the Miata to reduce noise.*

Fig. 18-3. *A stainless steel hose clamp holds the fuel pump within the rubber hoop.*

The pump/hose assembly will hang from the frame rail by a bolt positioned from inside the rear deck. A piece of tape covers a hole through which the bolt can be inserted. The bolt head must be downward. Use washers on all faces.

Install the pump/hanger assembly. Use the 5-inch bolt.

Remove the fuel line from the inlet side of the filter and route to the new pump inlet.

Route the new pump outlet to the fuel filter inlet.

Route the fuel lines over the cross member and anchor with tie wraps. Keep the lines away from heat, road debris, and any moving parts. Replace standard clamps with higher-strength spiral-lock clamps. See Fig. 18-4.

> **CAUTION** —
> *Fuel spillage will occur on removal of the fuel lines from the filter.*

Wiring the Fuel Pump

Roll back the carpet on the shelf behind the seats. Remove the service-hole cover. This is the cover anchored by six Phillips-head screws. See Fig. 18-5.

Locate the blue wire with the red stripe. Splice into this wire with the connector provided. This wire allows the OEM rollover fuel pump cutoff to be extended to the second pump.

Fig. 18-4. The higher-pressure fuel system requires replacing standard fuel-line clamps with higher-strength spiral-lock clamps.

Fig. 18-5. The power wire to maintain the rollover fuel pump cut-off to the second pump is accessed through the shelf behind the seats.

Route a 7-foot segment of wire downward between the tank and chassis. It is helpful to pull this wire through with a straightened coat hanger.

Replace the fuel tank service cover and carpet.

Add suitable end terminals to the power and ground wires. Crimp these carefully and test with a firm pull.

The fuel pump negative wire must be grounded. The rear bumper retaining bolt is a suitable location. Note the terminal designations on the pump.

Exhaust Manifold

Inspect the inside of the exhaust manifold for casting debris. Clean as necessary.

Install the two lower mount studs into the manifold with Never-Seize compound on the threads. Use the double-nut jam method. The front lower stud must be the shorter of the two. See Fig. 18-6.

Install the exhaust manifold onto the engine. Reuse the old gasket. If using a thin-walled box end wrench, the original center nut may be reinstalled. Otherwise, the center nut must be replaced with the thin nut provided, since wrench clearance is minimal. Reuse the remainder of the old locknuts. Attach the water tube bracket to an exhaust stud, as it was originally configured.

Fig. 18-6. *The turbo is held to the manifold by two studs and two through-bolts. The studs must be wrenched into place by the double-nut jam method.*

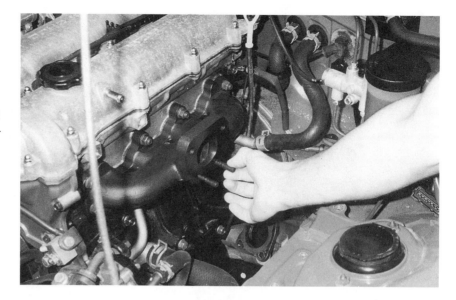

Fig. 18-7. *The exhaust manifold's compact dimensions require a slim-profile nut for the center fastener.*

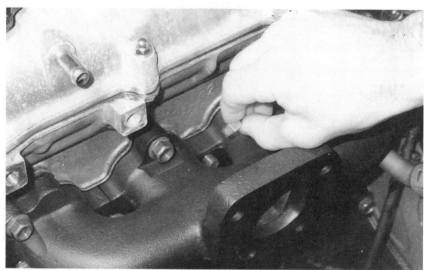

Turbine Outlet Pipe   Install three studs into the lower end of the turbine outlet pipe. Use Never-Seize compound. Reuse the original gasket. See Fig. 18-8.

Fig. 18-8. *Preparation of the turbine outlet pipe is limited to installation of the studs needed to fasten to the stock Miata exhaust header pipe.*

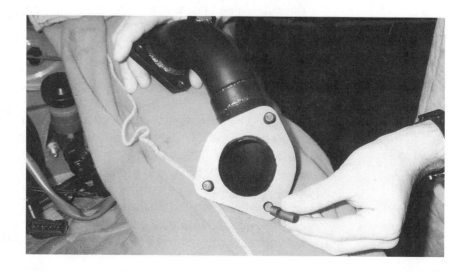

Unhook the oxygen sensor wire from its anchor at the bell housing spacer plate.

Insert the turbine outlet pipe into position. Leave the nuts loose until the pipe is attached to the turbine.

Attach the oxygen sensor to the tailpipe.

Reattach the exhaust clamp at the transmission bracket. Leave the bolts loose.

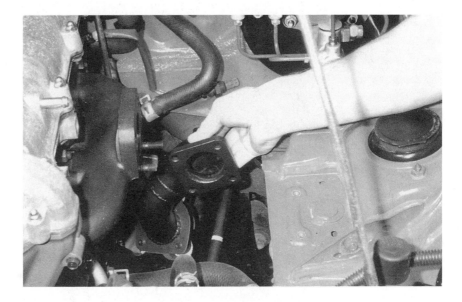

Fig. 18-9. The turbine outlet pipe must be placed into position before the turbo is installed.

Turbocharger

Attach three silicone signal-line hoses to the fittings on the turbo vane actuator. The center fitting "vent" will be the short line.

Remove the top fitting from the turbocharger oil reservoir. Add 120 cc of oil to the reservoir. Do not overfill. Replace the plug. Inspect the plugs in the oil reservoir to assure that the air breather plug is the uppermost of the two. These are pipe threads and need only be tightened until snug.

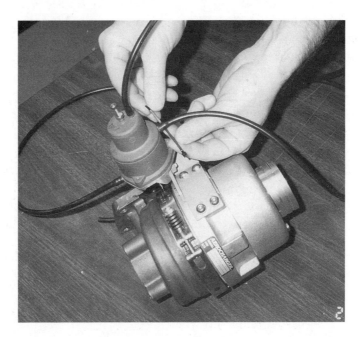

Fig. 18-10. Preparing the turbo for installation by adding signal lines to the vane position actuator

Fig. 18-11. *The oil reservoir is sealed with a special sintered brass "breather" plug.*

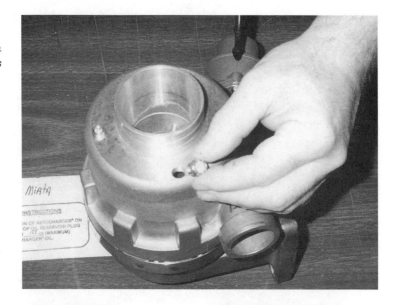

Fig. 18-12. *Turbo prep includes filling the reservoir with 120 cc of the special aircraft turbine engine oil.*

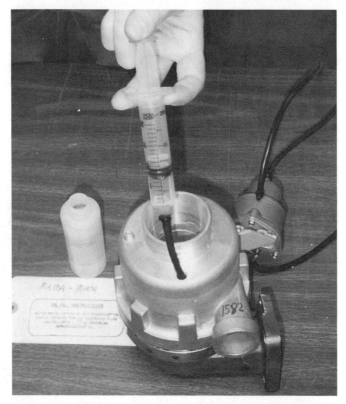

Attach the turbo to the exhaust manifold. The upper bolts must be inserted from the engine side. Use the mechanical locknuts.

The mechanical locknuts are critical, since engine vibrations tend to loosen fasteners. Use the gasket provided. Leave the nuts finger tight.

NOTE ——
When the turbo is in position, the compressor outlet should point straight up and the actuator downward and inboard. The actuator needs only adequate clearance to other objects. If the positions are incorrect, the turbo must be returned to the kit manufacturer for adjustment.

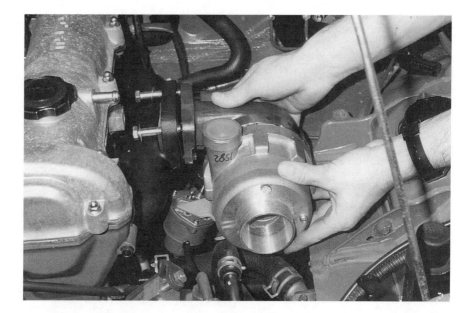

Fig. 18-13. *Note protection of the compressor outlet while the turbo is being fitted to the manifold. Every fastener must have a washer under the head and nut.*

Temporarily cover the compressor outlet with something— for example, the fuel pressure regulator baggie. Any foreign particle dropped into the compressor outlet will likely damage the turbo. Also stuff a clean rag in the compressor inlet. (Do as I say, not as I do in the photo.)

Attach the outlet pipe to the turbine. Insert the studs through the flange, placing the gasket in position, and anchor with the double-nut method. Use Never-Seize compound on all related threads.

Tighten all related fasteners: outlet pipe to turbo first, outlet pipe to tailpipe second, transmission anchor third, and turbo to manifold last.

Fig. 18-14. *With the turbo in place, fit the turbine outlet gasket and secure the fasteners to the outlet pipe.*

Intercooler

Install the intercooler in front of the cooling system radiator and mount it at two points. Attach one mount to the lower bolt of the vertical support bracket for the hood latch. Use the longer bolt provided. For proper alignment without binding, it may be necessary to add a spacer between the mounting plate and lug.

Fig. 18-15. *The inter-cooler is positioned in front of the cooling system radiator and AC condenser. The bottom is angled out-ward to cause the least blockage of airflow to the cooling system.*

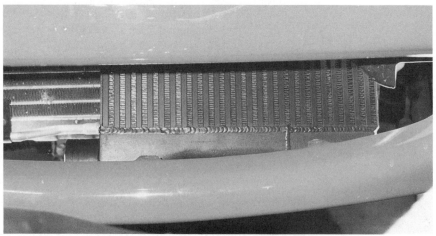

Fig. 18-16. *As installed, the inter-cooler receives substantial airflow through the standard air inlet.*

The second intercooler attachment is the frame end of the body support rod. Place the intercooler bracket between the support rod and the frame. Use the original fasteners.

> **NOTE** ——
> Do not replace the splash pan. This pan inhibits air flow to the radiator.

INTERCOOLER TUBES. Install the 10-32 hose barb into the aft side of the throttle body inlet casting. Seal with Loctite. Be very careful with the small threads, as they can easily strip in the casting. Do not permit Loctite to clog the hose barb.

Install the throttle body inlet casting. Point the casting inlet straight down.

Attach the hose from the idle air-control valve to the throttle inlet casting. Secure with the original clamp.

Assemble the remainder of the intercooler tubes. Leave all joints loose and adjust the position and fit of tubes for clearance and appearance, then tighten

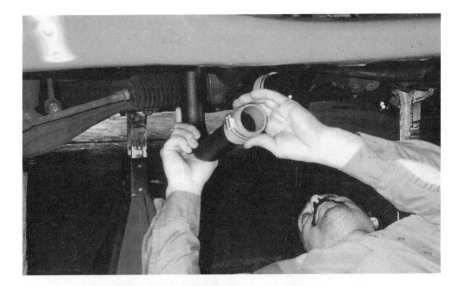

Fig. 18-17. *With the turbo and intercooler in position, the interconnecting tubes can be installed.*

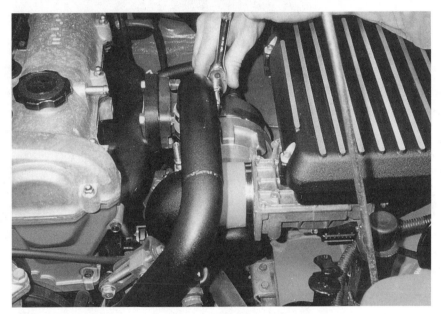

Fig. 18-18. *Tightening hose clamps on pressurized tubes should be done with a ratchet wrench. Screwdriver tight will almost assure a tube's popping off under boost.*

all hose clamps. Be certain each hose properly overlaps the inside tube and that the retaining clamp is completely over the tube.

> **CAUTION** —
> *The compressor outlet tube can rub the hood when the engine rocks if the tube is not pushed into the compressor outlet until it touches the compressor outlet boss.*

> **NOTE** —
> Do not replace the plastic inlet duct.

Compressor Inlet Install the brass fittings for the valve cover breather into the compressor inlet casting. Use a 90° el and point the hose barb upward.

Install the rubber O-rings into the grooves on the turbo. Lubricate the O-rings with a small amount of grease.

Remove the rag guarding the compressor inlet. Press the inlet casting onto the turbo and swivel the inlet to point directly outboard.

Air Filter Box

The filter box will attach to two points. One is a tab on the aft sheet metal gusset for the left front strut mount. This point is immediately below the front end of the brake master cylinder. Install the rubber isolator onto this tab. Use the nylon locknut and appropriate washers. Leave finger tight.

The second mount is an existing hole located 3-1/2 inches forward and 4-1/2 inches outboard of the left strut centerline. Drill this hole to 1/4 inch. Install a second isolator at this point.

Install the small hose barb into the threaded hole adjacent to the rear mount of the filter box.

Attach the flowmeter to the filter box. Reuse the original gasket, studs, and nuts.

Fig. 18-19. *The air filter bottom case serves as the airflow meter mount.*

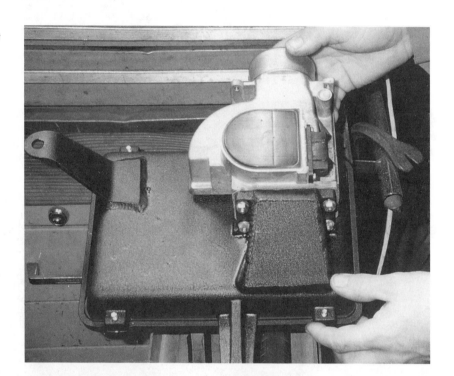

Fig. 18-20. *The flowmeter/filter case assembly mounts to the Miata's structure with rubber isolators to allow for engine rock.*

Press the filter element into the filter box. Bolt the upper and lower box halves together with the stainless steel cap screws. Position the cap such that the air inlet faces outboard.

Slip the 2 3/4-inch-diameter hose onto the compressor inlet casting.

Place two hose clamps onto the hose and leave them loose.

Attach the wire harness connector to the flowmeter. The wires are best routed beneath the filter box.

Insert the flowmeter into the hose on the inlet casting and position the filter box.

Attach the air filter assembly to the inner fender well at the two isolators. Adjust the position until all alignments are correct. One or both isolators may need spacing up. Use the nylon locknuts and appropriate washers. Check hood clearance prior to closing the hood.

Tighten all related clamps and fasteners.

Miscellaneous

Remove the restrictor from the original valve cover breather hose and place inside a 6-1/2-inch-long segment of 5/16-inch hose. Use a small amount of lubricant on the hose barbs for ease of assembly.

Route this hose from the hose barb on the compressor inlet casting to the valve cover breather.

Attach the heat shield to the cylinder head. Use suitable washers under the bolt heads.

Fig. 18-21. The valve cover breather has a small restrictor inside that must be placed inside the new breather hose. The breather must be placed before the turbo to avoid pressurizing the crankcase.

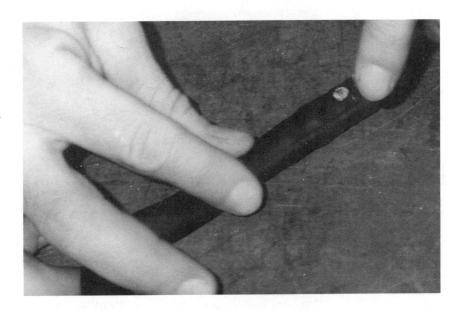

VATN Actuator Signal Lines

The line from the lower fitting of the actuator (small end) is the boost-pressure signal. This signal originates at the hose barb on the aft side of the throttle body inlet casting. Check this hose barb for possible Loctite blockage by blowing through the hose.

The upper fitting on the actuator is the vacuum signal. This line will get its signal from the hose exiting the top of the intake manifold approximately 1 inch after the throttle body. Sever this hose and insert the brass tee. Attach the actuator signal line to the leg of the tee.

The center fitting on the actuator is a breather only. It is connected to the fitting at the aft bottom of the air box.

> **CAUTION ——**
> *Check these lines carefully. If they are not correct, the turbo will be subject to overboosting. This may overrev the turbo and cause damage.*

> **NOTE ——**
> Prior to final assembly, blow through all actuator signal lines and fittings to assure that none are blocked, crimped, or otherwise plugged.

Relocation of Cruise Control Actuator

Vehicles equipped with cruise control must have the control actuator moved. A convenient location for the actuator is the small cavity just in front of the clutch master cylinder. A mount bracket is provided that attaches to the outboard master brake cylinder mount. Keep the actuator cable as straight as possible.

Fuel Pressure Regulator

Attach the regulator to the bracket.

Install the two fuel-line hose barbs. Use thread sealant. Do not use Teflon tape. These fittings should only be tightened snug.

> **CAUTION ——**
> *Do not excessively tighten the hose barbs, otherwise the casting may crack.*

Mount the regulator and bracket assembly to the firewall at the position shown. Assure clearance to the hood.

Fig. 18-22. The rising-rate fuel pressure regulator conveniently mounts to the firewall. Drilling the mount holes accurately requires a drill dimple.

Remove the original equipment fuel injection return line from the steel return line on the frame of the car. Route this line to the side fitting on the regulator. This line then connects the output of the stock regulator to the input of the new regulator. Secure with proper hose clamps.

> **CAUTION ——**
> *Fuel spillage will occur.*

Install a segment of the new high-pressure fuel line from the center fitting of the regulator to the steel line at the frame. Secure with proper hose clamps.

> **NOTE ——**
> These two preceding steps have inserted the regulator into the EFI return line.

Fig. 18-23. *Once the regulator is in place, fuel and signal lines complete its hookup.*

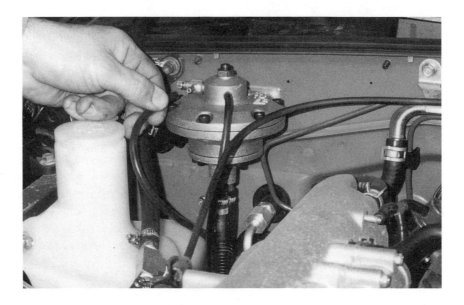

Locate and sever the vacuum signal line to the stock fuel pressure regulator.

Place a white plastic or brass tee in the signal line and route a vacuum hose from the leg of the tee to the new regulator. Insert the small plastic restrictor into this signal line.

Add the one-way check valve to the exit of the needle valve. This check valve eliminates vacuum leaks yet allows adjustment of the regulator by boost-signal leakage.

Assemble a brass tee from the items provided. Install this fuel pressure check gauge tee into the fuel rail inlet hose at the frame connection. This is the lower fuel line on the right side of the engine.

> **CAUTION** ——
> *The fuel inlet line will be under pressure and fuel will spill. Spillage can be reduced by using fuel-line clamps.*

Tape the fuel pressure check gauge to the windshield such that it can be observed while driving the car. Route a piece of the high-pressure fuel line from the brass tee to the fuel pressure check gauge.

Fig. 18-24. *For reasons of safety, the fuel pressure gauge, which is needed to complete the tuning process, should not be placed inside the cockpit. Tape the gauge to the outside of the windshield at a convenient location for viewing while driving.*

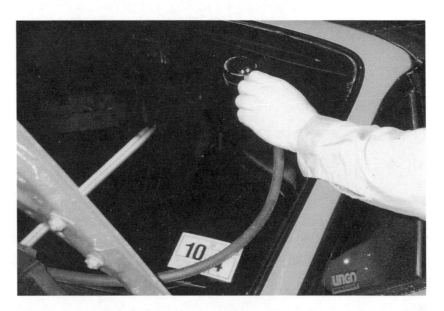

Boost Gauge   Attach the boost gauge and cup to the lower left windshield pillar. Use the sheet metal screws provided.

Route one wire to the red wire with black stripe at the dimmer switch. The switch pulls out of the dash easily with a screwdriver. The plug may be disconnected to ease splicing.

> **NOTE** ——
> If you prefer the gauge light to vary brightness with the instrument lights, wire it to the rheostat according to the factory manual.

Route the other gauge wire to a convenient black wire or ground.

The pressure line to the gauge can easily be routed through the firewall by making a small hole in the grommet located to the left of the throttle cable. A sharp bit turned slowly will make a hole in the grommet. Route the gauge line to the capped fitting located aft of the throttle body, atop the plenum.

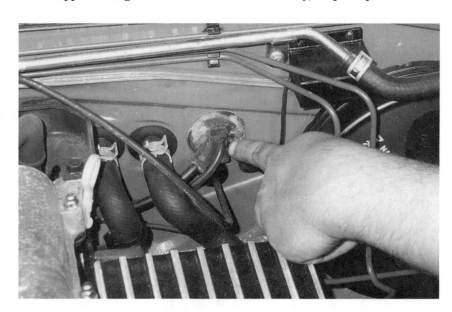

Fig. 18-25. The signal line for the boost gauge passes through the firewall at the speedometer cable grommet. A sharp bit turned slowly will make a hole in the grommet.

Ignition Retard   Install the MSD ignition retard unit in accordance with MSD's instructions.

Miscellaneous   Reconnect the battery. Clean the terminals if needed.

A vacuum check valve must be inserted into the hose to the vacuum canister. The canister is located 2 inches outboard of the throttle body. The check valve goes into the smaller of the two hoses. Sever the hose and insert the check valve with the white end toward the canister. This check valve permits a vacuum to be drawn on the canister, but the canister will not be pressurized under boost.

Testing   Start the engine and check for vacuum and fuel leaks. Correct as required.

Set the ignition timing to 10° BTDC. Open the connector on the wheel well on the driver's side and place a jumper between terminals "GND" and "TEN." Attach the timing light to the number one plug wire. Change timing by loosening the bolt on the right side of the crank angle sensor at the rear of the intake cam. Rotate the sensor until the 10° advance is achieved, as checked at the front engine pulley. When the timing is correct, tighten the bolt and remove the jumper wire.

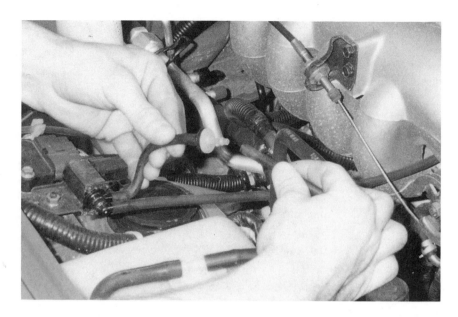

Fig. 18-26. *The charcoal canister must be protected from boost pressure. A one-way valve placed in the vacuum line allows the engine to purge the canister while blocking boost pressure.*

Several objectives must be met in the testing procedure:

Ascertain fuel pressure rise rate as a function of boost pressure. The needle valve is the fuel pressure adjustment. Adjust in one-twentieth-turn increments until the desired fuel pressure is achieved according to the following table:

Boost pressure (psi)	Fuel pressure (psi)
0	35–39
2	47–53
4	60–70
8	95–100

- Determine that no combustion roughness or engine knock occurs when operating at maximum boost.
- Boost pressure should be between 4 and 6 psi at full throttle at 2000 rpm. If less than this, call the manufacturer for consultation.
- Maximum boost pressure should be 7 to 8 psi.

> **CAUTION** —
> *Due to the sparse sound insulation on the Miata, knock is difficult to hear. Pay careful attention to the sound of detonation, as it is very damaging to the engine.*

If knock is detected, lift off the throttle immediately.

Drive the car a few miles prior to applying boost. If all systems are operating normally, proceed with the testing. Generally, use third or fourth gears, to keep events at a slower pace. Apply boost in small increments, so that no sudden changes occur.

Circumstances can combine to make the Aerocharger either less or more responsive than desired. If either case is perceived during testing, call the kit manufacturer for further guidance.

When the engine runs smoothly to the redline in fourth gear at 7 to 8 psi boost pressure, with correct fuel pressure and no hint of detonation or rough combustion, the installation may be considered complete.

Fig. 18-27. When testing and tuning are done, remove the fuel pressure gauge. The installation may be considered complete.

Remove the fuel pressure check gauge.

CAUTION —
Fuel spillage may occur.

Review the instructions and installation for any details overlooked, and correct as required.

General Rules of Operation

- Use 92+ fuel at all times. Higher, if available.
- Do not apply maximum boost for more than 15-second durations.
- If any sounds of rough combustion occur, cease using boost until the cause is identified and corrected.
- The oil must be checked every 10,000 miles in the turbo reservoir. Do not overfill. Oil refill interval will be 20,000 miles.
- Mobil Oil synthetic SHC630 is the only acceptable oil for the Aerocharger. This is available from the kit manufacturer or a Mobil Oil products distributor.
- Use extreme caution when driving the vehicle on wet pavement, as the rate of boost rise can cause an unexpected loss of traction.

The foregoing procedure is typical of the installation of an aftermarket turbocharger system. There are many reasons to respect the process. There are none to fear it.

SUPPLIERS

Advanced Engineering
310-327-9336
EFI systems, Fuel injectors,
Fuel pressure regulators,
Fuel pumps, Fuel system items,
Throttle bodies

Ak Miller
310-949-2858
Turbochargers, Wastegates

Alamo Motorsports
210-637-0373
Boost controllers,
Fuel pressure regulators, Fuel
system items, Intercoolers, Surge
valves

Allied Industries
909-279-5712
Flanges, Gaskets, U-bends

Applied Technologies
864-972-3800
Fuel injectors, Fuel pressure
regulators, Fuel system items,
Intercoolers, Mufflers

ARP Fasteners
805-278-7223
Fasteners

Auto Avionics
201-870-9541
Gauges, Instruments
(testing)

Auto Meter
815-895-8141
Gauges, Instruments
(testing)

Bell Engineering
210-349-6515
Fuel pressure regulators, Fuel
pumps, Fuel system items,
Intercoolers, Turbochargers,
Turbo kit makers, Wastegates

Borla
805-986-8600
Mufflers

Burns Stainless
714-631-5120
Flanges, Gaskets, Mufflers,
U-bends

Canton Racing
203-484-4900
Fuel system items

Carroll Supercharging
201-835-1705
Fuel pumps

Cartech Racing
210-308-8464
Fuel pressure regulators,
Turbo kit makers

Childs & Albert
805-295-1905
Fasteners, Turbo pistons

Coast Fuel Injection
408-287-7600
Fuel injectors, Fuel pressure
regulators, Fuel system
items

Competition Cams
800-999-0853
Turbo cams

Crane Cams
904-252-1151
Turbo cams

Crower
619-422-1191
Turbo cams

Cutler
305-653-9098
EFI systems, Fuel injectors, Fuel
pressure regulators, Fuel system
items, Intake manifolds, Throttle
bodies

Datcon Instruments
717-569-5713
Gauges, Instruments
(testing)

DFI
313-380-1322
EFI systems, Fuel injectors,
Fuel pressure regulators,
Fuel system items

Dinan Engineering
415-962-9401
Turbo kit makers

Duttweiler Auto
805-659-3648
EFI systems, Fuel injectors,
Fuel pressure regulators,
Intercoolers

DynoLab
206-243-8877
Instruments (testing)

Earl's Supply
310-609-1602
AN fittings, Fuel system items,
Hoses, Oil lines

Electromotive
703-378-2444
EFI systems, Fuel injectors,
Fuel pressure regulators,
Knock sensors

Eurasian
800-444-3271
Fuel pumps, Fuel system items

Faria Instruments
203-848-9271
Gauges, Instruments
(testing)

Fel-Pro Gaskets
708-674-7700
Gaskets

Flow Master
800-544-4761
Mufflers

Gale Banks Engineering
818-969-9605
Turbo kit makers

Genie
800-227-2242
Mufflers

Goodridge
310-533-1924
AN fittings, Fuel system items,
Hoses, Oil lines

GReedy Performance
714-588-8300
Air filters, Boost controllers,
Intercoolers, Surge valves,

Turbo kit makers
Hahn Racecraft
708-851-5444
Intercoolers, Turbochargers

Haltech EFI
214-831-9800
EFI systems, Fuel injectors,
Fuel pressure regulators

Horiba
313-213-6555
Instruments (testing)

**High Performance
Coatings**
800-456-4721
Coatings

HKS
310-328-8100
Air filters, Boost controllers,
Fuel pressure regulators,
Intercoolers, Mufflers, Surge
valves, Turbo kit makers,
Wastegates

Hose of North Texas
214-243-1393
AN fittings, Hoses, Oil lines

Isspro
503-232-0134
Gauges, Instruments
(testing)

J&M Supply
512-888-9388
Weld els

JE Pistons
714-898-9763
Turbo pistons

Jet Hot Coatings
610-277-5646
Coatings

J&S Electronics
714-534-6975
Knock sensors

Jim Wolf Racing
619-442-0680
Air filters, EFI systems, Fuel
injectors, Fuel pressure
regulators, Intercoolers

K&N Engineering
909-684-9762
Air filters

Keith Black Racing
310-861-4765
Turbo pistons

Kent Moore Tool Group
313-774-9500
Instruments (testing)

Land & Sea
603-329-5645
Instruments (testing)

Mallory
702-882-6600
Fuel pressure regulators

Manley Engineering
908-905-3366
Turbo pistons

Marren Motorsports
203-732-4565
EFI systems, Fuel injectors, Fuel
pressure regulators, Fuel pumps

Mechtech Motorsports
619-432-0555
Boost controllers, Fuel
pressure regulators, Intercoolers

Mikuni
818-885-1242
Carburetors, Intake manifolds

Mitsubishi Turbos
708-238-8510
Turbochargers

Mosselman Turbos
(Netherlands)
011-311-831-1840
Turbo kit makers

Motec
714-895-7001
EFI systems, Fuel injectors,
Fuel pressure regulators

MSD Ignitions
915-857-5200
Fuel injectors

ND Turbosystems
408-980-1691
Turbo kit makers

Neely Industries
817-274-4300
Lubricants (moly)

Octane Boost
214-289-0631
Fuel additives

Oeschner Supply
214-631-0402
Hoses

Omega Instruments
203-359-1660
Instruments (testing)

Paxton Products
805-987-5555
Fuel pressure regulators, Fuel
system items

Phillips Racing Fuels
918-661-7601
Racing fuel

PolyDyn Coatings
713-694-3296
Coatings

Precision Turbo
708-418-5227
Fuel injectors

Racing Beat
714-779-8677
Mufflers

RC Engineering
310-320-2277
Fuel injectors, Fuel pressure
regulators, Fuel pumps

Redline/Weber
310-604-0124
Carburetors, Fuel system items,
Intake manifolds

76 Racing Fuel
800-345-0076
Racing fuel

Spearco
818-901-7851
Intercoolers,
Turbo kit makers

Sterling Instruments
313-471-0990
Instruments (testing)

Sunoco Race Fuels
800-722-3427
Racing fuel

Super Chips
407-260-0838
Boost controllers

Swain Coatings
716-889-2786
Coatings

Tenant Industries
714-632-8430
Oil pumps

Thermo Tec
419-962-4556
Coatings

Tilton Engineering
805-688-2353
Oil pumps

ToyoMoto
305-378-9325
Turbo kit makers

Turbo City
714-639-4933
Gaskets, Gauges, Turbochargers,
Wastegates

Turbo Engineering
303-271-3997
Turbochargers

Turbonetics
805-529-8995
Flanges, Gaskets, Hoses,
Turbochargers, Wastegates

Turbo Performance Center
410-766-5215
EFI systems, Turbo kit
makers

Turbo Power
916-677-2233
Turbochargers

Turbo Technology
206-475-8319
Turbo kit makers

Turbo Tuf
201-773-4200
Mufflers

TWM Induction
805-967-9478
Air filters, Carburetors, Fuel
injectors, Fuel pumps, Fuel
system items, Intake manifolds,
Throttle bodies

VP Racing Fuels
812-238-2084
Racing fuel

VDO
703-665-0100
Gauges, Instruments
(testing)

Vericom
619-933-4256
Instruments (testing)

Vinson Supply
214-369-1224
Weld els

Warner Ishi
217-774-9571
Turbochargers

Westberg Manufacturing
707-938-2121
Gauges

Wiseco Manufacturing
216-951-6600
Turbo pistons

Worldwide Racing Fuels
800-648-2262
Racing fuel

GLOSSARY

ABSOLUTE PRESSURE. This term refers to pressure measured on the scale that has its zero point at approximately 14.7 psi (at sea level) below atmospheric pressure. It is a true measurement of all the pressure, rather than just the pressure above atmospheric. See Gauge pressure.

ABSOLUTE TEMPERATURE. Similar to absolute pressure, absolute temperature has its zero point where no heat exists. This is approximately 460°F below 0°F. An absolute degree is the same size as a Fahrenheit degree. The freezing point of water (32°F) is about 492°F above absolute zero, or 492° absolute.

AIR/FUEL RATIO (AFR). AFR is the ratio of the weight of air to the weight of fuel in a combustible mixture. AFR is critical in the proper functioning of an engine.

AMBIENT. Ambient refers to the surrounding atmospheric pressure and temperature.

ATMOSPHERIC. This word has recently taken on the connotation of an engine operating without any form of supercharger. My lawn mower has an atmospheric engine.

BLOW-THROUGH. This indicates that the throttle is on the outlet side of the turbo compressor. See **DRAW-THROUGH.**

BOOST. Boost is pressure above atmospheric, measured in the intake manifold. This book will use pounds per square inch above atmospheric pressure.

BOOST THRESHOLD or **BOOST POINT.** This is the lowest engine rpm at which boost from the turbocharger will increase power over the engine's atmospheric equivalent. More simply, the lowest rpm at which noticeable boost (usually 1–2 psi) can be achieved.

BYPASS VALVE. The bypass valve permits a bleed of flow around the turbo when the engine is not under boost.

CLEARANCE VOLUME. Combustion chamber volume above the piston at top dead center is called clearance volume.

COMPRESSION RATIO. This is displacement volume plus clearance volume divided by clearance volume.

COMPRESSOR. In this book, the compressor is the air pump itself—the front half of the turbo, through which intake air passes. It is also frequently referred to as the "cold" side.

COMPRESSOR EFFICIENCY (E_c). Efficiency is the ratio of what really happens to what should happen. In the case of the compressor, measurement of the temperature gain caused by compressing the air exceeds what thermodynamics says it should be. Compressor efficiency converts calculated temperature gains to real temperature gains.

COMPRESSOR SURGE. Compressor surge occurs when the throttle is slammed shut and air is caught between a pumping turbo and the throttle plate. This air blasts its way backward out the front of the turbo. When this happens, there is suddenly room for more air in the manifold, and air is pumped back in by the still-spinning turbo. The throttle is still closed, so the air again blasts back out through the turbo. This continues until the turbo loses enough speed for leakback around the compressor to dampen the air oscillations. Compressor surge can also occur under boost if too much boost pressure is present with low airflow through the system.The chirping sound heard from the turbo when lifting off the throttle while operating under boost results from this oscillating air volume. This noise is suppressed by the bypass valve

CROSSOVER POINT. This is the point at which manifold boost pressure equals turbine inlet pressure.

DETONATION. Detonation is spontaneous combustion of the air/fuel mixture ahead of the flame front. When pressure and temperature exceed that required for controlled combustion, the mixture autoignites. The metallic pinging sound is the resulting explosion's shock wave colliding with the cylinder walls.

Note: Ping, knock, and detonation are equivalent terms. Pre-ignition is an altogether different beastie. Do not call one the other.

DISPLACEMENT VOLUME. Displacement volume may be defined in several ways: (1) the swept volume of the cylinder; (2) the area of the bore times the length of the stroke; (3) total engine displacement divided by the number of cylinders.

DRAW-THROUGH. This indicates that the throttle is on the inlet side of the turbo compressor. See **BLOW-THROUGH.**

END GAS. The end gas is the last part of the air/fuel mixture to burn. Its importance to a turbocharged engine is paramount, because it is this end gas in which detonation usually occurs.

GAUGE PRESSURE. Gauge pressure is the scale that reads zero at atmospheric pressure. All references to boost pressure in this book will refer to gauge pressure. For example, 5 psi boost would be 5 psi above atmospheric pressure.

IN. HG. This phrase reads "inches of mercury" and is a measure of pressure on yet a different scale. In this book, in. hg will refer to vacuum in the intake manifold, and the scale works downward toward atmospheric pressure. For example, idle speed vacuum is usually about 18 in. hg, and as throttle is applied, the vacuum goes toward 0 gauge, which is atmospheric pressure.

INTERCOOLER. An intercooler is a heat exchanger placed between the turbo and engine to remove heat from air exiting the turbo when operating under boost. Intercoolers are also called charge air coolers.

INTERCOOLER EFFICIENCY (E_i). An intercooler's efficiency is measured by how much heat it removes relative to the heat added by the compressor.

INERTIAL LOAD. Inertial loads are those created by weight and acceleration. A heavier piston creates a greater inertial load. Likewise, an increase in rpm means greater acceleration and, thus, a greater inertial load.

LAG. Lag is the delay between a change in throttle and the production of noticeable boost when engine rpm is in a range in which boost can be achieved.

LEAN. Lean means not enough fuel to achieve a the correct air/fuel ratio for the existing conditions.

NONSEQUENTIAL FUEL INJECTION. EFI that pulses independently of the intake valve position is nonsequential.

OEM. Original Equipment Manufacturer; the company that built it in the first place.

POWER. Strictly speaking, power is the result of how fast a certain amount of work is done. In the automotive context, power is the product of torque at any specific rpm times that rpm.

POWER LOAD. This is the load induced into all engine components by pressure created by the burning gases.

PRE-DETONATION. This is a meaningless phrase and should not be included here or anywhere else.

PRE-IGNITION. Pre-ignition refers to spontaneous combustion of the air/fuel mixture prior to the spark.

PRESSURE RATIO. The ratio of absolute boost pressure to atmospheric pressure is called the pressure ratio.

PULSE DURATION. The amount of time, measured in thousandths of a second (msec), that an electronic fuel injector is held open on any single pulse. Pulse duration is a relative measurement of the amount of fuel delivered to one cylinder per combustion cycle.

REVERSION. Reversion occurs when some of the burned exhaust gases are pushed back into the combustion chamber and intake system during valve overlap. This is caused by exhaust manifold pressure exceeding intake pressure or by shock waves in the exhaust ports and manifolds.

RICH. Rich is the condition that exists when too much fuel is present to achieve a maximum-power air/fuel ratio.

SEQUENTIAL FUEL INJECTION. A fuel injector pulse timed to discharge fuel when the intake valve is in the most advantageous position is called sequenced. It pulses the injectors in the same sequence as the firing order.

SUPERCHARGE. To force more air into an engine than the engine can breathe by itself is to supercharge it. A supercharger is the device that does this. [It may be driven by a belt, gears, or a turbine. When driven by a turbine, it is called a turbocharger.

THERMAL EFFICIENCY. See **COMPRESSOR EFFICIENCY**, **INTERCOOLER EFFICIENCY**.

THERMAL LOAD. In this book, thermal load will take the rather narrow definition of heat added to the system by the turbocharger. This comes from heat produced in the air that is compressed by the turbo and the mixture heat increase due to reversion.

THROTTLE RESPONSE. A change in the speed or torque of an engine brought about by a change in throttle position is called throttle response. Throttle response should not be confused with turbo response.

TORQUE. The amount of twisting force provided by a turning shaft is called torque. It is measured in foot-pounds, inch-pounds, or newton-meters.

TURBINE. The turbine is the fan driven by the engine's exhaust gases. It is often called the "hot" side of the turbocharger.

TURBOCHARGER. A turbocharger is a supercharger driven by a turbine.

UNDER BOOST. When a system has greater-than-atmospheric pressure in the intake manifold, it is operating under boost.

VOLUMETRIC EFFICIENCY (E_v). This is the ratio of the number of molecules of air that actually get into a combustion chamber to the number of molecules in an equal volume at atmospheric pressure. For atmospheric engines, this ratio is almost always less than one. Supercharged engines are capable of operating at ratios greater than one.

WASTEGATE. The wastegate is a boost-pressure-actuated valve that allows only enough exhaust gas into the turbine to achieve desired boost. The wastegate routes the remainder of the exhaust gas around the turbine and out the tailpipe.

INDEX

WARNING —

• *Automotive service, repair, and modification is serious business. You must be alert, use common sense, and exercise good judgement to prevent personal injury.*

• *Before using this book or begining any work on your vehicle, thoroughly read the Warning on the copyright page, and any Warnings and Cautions listed on the inside front cover.*

WARNING —

• *Automotive service, repair, and modification is serious business. You must be alert, use common sense, and exercise good judgement to prevent personal injury.*

• *Before using this book or begining any work on your vehicle, thoroughly read the Warning on the copyright page, and any Warnings and Cautions listed on the inside front cover.*

Selected Books and Repair Information From Bentley Publishers

Engineering

Supercharged! Design, Testing, and Installation of Supercharger Systems *Corky Bell* ISBN 0-8376-0168-1

Bosch Fuel Injection and Engine Management *Charles O. Probst, SAE* ISBN 0-8376-0300-5

Scientific Design of Exhaust and Intake Systems *Phillip H. Smith and John C. Morrison* ISBN 0-8376-0309-9

The Leading Edge: Aerodynamic Design of Ultra-Streamlined Land Vehicles *Goro Tamai* ISBN 0-8376-0860-0

Driving

The Unfair Advantage *Mark Donohue* ISBN 0-8376-0073-1(hc); 0-8376-0069-3(pb)

Going Faster! Mastering the Art of Race Driving *The Skip Barber Racing School* ISBN 0-8376-0227-0

A French Kiss With Death: Steve McQueen and the Making of *Le Mans* *Michael Keyser* ISBN 0-8376-0234-3

The Speed Merchants: A Journey Through the World of Motor Racing 1969–1972 *Michael Keyser* ISBN 0-8376-0232-7

Sports Car and Competition Driving *Paul Frère* with foreword *by Phil Hill* ISBN 0-8376-0202-5

The Technique of Motor Racing *Piero Taruffi* ISBN 0-8376-0228-9

Think To Win: The New Approach to Fast Driving *Don Alexander with foreword by Mark Martin* ISBN 0-8376-0070-7

Other Enthusiast Titles

Mercedes-Benz E-Class Owner's Bible™ 1986–1995 *Bentley Publishers* ISBN 0-8376-0230-0

Civic Duty: The Ultimate Guide to the Honda Civic *Alan Paradise* ISBN 0-8376-0215-7

Road & Track Illustrated Automotive Dictionary *John Dinkel* ISBN 0-8376-0143-6

Harley-Davidson Evolution V-Twin Owner's Bible™ *Moses Ludel* ISBN 0-8376-0146-0

Jeep Owner's Bible™ *Moses Ludel* ISBN 0-8376-0154-1

Audi

Audi A4 Repair Manual: 1996–2001, 1.8L turbo, 2.8L, including Avant and quattro *Bentley Publishers* ISBN 0-8376-0371-4

Audi A4 1996–2001, S4 2000–2001 Official Factory Repair Manual on CD-ROM *Bentley Publishers* ISBN 0-8376-0833-3

Audi A6 Sedan 1998–2002, Avant 1999–2002, allroad quattro 2001–2002, S6 Avant 2002 Official Factory Repair Manual on CD-ROM *Bentley Publishers* ISBN 0-8376-0836-8

BMW

BMW 3 Series Enthusiast's Companion™ *Jeremy Walton* ISBN 0-8376-0220-3

BMW 3 Series (E46) Service Manual: 1999–2001, 323i, 325i, 325xi, 328i, 330i, 330xi Sedan, Coupe, Convertible, Sport Wagon *Bentley Publishers* ISBN 0-8376-0320-X

BMW 3 Series (E36) Service Manual: 1992–1998, 318i/is/iC, 323is/iC, 325i/is/iC, 328i/is/iC, M3 *Bentley Publishers* ISBN 0-8376-0326-9

BMW 5 Series Service Manual: 1989–1995 525i, 530i, 535i, 540i, including Touring *Bentley Publishers* ISBN 0-8376-0319-6

BMW 7 Series Service Manual: 1988–1994, 735i, 735iL, 740i, 740iL, 750iL *Bentley Publishers* ISBN 0-8376-0328-5

Chevrolet

Zora Arkus-Duntov: The Legend Behind Corvette *Jerry Burton* ISBN 0-8376-0858-9

Corvette from the Inside: The 50-Year Development History *Dave McLellan* ISBN 0-8376-0859-7

Corvette by the Numbers: The Essential Corvette Parts Reference 1955–1982: *Alan Colvin* ISBN 0-8376-0288-2

Chevrolet by the Numbers 1965–1969: The Essential Chevrolet Parts Reference *Alan Colvin* ISBN 0-8376-0956-9

Camaro Exposed: 1967–1969, Designs, Decisions and the Inside View *Paul Zazarine* ISBN 0-8376-0876-7

Corvette Fuel Injection & Electronic Engine Management 1982–2001: *Charles O. Probst, SAE* ISBN 0-8376-0861-9

Corvette 427: Practical Restoration of a '67 Roadster *Don Sherman* ISBN 0-8376-0218-1

Ford

The Official Ford Mustang 5.0 Technical Reference & Performance Handbook: 1979–1993 *Al Kirschenbaum* ISBN 0-8376-0210-6

Ford F-Series Pickup Owner's Bible™ *Moses Ludel* ISBN 0-8376-0152-5

Ford Fuel Injection and Electronic Engine Control: 1988–1993 *Charles O. Probst, SAE* ISBN 0-8376-0301-3

Porsche

Porsche Carrera 964 and 965, 1989–1994 Technician's Handbook: Without Guesswork™ *Bentley Publishers* ISBN 0-8376-0292-0

Porsche 911 Carrera Service Manual: 1984–1989 *Bentley Publishers* ISBN 0-8376-0291-2

Porsche 911 SC Coupe, Targa, and Cabriolet Service Manual: 1978–1983 *Bentley Publishers* ISBN 0-8376-0290-4

Volkswagen

Volkswagen Sport Tuning for Street and Competition *Per Schroeder* ISBN 0-8376-0161-4

Battle for the Beetle *Karl Ludvigsen* ISBN 0-8376-0071-5

New Beetle Service Manual: 1998–2002 1.8L turbo, 1.9L TDI diesel, 2.0L gasoline *Bentley Bpublishers* ISBN 0-8376-0376-5

New Beetle 1998–2002 Official Factory Repair Manual on CD-ROM *Bentley Publishers* ISBN 0-8376-0838-4

Passat Service Manual: 1998–2002, 1.8L turbo, 2.8L V6, 4.0L W8, including wagon and 4MOTION *Bentley Publishers* ISBN 0-8376-0393-5

Passat 1998–2002 Official Factory Repair Manual on CD-ROM *Bentley Publishers* ISBN 0-8376-0837-6

Jetta, Golf, GTI Service Manual: 1999–2002 2.0L Gasoline, 1.9L TDI Diesel, 2.8L VR6, 1.8L Turbo *Bentley Publishers* ISBN 0-8376-0388-9

New Beetle Service Manual: 1998–1999 2.0L Gasoline, 1.9L TDI Diesel, 1.8L Turbo *Bentley Publishers* ISBN 0-8376-0385-4

Jetta, Golf, GTI, Cabrio Service Manual: 1993–1999, including Jetta_III and Golf_III *Bentley Publishers* ISBN 0-8376-0366-8

Jetta, Golf, GTI 1993–1999, Cabrio 1995–2002 Official Factory Repair Manual on CD-ROM *Bentley Publishers* ISBN 0-8376-0834-1

Eurovan Official Factory Repair Manual: 1992–1999 *Volkswagen of America* ISBN 0-8376-0335-8

Eurovan 1992–2002 Official Factory Repair Manual on CD-ROM *Bentley Publishers* ISBN 0-8376-0835-X

Jetta, Golf, GTI Service Manual: 1985–1992 Gasoline, Diesel, and Turbo Diesel, including 16V *Bentley Publishers* ISBN 0-8376-0342-0

Super Beetle, Beetle and Karmann Ghia Official Service Manual: Type 1, 1970–1979 *Volkswagen of America* ISBN 0-8376-0096-0

ART CREDITS

ABOUT THE AUTHOR

Corky Bell was born in Albuquerque and raised somewhere between Illinois, Florida, Louisiana, Texas, New Mexico, and Europe. After receiving a degree in mechanical engineering from Texas A&M, he worked as an engineer at Bell Helicopter for twelve years. He opened Cartech in Dallas in 1977, after his interest in turbocharging grew from a hobby into a business. He subsequently moved Cartech to San Antonio and in 1992 formed Bell Engineering, to expand the scope of business by providing engineering and fabrication services for light aircraft.

For sixteen years he enjoyed the wonderful opportunity to play amateur auto racer (SCCA and IMSA), which left him with lots of hard-earned automotive experience, many fond memories, and many good friends.

Married for twenty-seven years, with two daughters, he lives with his family in the great Texas hill country north of San Antonio.